GnuCash Help Manual

The GnuCash Documentation Team

GnuCash Help Manual

by The GnuCash Documentation Team

This manual describes how to use the GnuCash Financial software.

Copyright © 2002-2017 GnuCash Documentation Team

Feedback

To report a bug or make a suggestion regarding this package or this manual, follow the directions at the GNOME Bug Tracking System [http://bugzilla.gnome.org].

Table of Contents

List of Figures

List of Tables

About the Author

The GnuCash Documentation Team is a self-designated group of GnuCash users and developers who have volunteered to write this documentation for the benefit of the broader user base. People who are interested in joining this group are encouraged to express their interest on the GnuCash lists (gnucash-users and gnucash-devel) for further direction.

Contributors on the team so far have been: Yawar Amin, J. Alex Aycinena, Frank Ellenberger, Chris Good, Dave Herman, Geert Janssens, Chris Lyttle, Cristian Marchi, John Ralls, Robert Ratliff, Mark Simpson, and Christian Stimming.

Chapter 1. Introduction to GnuCash

What is GnuCash?

GnuCash is a personal and small business finance application. It's designed to be easy to use, yet powerful and flexible. GnuCash allows you to track your income and expenses, reconcile bank accounts, monitor stock portfolios and manage your small business finances. It is based on professional accounting principles to ensure balanced books and accurate reports.

Chapter 2. Using This Document & Getting Help

This document is organized in two dimensions;

- From the GUI (Graphical User Interface) explaining the available options and their functions, with links to deeper descriptions and usage. Chapter 4, *GnuCash Windows & Menus Options Overview*

- By classifying Operations, Tasks, or Functions based on whether it is an Account, Transaction, Reporting or other oriented operation. Examples are;

  - Account Actions - Chapter 5, *Setting Up, Editing & Working with Accounts*

  - Transaction/Register Actions - Chapter 6, *Common Transaction Operations*

  - Tools and Assistants - Chapter 8, *Tools & Assistants*

  - Reporting & Charting - Chapter 9, *Reports And Charts*

  - Customization - Chapter 10, *Customizing GnuCash*

Accessing Help

This window is accessed by going to the Help menu and selecting either the Tutorial and Concepts Guide or the Contents (F1). the section called "Account Tree - Help Menu"

The Help Window has a *Toolbar* for navigation. The *Toolbar* is described below;

- Back Used to navigate to topics previously viewed.

- Forward Used to navigate to topics previously viewed.

- Help Used to access various GNOME Help files.

- Search Enter search term to search GNOME Help files. Does not search GnuCash Help file.

The right side of the Help Window displays the currently opened help page. The left side of the Help Window contains the help Topics list tab. Selecting one of the help topics will load that page on the right side.

GnuCash Tutorial and Concepts Guide

This guide is the counterpart to this help. It explains the concepts used in GnuCash and has a tutorial that takes you through using GnuCash to manage your accounts. It will appear if you choose Open the new user tutorial in the Welcome to GnuCash! menu.

To open this Guide manually go to Help → Tutorial and Concepts Guide.

It is strongly recommended to read this guide if you are new to GnuCash or unfamiliar with accounting concepts.

GnuCash Wiki

An immense amount of less-formal documenation, both of GnuCash itself and its maintenance and development may be found in the GnuCash Wiki [https://wiki.gnucash.org/wiki]; the Frequently Asked Questions [https://wiki.gnucash.org/wiki/FAQ] page should be a first stop whenever you encounter difficulty using GnuCash.

GnuCash On-line Assistance

Mailing List

The primary source of user support is the user mailing list [mailto:gnucash-user@gnucash.org]. If you prefer a web forum-like presentation, you can use it via Nabble [http://gnucash.1415818.n4.nabble.com/Gnu-Cash-User-f1415819.html]. One must subscribe [https://lists.gnucash.org/mailman/listinfo/gnucash-user] before posting, even if using Nabble.

IRC

Several of the developers monitor the #gnucash channel at irc.gnome.org. They're usually doing something else, too, and of course aren't always at their computers. Log in, ask your question, and stay logged in; it may be several hours before your question is noticed and responded to. To see if you missed anything check the IRC logs [https://code.gnucash.org/logs].

The GnuCash web site [http://www.gnucash.org] has more details on these channels. You will also find pointers there to additional useful resources such as the bug tracking system.

Chapter 3. Getting Started

Running GnuCash

GnuCash can be run from your desktop main menu by selecting the associated menu entry.

Alternatively it can be run from a shell (command line) with the command **gnucash**.

During the loading of the GnuCash main window you will see the *GnuCash Splash Screen* where some information about the program itself and the loading process are displayed.

Welcome to GnuCash dialog

Next you will be presented with the Welcome to GnuCash! dialog with three choices:

- Create a new set of accounts: Runs the New Account Hierarchy Setup assistant (see the section called "New Account Hierarchy Setup"). Select this option if you want to be assisted in creating a set of accounts.

- Import my QIF files: Runs the Import QIF Files assistant (see the section called "Import QIF Files"). Select this option if you already have Quicken files (`.qif` files) from another financial application and wish to import them into GnuCash.

- Open the new user tutorial: Opens the GnuCash Tutorial and Concepts Guide. Select this option if you are completely new to GnuCash and accounting concepts.

  ### Note

  It is possible to run these items after you have made a choice here, but the Welcome to GnuCash! screen will not reappear. To try one of the other choices later, read the section called "New Account Hierarchy Setup", the section called "Import QIF Files" and the section called "GnuCash Tutorial and Concepts Guide" to see how to start them from the GnuCash menu.

This screen is intended for you to use to get up and running quickly. The Cancel button is used to exit the screen. It will then prompt you with Display Welcome Dialog Again?. If you do not want to see the Welcome to GnuCash! menu again click the No button. Click the Yes button or press the keyboard **Enter** key for the default which is to have the Welcome to GnuCash! screen run again.

Note

Selecting either of these options will leave you with a minimum GnuCash main window. Operations in this window are described in Chapter 4, *GnuCash Windows & Menus Options Overview*.

New Account Hierarchy Setup

This assistant helps you to create a set of GnuCash accounts. It will appear if you choose Create a new set of accounts in the Welcome to GnuCash! menu.

This will create a new blank GnuCash file and then automatically start the New Account Hierarchy Setup assistant.

Tip

To start this assistant manually, go to File → New if you need to create a new file. If you want to run the assistant within the opened file, go to Actions → New Account Hierarchy... when the accounts tree tab is displayed.

1. The New Account Hierarchy Setup assistant opens with a screen that briefly describes what this assistant does. The three buttons at the very bottom of the screen will not change while using the assistant.

   - Cancel: exit the process and cancel creating a new set of accounts.

   ## Warning

   If you click this button, any selections you have made up to this point will be lost.

   - Back: brings up the previous screen so that you can change a previous selection until the first screen.

   - Forward: brings up the next screen so you can continue through the assistant.

2. The next screen allows you to Choose Currency to use as default for your accounts.

   - The Currency: drop down list defaults to the currency configured in the Accounts tab under GnuCash Preferences (see the section called "Accounts"). If you wish your accounts to use a different default currency, select one from the list.

   - The Forward button is used to confirm your selection and continue to the next screen.

3. The next screen is used to Choose accounts to create.

   You will see a screen divided into three parts.

   - The left upper portion has a list of Categories for commonly used hierarchies of accounts. Select from this list the types of accounts you wish to use. You can select as many of the categories of accounts as you wish.

   - The left lower section has a Category Description that displays a detailed description of the category currently highlighted.

   - The right side has a list of the Accounts that will be created from the selected category.

   - The Select All button allows you to include all of the account categories.

   - The Clear All button allows you to deselect all of the categories selected.

4. The next screen allows you to Setup selected accounts by entering the opening balances and by selecting if the account is a placeholder.

   ## Note

   Equity accounts do not have opening balances so the opening balance value for this kind of accounts is locked and set to zero by GnuCash

   ## Note

   Placeholder accounts are used to create a hierarchy of accounts and normally do not have transactions or opening balances.

Follow the instructions in the display on how to select the account and entering an opening balance for the account. A single click is used to highlight an account.

- The left side of the screen has a list of Account Names. Select an account by "clicking" once in the Account Names column with the account highlighted. This will open the account name for changes.

- The right side of the screen has a check-box to make an account a Placeholder and a box to add the Opening Balance for the selected account. Again a single click in the Opening Balance or Placeholder column will open the field for changes.

5. The Finish account setup is the last screen and gives you a final list of the three choices to finish the assistant.

- Cancel: exits the assistant and cancels creating a new set of accounts.

Warning

If you click this button, any selections you have made up to this point will be lost.

- Back: brings up the previous screen so that you can change a previous selection until the first screen.

- Apply: creates the accounts you have selected.

You should now have a hierarchy of accounts in your main GnuCash account window.

Import QIF Files

This Assistant helps you import Quicken QIF files. It will appear if you choose Import my QIF files in the Welcome to GnuCash! menu.

To start this assistant manually go to File → Import ... → Import QIF....

In the following all the screens that you can see in this assistant are described in order of appearance.

1. The Import QIF files assistant opens with a screen that briefly describes what this assistant does and requests the file(s) to import. The three buttons at the very bottom of the screen will not change while using the assistant.

- Cancel: exit the process and cancel importing QIF files.

Warning

If you click this button, any selections you have made up to this point will be lost.

- Back: brings up the previous screen so that you can change a previous selection until the first screen.

- Forward: brings up the next screen so you can continue through the assistant.

2. The next screen allows you to Select a QIF file to load. The Select... button on this screen is used to access the list of files. The Select... button brings up the Select QIF File dialog.

Navigate to where you have stored your QIF files and select the first one then click Import. The next screen will display it in the Select a QIF File to Load field.

Note

If the file you are loading does not have an QIF date listed in it you will see the Set a date format for this QIF file screen. Select the proper format from the pull down list and continue.

Note

If the file you are loading does not have an account name listed in it you will see the Set the default QIF account name screen. Otherwise you will skip this screen and go on to the screen in the next section that shows loaded QIF files.

- The Account name: field is used to set an account name for this QIF file.

3. The next screen shows you the QIF files you have loaded. You can use this screen to return to the previous screen and load more QIF files. It will also let you unload any files you have loaded by mistake.

- The top panel shows the list of QIF Files you have loaded.

- The Load another file button takes you back to the previous screen to load another QIF file.

- The Unload selected file button allows you to select a file from the top panel and remove it from the list.

When you have selected all the QIF files to be imported, click the Forward button.

4. Depending on the type of data contained in the QIF files to be imported, you may see only one or all of the following screens:

Accounts and stock holdings   This screen gives a description of the Accounts and stock holdings matching process on the following Match QIF accounts with GnuCash accounts screen.

Tip

This and other informational screens in the Import QIF files assistant can be turned off in the Online Banking tab (see the section called "Online Banking") under GnuCash Preferences.

The next screen lets you Match QIF accounts with GnuCash accounts. You will see a list of QIF account names on the left and suggested GnuCash account names on the right. The New? column indicates if the GnuCash account name will be created by the QIF Import.

To change the GnuCash account to a different one select the QIF account. A screen will pop up to select another account or create a new one.

- Select an account from the list to choose a already existing account.

- The New Account button allows you to add a new account name as a sub-account (child of selected) of the selected account.

- The OK button is used to confirm your selection.

- The Cancel button is used to exit the dialog without using any changes you have made.

Income and Expense categories

This screen gives a description of the Income and Expense categories matching process on the following Match QIF categories with GnuCash accounts screen.

Tip

This and other informational screens in the Import QIF files assistant can be turned off in the Online Banking tab (see the section called "Online Banking") under GnuCash Preferences.

The next screen lets you Match QIF categories with GnuCash accounts. You will see a list of QIF category names on the left and suggested GnuCash account names on the right. The New? column indicates if the GnuCash account name will be created by the QIF Import.

To change the GnuCash account to a different one select the QIF category. A dialog will pop up to select another account or create a new one.

- Select an account from the list to choose a already existing account.

- The New Account button allows you to add a new account name as a sub-account (child of selected) of the selected account.

- The OK button is used to confirm your selection.

- The Cancel button is used to exit the dialog without using any changes you have made.

Payees and memos

This screen gives a description of the Payees and memos matching process on the following Match payees/memos to GnuCash accounts screen.

Tip

This and other informational screens in the Import QIF files assistant can be turned off in the Online Banking tab (see the section called "Online Banking") under GnuCash Preferences.

The next screen lets you Match payees/memos to GnuCash accounts. You will see a list of QIF payee/memo names on the left and suggested GnuCash account names on the right. The default GnuCash account used is called Unspecified. The New? column indicates if the GnuCash account name will be created by the QIF Import.

To change the GnuCash account to a different one select the QIF payee/memo. A dialog will pop up to select another account or create a new one.

- Select an account from the list to choose a already existing account.

- The New Account button allows you to add a new account name as a sub-account of the selected account.

- The OK button is used to confirm your selection.

- The Cancel button is used to exit the dialog without using any changes you have made.

5. The next screen allows you to Enter the QIF file currency. The drop down list defaults to the currency configured in the Accounts tab (see the section called "Accounts") under GnuCash Preferences. If you wish the new accounts to use a different currency, select one from the list.

When you have selected the currency, click the Forward button.

6. Depending on the type of data contained in the QIF files to be imported, you may or may not see one or more of the following screens:

Tradable Commodities

This screen gives a description of the Tradable Commodities process on the screen.

Tip

This and other informational screens in the Import QIF files assistant can be turned off in the Online Banking tab (see the section called "Online Banking") under GnuCash Preferences.

A series of screens, one for each of the stock, mutual fund, or commodity, displays the exchange, full name, and symbol for each of the commodities listed in the QIF file you are importing so that you can check them before proceeding.

Match duplicate transactions

This screen gives a description of the Match duplicate transactions process on the following Select possible duplicates screen.

Tip

This and other informational screens in the Import QIF files assistant can be turned off in the Online Banking tab (see the section called "Online Banking") under GnuCash Preferences.

The next screen lets you Select possible duplicate transactions. Imported transactions are shown on the left panel and possible matches to each selected transaction are shown on the right.

• The left panel shows the list of Imported transactions to select from for matching duplicates

• The right panel shows the list of *possible* duplicates for the selected imported transaction. Select the one that most closely matches

7. The last screen, Update your GnuCash accounts, gives you a list of three choices to finish the assistant.

• Cancel: exit the process and cancel importing QIF files.

Warning

If you click this button, any selections you have made up to this point will be lost.

• Back: brings up the previous screen so that you can change a previous selection until the first screen.

• Forward: imports the data and creates the accounts you have specified.

You should now have successfully imported your accounts.

Tip

Imported transactions might need to be **reconciled**. This process is described in the GnuCash Tutorial and Concepts guide.

Tip of The Day

The Tip of the Day screen starts whenever you start GnuCash unless it has been disabled in the GnuCash Preferences. It gives tips on features and using GnuCash. You can use the three buttons at the bottom of the screen to look through the tips.

Close   Dismiss the Tip of the Day screen

Prev   Shows the previous tip

Forward   Shows the next tip

The Show tips at startup check-box is used to enable or disable the Tip of the Day from running at GnuCash start-up.

It is also possible to configure the Tip of the Day to run at start-up under the General tab in GnuCash Preferences. The Tip of the Day can also be manually run by going to Help → Tip of the Day.

Chapter 4. GnuCash Windows & Menus Options Overview

The main GnuCash window displays the accounts, reports, menu selections and tools you may use to process your financial data. This section gives you an overview of the different windows and sections of windows that you will see in GnuCash.

Links in the various tables will lead to additional details on the topic.

GnuCash Windows and Menus

Main GnuCash Window

You can access commonly used sub-windows and tools through this window.

Figure 4.1. The Main GnuCash Window

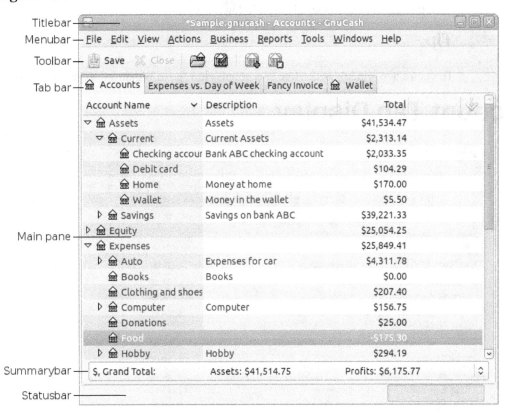

The parts in which the main GnuCash window is divided.

When you start GnuCash, after a couple of windows (Splash screen, Tip of the Day) the main window will be displayed. This window is divided into the following sections (see Figure 4.1, "The Main GnuCash Window" for reference):

Titlebar	Displays the name of the currently opened file and the active tab's name
Menubar	Displays the available menu entries

Toolbar	Displays the available *Toolbar* buttons
Tab bar	Lists the open reports, registers and tree of accounts
Main pane	The major display space showing the content of the currently selected tab
Summarybar	Displays a financial summary
Statusbar	Gives a description of the active menu item and shows a progress bar

Note

The contents and options within the various sub-menus of the different sections of the main Gnu-Cash window will vary upon the active display window.

The tree of accounts is labeled Accounts in the *Tab bar*, and displays all your accounts and their balances, grouped according to standard accounting practice.

Tip

To open an additional view of the tree of accounts go to View → New Accounts Page. This will open the account tree in the existing window.

Tip

To open a new window with a tree of accounts view, go to Windows → New Window with Page.

Account Tab Display

Figure 4.2. The *Account Tree* Display.

This is an image of the Accounts tab.

Account Tree - Menus

The *Menubar* for the Accounts Tree window contains the following options.

Account Tree - File Menu

The following table describes the options in the File Menu.

Clicking on the File option of the *Menubar* will "pull down" a menu of options described in Table 4.1, "Account Tree - File Menu - Access to file, account operations and printing.".

Table 4.1. Account Tree - File Menu - Access to file, account operations and printing.

Menu Item	Description	
New File (**Ctrl+N**)	Creates a new data file (starts with new accounts and data.)	
Open... (**Ctrl+O**)	Opens an already existing GnuCash data file.	
Import →	Opens the Import sub-menu to import files from other financial programs.	
	Import QIF...	Starts the QIF file Import process.
	Import OFX/QFX...	Starts the OFX/QFX file Import process.
	Import Accounts from CSV...	Starts the CSV Account file import process. The file to import must be in the same format as the one exported by GnuCash.
	Import Transactions from CSV...	Starts the CSV Transactions file import process. The file to import must be a delimited file.
	Replay GnuCash .log file...	Starts the replaying of a GnuCash log file. Used for data recovery from "crashes".
	Import MT940	.
	Import MT942	.
	Import DTAUS	.
	Import DTAUS and send	.
	Import Bills & Invoices...	Open the Import Transactions from text file window.
	Import Customers and Vendors ...	Open the Import Customers and Vendors from text file window.
Save (**Ctrl+S**)	Saves the currently open file.	
Save As... (**Shift+Ctrl+S**)	Saves the currently opened file with a different name. **Warning** Do NOT store your data file in `~/.gnucash/books`.	
Revert	Reload the last saved version of the currently opened file. Useful if you need to discard changes made to the data and not yet saved.	
Print	*Grayed out option.*	
Page Setup... (**Shift+Ctrl+P**)	Lets you choose the paper size, layout and margins for printing.	

Menu Item	Description	
Export →	Opens the Export sub-menu.	
	Export Accounts Tree to CSV	Exports your account hierarchy to a delimited CSV file. Does not export data.
	Export Transactions to CSV	Exports transactions to a delimited CSV file.
	Export Accounts	Exports your account hierarchy to a new GnuCashfile. Does not export data.
Properties (**Alt+Enter**)	Sets options for this GnuCash data file.	
Recently opened files	Numbered list of most recently opened GnuCash data files.	
Close (**Ctrl+W**)	Close the current tab. ### Note In the initial Account tree this item is not available - it will be grayed out.	
Quit (**Ctrl+Q**)	Exits GnuCash.	

Account Tree - Edit Menu

Table 4.2. Account Tree - Edit Menu - Access to file and account editing operations and preferences.

Menu Item	Description
Cut (**Ctrl+X**)	Performs a standard *Cut* operation.
Copy (**Ctrl+C**)	Performs a standard *Copy* operation.
Paste (**Ctrl+V**)	Performs a standard *Paste* operation.
Edit Account (**Ctrl+E**)	Modify name or characteristic of selected account. the section called "Editing an Account"
Delete Account... (**Delete**)	Remove an account. See the section called "Deleting an Account"
Renumber Subaccounts...	Starts the Renumber Account assistant. See the section called "Renumbering Subaccounts". ### Note This item is selectable only if you have highlighted an account with at least one subaccount in the accounts tree.
Open Account	Opens the register window for the currently selected account.
Open Subaccount	Opens a register window that displays all the transactions for the selected account and for all its subaccounts.

Menu Item	Description
Find... (**Ctrl+F**)	Set criteria for a search for a specific transaction. See the section called "Find" for specifics on searches.
Preferences (GnuCash → Preferences on Mac OS X).	Customize GnuCash for location, style, and numerous other preferences. See the section called "Setting Preferences".
Style Sheets	Modify/customize Style Sheets. See the section called "Changing Style Sheets".
Tax Report Options	Set tax characteristics on account(s) (US). Assign tax form and line to account. See the section called "Setting Tax Report Options"

Account Tree - View Menu

Table 4.3. Account Tree - View Menu - Changes display window view.

Menu Item	Description
Toolbar	Check-box to enable/disable display of *Toolbar*.
Summarybar	Check-box to enable/disable display of *Summarybar*.
Statusbar	Check-box to enable/disable display of *Statusbar*.
Filter by ...	Set filter for accounts displayed in the Account Tree display.
Refresh (**Ctrl+R**)	Repaint the display screen.
New Accounts Page	Open a new tab that displays the account tree.

Account Tree - Actions Menu

Table 4.4. Account Tree - Actions Menu - Setup scheduled transactions, repair accounts, perform stock splits, transfer and reconcile transactions.

Menu Item	Description	
Online Actions →	This menu item (and sub-menu) is shown only if Online Banking was enabled for GnuCash	
	Get Balance	
	Get Transactions	Download transactions from online accounts
	Issue Transaction...	Upload transaction(s) to online account ??
	Issue SEPA Transaction...	
	Internal Transaction...	
	Direct Debit...	
	Show log window...	Open the Online Banking Connection Window
Scheduled Transactions →	Scheduled Transactions sub-menus	

Menu Item	Description	
	Scheduled Transaction Editor	Invoke tool to edit scheduled transactions. See the section called "Edit Scheduled Transaction Window"
	Since Last Run...	Display Scheduled transactions since last running of GnuCash. the section called "Since Last Run Assistant"
	Mortgage & Loan Repayment...	Starts the Mortgage & Loan Repayment assistant for setting up repayments. the section called "Mortgage & Loan Repayment Assistant"
Budget →	Budget sub-menus	
	New Budget	Opens the window to create a new budget.
	Open Budget	Opens an existing budget.
	Copy Budget	Copy a budget.
New Account...	Creates a new account and opens the account properties window.	
New Account Hierarchy...	Starts the New Account Hierarchy Setup assistant.	
Transfer... (**Ctrl+T**)	Starts the Transfer assistant for transfer between accounts.	
Reconcile...	Open the Reconcile window. the section called "Reconciling an Account to a Statement"	
Auto clear...	Opens the auto-clear screen where you can fill up the automatic clear information.	
Stock Split...	Starts the Stock Split assistant. Additional details the section called "Recording a Stock Split"	
View Lots...	Opens the Lots in Account form.	
Check & Repair →	Check & Repair Submenus	
	Check & Repair Account	Check for and repair unbalanced transactions and orphan splits in this account.
	Check & Repair Subaccounts	Check for and repair unbalanced transactions and orphan splits in this account and its subaccounts.
	Check & Repair All	Check for and repair unbalanced transactions and orphan splits in all accounts.
Reset Warnings...	GnuCash gives warnings when certain operations are attempted, such as removing a transaction or removing the splits of a transaction. The warning message gives you the option to not give you these warnings when attempting the operation. Check-boxes labeled Remember and don't ask me again and Remember and don't ask me again this session allow disabling the warnings. This option resets the warnings to the default, i.e. display all warnings.	

Menu Item	Description	
	Tip Warnings may be selectively enabled.	
Rename Page	Open the form to rename the current page/tab.	

Account Tree - Business Menu

Table 4.5. Account Tree - Business Menu - Access small business features of GnuCash.

Menu Item	Description	
Customer →	Select customer related activities.	
	Customers Overview	Open a customers overview page.
	New Customer...	Start the form to create a new customer.
	Find Customer...	Start the assistant to search for a customer.
	New Invoice...	Start the form to create a new invoice.
	Find Invoice...	Start the assistant to search for an invoice.
	New Job...	Start the form to create a new job.
	Find Job...	Start the assistant to search for a job.
	Process Payment...	Starts the Process Payment assistant. Requires an account of type "A/Payable" before running assistant.
Vendor →	Select vendor related activities.	
	Vendors Overview	Open a vendors overview page.
	New Vendor...	Start the form to create a new vendor.
	Find Vendor...	Start the assistant to search for a vendor.
	New Bill...	Start the form to create a new bill.
	Find Bill...	Start the assistant to search for a bill.
	New Job...	Start the form to create a new job.
	Find Job...	Start the assistant to search for a job.

Menu Item	Description	
	Process Payment...	Starts the Process Payment assistant. Requires an account of type "A/Payable" before running assistant.
Employee →	Select employee related activities.	
	Employees Overview	Open an employees overview page.
	New Employee...	Start the form to create a new employee.
	Find Employee...	Start the assistant to search for an employee.
	New Expense Voucher...	Start the form to create a new expense voucher.
	Find Expense Voucher...	Start the assistant to search for an expense voucher.
	Process Payment...	Starts the Process Payment assistant. Requires an account of type "A/Payable" before running assistant.
Sales Tax Table	View and edit the list of tax tables.	
Billing Terms Editor	View and edit the list of Billing Terms.	
Bills Due Reminder	View and edit the list of Bills Due Reminder.	

Account Tree - Reports Menu

This is a brief listing of each of the available reports and graphs. See the section called "Reports Listed By Class" for specific report details. Each report or graph may be customized by selecting a different *Stylesheet* or by pressing the Options button in the *Toolbar*.

Table 4.6. Account Tree - Reports Menu - Access GnuCash Reports and Charts.

Menu Item	Description	
Assets & Liabilities →		
	Advanced Portfolio	
	Asset Barchart	
	Asset Piechart	
	Average Balance	
	Balance Sheet	
	Balance Sheet using eguile-gnc	
	General Journal	
	General Ledger	
	Investment Portfolio	
	Liability Barchart	

Menu Item	Description	
	Liability Piechart	
	Net Worth Barchart	
	Net Worth Linechart	
	Price Scatterplot	
Business Reports →		
	Customer Report	
	Customer Summary	
	Easy Invoice	
	Employee Report	
	Fancy Invoice	
	Job Report	
	Payable Aging	
	Printable Invoice	
	Receivable Aging	
	Tax Invoice	
	Vendor Report	
Income & Expense →		
	Cash Flow	
	Equity Statement	
	Expense Barchart	
	Expense Piechart	
	Expenses vs. Day of Week	
	Income & Expense Chart	
	Income Barchart	
	Income Piechart	
	Income Statement	
	Income vs. Day of Week	
	Profit & loss	
	Trial Balance	
Sample & Custom →		
	Welcome Sample Report	
	Custom Multicolumn Report	
	Sample Report With Examples	
Budget →		
	Budget Balance Sheet	
	Budget Barchart	
	Budget Flow	

Menu Item	Description
	Budget Income Statement	
	Budget Profit & Loss	
	Budget Report	
Account Summary	Report showing the balance of selected accounts.
Future Scheduled Transactions Summary	Report showing a summary of future transactions.
Tax Schedule Report & TXF Export	Create a Tax report (US) and/or export data for tax preparation software. (TXF)
Transaction Report	
Saved Report Configurations	Open the screen to manage saved user configured reports.

Account Tree - Tools Menu

Table 4.7. Account Tree - Tools Menu - Access to miscellaneous tools and editors

Menu Item	Description
Online Banking Setup ...	Starts the Online banking setup assistant, if Gnu-Cash was built to support on-line banking. the section called "HBCI (Online Banking) Setup Assistant"
Price Editor	Tool to enter or modify Stock/Fund prices. Details at the section called "Price Editor"
Security Editor	Tool to enter or modify Stock or commodities. Details at the section called "Security Editor"
Loan Repayment Calculator	Details at the section called "Loan Repayment Calculator"
Close Book	Open a screen where you can enter the required information to close the current accounting period. See the section called "Close Book".
General Journal	See the section called "General Journal"

Account Tree - Windows Menu

Table 4.8. Account Tree - Windows Menu

Menu Item	Description
New Window	Opens a new GnuCash empty window.
New Window with Page	Moves the current tab into a new window.
Opened windows	A numbered list of open windows.

Account Tree - Help Menu

Table 4.9. Account Tree - Help Menu - Access to this help and the Tutorial and Concepts Guide.

Menu Item	Description
Tutorial & Concepts Guide	Explanation of accounting principles and how to apply them in GnuCash
Tips Of The Day	Shows short notes about features you might otherwise miss.
Contents	Open this document.
About	Show the information screen with GnuCash version, license and credits

Account Tree - *Toolbar* Icons/Buttons

The GnuCash main Window has a number of buttons in the *Toolbar* to quickly access some common functions used with the specific active tab. The *Toolbar* can be hidden or shown by selecting View → Toolbar. The specific options displayed in the *Toolbar* vary with the functions available to the "active tab".

A brief description of the function of a *Toolbar* button is displayed when the mouse pointer is placed over the icon for a couple of seconds.

Table 4.10. Account Tree - Window *Toolbar*

Toolbar Buttons	Description
Save (**Ctrl+S**)	Perform a save on the data file, commit all transactions to the data file.
Close (**Ctrl+W**)	Close the currently active account page **Note** This icon is not available for the first accounts tab. It is available for additional account tree displays.
Open	Open a transaction register of the selected account.
Edit	Edit the characteristics for the selected account. the section called "Editing an Account"
New	Start the assistant for creating a new account. the section called "Creating a New Account"
Delete	Remove the selected account. the section called "Deleting an Account"

Tab bar

The *Tab bar* displays "file/notebook folder" style tabs for open transaction registers, reports and the account tree.

Main pane - Account tree

The account tree displays the list of your accounts in hierarchical format. This enables you to organize your accounts by type.

Tip

The triangle shape (or plus sign) beside the account name is used to open and close the account tree. When you click on the triangle (plus sign), it changes from a rightward-pointing into a downward-pointing sign (minus sign) to indicate that the tree is opened. You will then see offset below the account name either a list of the sub account(s) or another triangle (plus sign) to the left of an account. This indicates another lower level of the account tree.

In the main pane are also shown, by default, four columns: Account Name, Type, Description and Total. For each account, this informations, if available, is displayed in the same row of the account.

Tip

The columns shown for each account in the Account Tree can be customized to suit your needs. Click on the arrow icon on the far right of the Account Tree window to display a drop down list of column options. Click on a column description to add it to the Account Tree window. Click again on the column description to hide it.

The default display for the account tree window is in Notebook mode. This is indicated by the tab in the tab row of the main window. Other tabs will appear beside this one when you open reports, account registers or additional account trees.

Summarybar

The *Summarybar* displays balances appropriate for the opened account type at a glance. Usually accounts display today's account balance, any balance for future dates, a balance for cleared items and a reconciled balance. Stock accounts, however, display shares totals and their value. The *Summarybar* can be hidden or shown by selecting View → Summarybar.

Statusbar

The *Statusbar* displays informations about the currently highlighted menu item. It also shows a progress bar when opening or saving a GnuCash data file or generating reports. The *Statusbar* can be hidden or shown by selecting the Statusbar item on the View menu.

Account Register/General Journal

Account Register & General Journal Window

This window is used to enter and edit your account data. It also provides tools for scheduling future transactions, finding and reporting on transactions and printing checks.

To open the Account Register Window for an account, select the account in the Account Tree then go to File → Open Account or press **Ctrl+O**. This will open a new window with the Account Register. Pressing the Open button on the *Toolbar* in the Account Tree Window or the Jump button in the Account Register Window are alternate methods.

Figure 4.3. The *Account Register* Display.

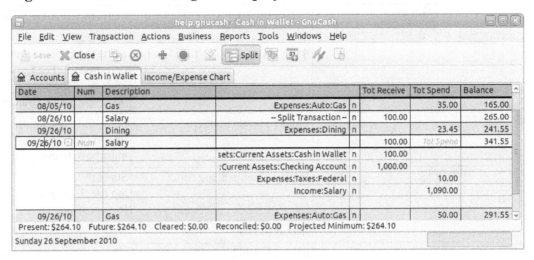

This is an image of the *Account Register* tab.

Tip

Appearance of the Account Register Display is highly customizable (see Tutorial and Concepts Guide, Choosing a Register Style [https://www.gnucash.org/docs/v2.6/C/gnucash-guide/txns-register-oview.html#txns-regstyle1]).

Note

The methods to enter transactions are described in detail in Chapter 6, *Common Transaction Operations*.

Account Register Menus

The *Menubar* for the Transaction Register window contains the following options.

Account Register - File Menu

The following table describes the options in the File.

Clicking on File in the *Menubar* will "pull down" a menu of choices described in Table 4.11, "Account Register - File Menu - Access to file and account operations and printing.".

Table 4.11. Account Register - File Menu - Access to file and account operations and printing.

Menu Item	Description	
New File (**Ctrl+N**)	Creates a new data file (starts with new accounts and data.)	
Open... (**Ctrl+O**)	Opens an already existing GnuCash data file.	
Import →	Opens the Import sub-menu to import files from other financial programs.	
	Import QIF ...	Starts the QIF file Import process.

Menu Item	Description	
	Import OFX/QFX ...	Starts the OFX/QFX file Import process.
	Import Accounts from CSV...	Starts the CSV Account file import process. The file to import must be in the same format as the one exported by GnuCash.
	Import Transactions from CSV...	Starts the CSV Transactions file import process. The file to import must be a delimited file.
	Replay GnuCash .log file...	Starts the replaying of a GnuCash log file. Used for data recovery from "crashes".
	Import MT940	.
	Import MT942	.
	Import DTAUS	.
	Import DTAUS and send	.
	Import Bills & Invoices...	Open the Import Transactions from text file window.
	Import Customers and Vendors ...	Open the Import Customers and Vendors from text file window.
Save (**Ctrl+S**)	Saves the currently open file.	
Save As... (**Shift+Ctrl+S**)	Saves the currently opened file with a different name. ## Warning Do NOT store your data file in ~/.gnucash/books.	
Print Checks... (**Ctrl+P**)	Starts the Print Checks assistant. See the section called "Printing Checks".	
Page Setup... (**Shift+Ctrl+P**)	Let you choose the paper size, layout and margins for printing.	
Export →	Exports ...	
	Export Accounts Tree to CSV	Exports your account hierarchy to a delimited CSV file. Does not export data.
	Export Transactions to CSV	Exports transactions to a delimited CSV file.
	Export Accounts	Exports your account hierarchy to a new GnuCashfile. Does not export data.
Properties (**Alt+Enter**)	Sets options for this GnuCash data file.	
Recently opened files	Numbered list of most recently opened GnuCash data files.	
Close (**Ctrl+W**)	Closes the currently opened transaction register.	
Quit (**Ctrl+Q**)	Exits GnuCash.	

Account Register - Edit Menu

Table 4.12. Account Register - Edit Menu - Access to file and account editing operations and preferences.

Menu Item	Description
Cut (**Ctrl+X**)	Performs a standard *Cut* operation.
Copy (**Ctrl+C**)	Performs a standard *Copy* operation.
Paste (**Ctrl+V**)	Performs a standard *Paste* operation.
Assign as payment...	Assign as payment the selected transaction.
Edit Account	Open form to edit/modify account characteristics and parameters.
Find... (**Ctrl+F**)	Set criteria for a search for a specific transaction. See the section called "Find" for specifics on searches.
Preferences (GnuCash → Preferences on Mac OS X).	Customize GnuCash for location, style, and numerous other preferences. See the section called "Setting Preferences".
Style Sheets	Modify/customize Style Sheets.
Tax Report Options	Set tax characteristics on account(s) (US). Assign tax form and line to account. See the section called "Setting Tax Report Options".

Account Register - View Menu

Table 4.13. Account Register - View Menu - Changes GnuCash display window characteristics.

Menu Item	Description	
Toolbar	Check-box to enable/disable display of *Toolbar*.	
Summarybar	Check-box to enable/disable display of Summary Bar.	
Statusbar	Check-box to enable/disable display of Status Bar.	
Basic Ledger	Radio button to select register display mode. See Tutorial and Concepts Guide, Choosing a Register Style [https://www.gnucash.org/docs/v2.6/C/gnucash-guide/txns-register-oview.html#txns-regstyle1].	
Auto-Split Ledger	Radio button to select register display mode.	
Transaction Journal	Radio button to select register display mode.	
Double Line	Check-box to enable/disable display of Double Line display.	
Sort by...	Set the sort order of the transactions display. Requires a click to start options form. Option form requires Cancel/OK to close.	
	Standard Order	Keep normal account order
	Date	Sort by date
	Date of Entry	Sort by date of entry.

Menu Item	Description	
	Statement Date	Sort by the statement date (unreconciled items last).
	Number	Sort by number.
	Amount	Sort by amount.
	Memo	Sort by memo.
	Description	Sort by Description.
	Action	Sort by action field.
	Notes	Sort by notes field.
	Reverse Order	Reverse the sort order.
	Save Sort Order	Save the sort order between sessions.
Filter by ...	Set filtering for accounts displayed in the Account Tree or transactions in Register display.	
Refresh (**Ctrl+R**)	Repaint the display screen.	
New Accounts Page	Open a new tab that displays the account tree.	

Account Register - Transaction Menu

Table 4.14. Account Register - Transaction Menu - access to transaction tools.

Menu Item	Description
Cut Transaction	Cut the selected transaction into the clipboard.
Copy Transaction	Copy the selected transaction into the clipboard.
Paste Transaction	Paste the selected transaction from the clipboard.
Duplicate Transaction	Insert in the register a copy of the selected transaction.
Delete Transaction	Delete the selected transaction.
Remove Other Splits	Remove all splits from the selected transaction.
Enter Transaction	Enter in the register the transaction you are currently working on.
Cancel Transaction	Blanks all fields in the selected transaction if it has not yet been recorded.
Void Transaction	Void the selected transaction.
Unvoid Transaction	Unvoid the selected transaction.
Add Reversing Transaction	Add a copy of the selected transaction with an inverted amount.
Associate File with Transaction	Associate a file with the selected transaction.
Associate Location with Transaction	Associate a URL with the selected transaction.
Open Associated File/Location	Open the file or location associated with the transaction. Available if a file or location was associated with the currently selected transaction.

Account Register - Actions Menu

Table 4.15. Account Register - Actions Menu - Setup scheduled transactions, repair accounts, perform stock splits, transfer and reconcile transactions.

Menu Item	Description	
Online Actions →	This menu item (and sub-menu) is shown only if Online Banking was enabled for GnuCash	
	Get Balance	
	Get Transactions	Download transactions from online accounts
	Issue Transaction...	Upload transaction(s) to online account ??
	Issue SEPA Transaction...	
	Internal Transaction...	
	Direct Debit...	
	Show log window...	Open the Online Banking Connection Window
Scheduled Transactions →	Scheduled Transactions sub-menus	
	Scheduled Transaction Editor	Invoke tool to edit scheduled transactions. See the section called "Edit Scheduled Transaction Window"
	Since Last Run...	Display Scheduled transactions since last running of GnuCash. the section called "Since Last Run Assistant"
	Mortgage & Loan Repayment...	Starts the Mortgage & Loan Repayment assistant for setting up repayments. the section called "Mortgage & Loan Repayment Assistant"
Budget →	Budget sub-menus	
	New Budget	Opens the window to create a new budget.
	Open Budget	Opens an existing budget.
	Copy Budget	Copy a budget.
Transfer... (**Ctrl+T**)	Starts the Transfer assistant for transfer between accounts.	
Reconcile...	Start the Reconcile process for the selected account. the section called "Reconciling an Account to a Statement"	
Stock Split...	Starts the Stock Split assistant. Additional details the section called "Recording a Stock Split"	
View Lots...	Opens the Lots in Account form.	
Blank Transaction	Move to the blank transaction at the bottom of the register	

Menu Item	Description	
Split Transaction	Expand the currently selected transaction to show splits.	
Edit Exchange Rate	Edit the exchange rate for the current transaction.	
Schedule...	Create a Scheduled Transaction with the current transaction as a template.	
Jump	Jump to the corresponding transaction in the other account.	
Check & Repair →	Check & Repair Submenus	
	All Transactions	Check for and repair unbalanced transactions and orphan splits in this account.
	This Transaction	Check for and repair splits in this transaction.
Reset Warnings...	GnuCash gives warnings when certain operations are attempted, such as removing a transaction or removing the splits of a transaction. The warning message gives you the option to not give you these warnings when attempting the operation. Check-boxes labeled Remember and don't ask me again and Remember and don't ask me again this session allow disabling the warnings. This option resets the warnings to the default, i.e. display all warnings. **Tip** Warnings may be selectively enabled.	
Rename Page	Open the form to rename the current page/tab.	

Account Register - Business Menu

The items shown in the Business menu are the same as listed in Table 4.5, "Account Tree - Business Menu - Access small business features of GnuCash.".

Account Register - Reports Menu

The items shown in the Reports menu are the same as listed in Table 4.6, "Account Tree - Reports Menu - Access GnuCash Reports and Charts." plus the two types of report listed in the following.

- Account report

- Account Transaction Report

Account Register - Tools Menu

The items shown in the Tools menu are the same as listed in Table 4.7, "Account Tree - Tools Menu - Access to miscellaneous tools and editors".

Account Register - Windows Menu

The items shown in the Windows menu are the same as listed in Table 4.8, "Account Tree - Windows Menu".

Account Register - Help Menu

The items shown in the Help menu are the same as listed in Table 4.9, "Account Tree - Help Menu - Access to this help and the Tutorial and Concepts Guide.".

Account Register - *Toolbar* Icons/Buttons

The GnuCash main Window has a number of icons/buttons in the *Toolbar* to quickly access some common functions used with the specific active tab. The *Toolbar* can be hidden or shown by selecting the Toolbar item on the View menu.

Note

The specific options displayed in the *Toolbar* varies by the functions available to the active tab.

A brief description of the function of a button is displayed when the mouse pointer is placed over the button for a couple of seconds.

Table 4.16. Account Register (Transaction Register) Window *Toolbar*

Toolbar Buttons	Description
Save (**Ctrl+S**)	Perform a save on the data file, commit all transactions to the data file.
Close	Close this register.
Duplicate	Make a copy of the current transaction.
Delete	Delete the current transaction in this register.
Enter	Record the current transaction.
Cancel	Cancel the current transaction.
Blank	Move to a blank transaction at bottom of register.
Split	Show all splits in the current transaction. Not highlighted if View → Auto-Split Ledger is enableb.
Jump	Jump to the corresponding transaction in the other account
Schedule	Create a Scheduled Transaction with the current transaction as a template.
Transfer	Start the transfer assistant to transfer funds from one account to another.
Reconcile	Start the Reconcile process for the selected account. the section called "Reconciling an Account to a Statement"

Tab Bar

The *Tab bar* displays "notebook/file folder" style tabs for open transaction registers, account trees and reports.

List of Transactions

The List of Transactions displays transactions you have entered and a running balance. It also provides a blank transaction to enter new transactions. The column headings vary according to what type of account you have opened. Common headings are Date, Description, Transfer and Balance.

The View menu can be used to alter the appearance of the List of Transactions. Possible changes are limiting the number of transactions shown, using a different sort order and changing the style to more easily see transactions. The Split button also provides quick access to view all the parts of a transaction.

Summarybar

The *Summarybar* displays balances appropriate for the opened account type at a glance. Usually accounts display Present (today's) account balance, any balance for Future dates, a balance for Cleared items, a Reconciled balance and a Projected Minimum balance. Stock accounts, however, display shares totals and their value. The *Summarybar* can be hidden or shown by selecting the View → Summarybar item.

Statusbar

The *Statusbar* works the same as described in the section called "Statusbar".

Report Window

Report Display Window

This window is shown whenever a report or chart is selected from the Reports menu.

To open the report window, select a report from the Reports item in the *Menubar*. This will open a new window with the report displayed. It provides a web browser type display with active links to account data.

Note

Depending on the report there may be a delay while the report is generated. An approximation of the progress to completion is displayed in the *Statusbar*, if has not been opted out of displaying.

Figure 4.4. The *Report Window*

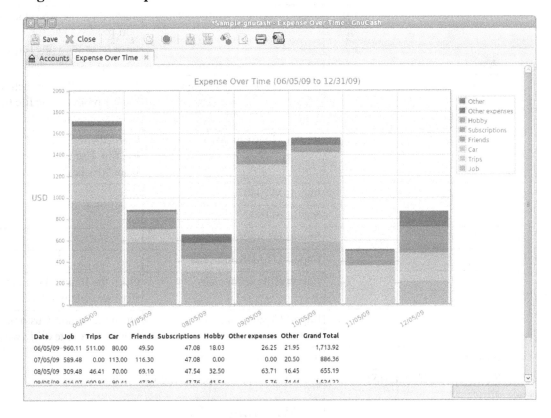

This is an image of the Income/Expense Chart.

Report Menus

The *Menubar* for the report window contains the following options.

Reports - File Menu

The following table describes the options in the File Menu.

Clicking on the File option of the *Menubar* will "pull down" a menu of options described in Table 4.17, "Report - File Menu - Access to file and account operations and printing.".

Table 4.17. Report - File Menu - Access to file and account operations and printing.

Menu Item	Description	
New File (**Ctrl+N**)	Creates a new data file (starts with new accounts and data.)	
Open... (**Ctrl+O**)	Opens an already existing GnuCash data file.	
Import →	Opens the Import sub-menu to import files from other financial programs.	
	Import QIF ...	Starts the QIF file Import process.
	Import OFX/QFX ...	Starts the OFX/QFX file Import process.

Menu Item	Description	
	Import Accounts from CSV...	Starts the CSV Account file import process. The file to import must be in the same format as the one exported by GnuCash.
	Import Transactions from CSV...	Starts the CSV Transactions file import process. The file to import must be a delimited file.
	Replay GnuCash .log file...	Starts the replaying of a GnuCash log file. Used for data recovery from "crashes".
	Import MT940	.
	Import MT942	.
	Import DTAUS	.
	Import DTAUS and send	.
	Import Bills & Invoices...	Open the Import Transactions from text file window.
	Import Customers and Vendors ...	Open the Import Customers and Vendors from text file window.
Save (**Ctrl+S**)	Saves the currently open file.	
Save As... (**Shift+Ctrl+S**)	Saves the currently opened file with a different name. ## Warning Do NOT store your data file in `~/.gnucash/books`.	
Revert	Reload the last saved version of the currently opened file. Useful if you need to discard changes made to the data and not yet saved.	
Print Report... (**Ctrl+P**)	Print the selected report.	
Page Setup... (**Shift+Ctrl+P**)	Let you choose the paper size, layout and margins for printing.	
Export as PDF →	Exports the displayed report as a PDF file.	
Export →	Opens the Export sub-menu.	
	Export Accounts Tree to CSV	Exports your account hierarchy to a delimited CSV file. Does not export data.
	Export Transactions to CSV	Exports transactions to a delimited CSV file.
	Export Report	Export the current report in an HTML formatted file.
	Export Accounts	Exports your account hierarchy to a new GnuCashfile. Does not export data.
Properties (**Alt+Enter**)	Sets options for this GnuCash data file.	
Recently opened files	Numbered list of most recently opened GnuCash data files.	
Close (**Ctrl+W**)	Closes the current report.	

Menu Item	Description
Quit (**Ctrl+Q**)	Exits GnuCash.

Report - Edit Menu

Table 4.18. Reports - Edit Menu - Access to file and account editing operations and preferences.

Menu Item	Description
Cut (**Ctrl+X**)	Performs a standard *Cut* operation.
Copy (**Ctrl+C**)	Performs a standard *Copy* operation.
Paste (**Ctrl+V**)	Performs a standard *Paste* operation.
Find... (**Ctrl+F**)	Set criteria for a search for a specific transaction. See the section called "Find" for specifics on searches.
Preferences (GnuCash → Preferences on Mac OS X).	Customize GnuCash for location, style, and numerous other preferences. See the section called "Setting Preferences".
Style Sheets	Modify/customize Style Sheets.
Report Options	Open form to edit/modify report selection criteria, stylesheets, date ranges, and many other parameters.
Tax Report Options	Set tax characteristics on account(s) (US). Assign tax form and line to account. See the section called "Setting Tax Report Options".

Report - View Menu

Except Filter By..., the items shown in the View menu are the same as listed in Table 4.3, "Account Tree - View Menu - Changes display window view."

Report - Actions Menu

Table 4.19. Reports - Actions Menu - Setup scheduled transactions.

Menu Item	Description	
Online Actions →	This menu item (and sub-menu) is shown only if Online Banking was enabled for GnuCash	
	Show log window...	Open the Online Banking Connection Window
Scheduled Transactions →	Scheduled Transactions sub-menus	
	Scheduled Transaction Editor	Invoke tool to edit scheduled transactions. See the section called "Edit Scheduled Transaction Window"
	Since Last Run...	Display Scheduled transactions since last running of GnuCash.

Menu Item	Description	
		the section called "Since Last Run Assistant"
	Mortgage & Loan Repayment...	Starts the Mortgage & Loan Repayment assistant for setting up repayments. the section called "Mortgage & Loan Repayment Assistant"
Budget →	Budget sub-menus	
	New Budget	Opens the window to create a new budget.
	Open Budget	Opens an existing budget.
	Copy Budget	Copy a budget.
Reset Warnings...	GnuCash gives warnings when certain operations are attempted, such as removing a transaction or removing the splits of a transaction. The warning message gives you the option to not give you these warnings when attempting the operation. Check-boxes labeled Remember and don't ask me again and Remember and don't ask me again this session allow disabling the warnings. This option resets the warnings to the default, This option resets the warnings to the default, i.e. display all warnings. **Tip** Warnings may be selectively enabled.	
Rename Page	Lets you type a new name for the current page or tab.	

Report - Business Menu

The items shown in the Business menu are the same as listed in Table 4.5, "Account Tree - Business Menu - Access small business features of GnuCash.".

Report - Reports Menu

The items shown in the Reports menu are the same as listed in Table 4.6, "Account Tree - Reports Menu - Access GnuCash Reports and Charts." with the addition of:

Table 4.20. Report - Reports Menu.

Menu Item	Description
Save Report Configuration	Save the current report configuration. If you are not working with a saved report configuration, you will be asked to give it a name. You will be able to run the exact same report again by using the Reports → Saved Report Configurations menu item.
Save Report Configuration As...	Save the current report configuration with a new name.

Report - Tools Menu

The items shown in the Tools menu are the same as listed in Table 4.7, "Account Tree - Tools Menu - Access to miscellaneous tools and editors".

Report - Windows Menu

The items shown in the Windows menu are the same as listed in Table 4.8, "Account Tree - Windows Menu".

Report - Help Menu

The items shown in the Help menu are the same as listed in Table 4.9, "Account Tree - Help Menu - Access to this help and the Tutorial and Concepts Guide.".

Reports - *Toolbar* Icons/Buttons

The Report Window has a *Toolbar* to quickly access the functions used with reports. The *Toolbar* can be hidden or shown by selecting View → Toolbar.

Table 4.21. Reports - *Toolbar* Buttons

Toolbar Button	Description
Save (**Ctrl+S**)	
Close (**Ctrl+W**)	Closes the displayed report.
Back	Move back one step in the history.
Forward	Move forward one step in the history.
Reload	Reload (rerun) current report.
Stop	Stops the HTML requests.
Save Report Configuration	Saves the displayed report. You will be able to run the exact same report again by using the Reports → Saved Report Configurations menu item.
Save Report Configuration As...	Saves the displayed report in a configuration file with a given name. You will then be able to run the exact same report again by using the Reports → Saved Report Configurations menu item.
Export	Exports HTML formatted report to a file.
Options	Edit options specific to selected report.
Print (**Ctrl+P**)	Queues the current report for printing.
Export as PDF	Exports the selected report as a PDF file.

Tab Bar

The *Tab bar* displays "notebook/file folder"-style tabs for open transaction registers, account trees and reports.

Report Main Display

This is where the report or chart you have selected is shown. The properties of this window are editable in two ways. Selecting the Options button on the *Toolbar* lets you edit what the report is showing and which accounts the information is drawn from. Selecting Edit → Style Sheets... lets you select the properties of the page that displays your report.

The report is able to act like a web browser if your report contains links to external web pages. The *Toolbar* buttons allow you to move Back and Forward through web pages. It will also open account registers when you click on links to accounts contained in the report.

You can also Export your report to a file and Print the report through the *Toolbar* buttons.

Summarybar

The *Summarybar* is not displayed when viewing a report window.

Statusbar

The *Statusbar* works the same as described in the section called "Statusbar".

Reconcile Window

To simplify navigation the following are the topics covered in this section; the section called "Reconcile Display Window", the section called "Menus", the section called "*Toolbar* Buttons".

The detailed explanation of reconciling an account is described in the section called "Reconciling an Account to a Statement".

Reconcile Display Window

To open the Reconcile window, click Actions → Reconcile... from the *Menubar* or the Reconcile button from the *Toolbar* in a register window. This will open a Reconcile screen in which you need to enter the Statement Date and the Ending Balance. If you select the Include subaccounts option, all transactions in the subaccounts of the selected account will also be counted for the reconcile operation. Pressing the OK button will open a Reconcile window allowing you to compare deposit and withdrawal transactions to your statement.

Table 4.22. Components of the Reconcile Window.

Component	Description
Menubar	Contains the Menus used in the Reconcile Window.
Toolbar (Icons and/or Text)	Contains buttons used to access common Reconcile Account Window tasks.
Funds In	This pane in the left contains a list of funds deposited in the account.
Funds Out	This pane in the right contains a list of funds withdrawn from the account.
Balance Pane	This pane in the lower right contains a list of balances useful for reconciling.

Menus

The following tables describe menus in the Reconcile Window.

Table 4.23. Reconcile Menu - Access to Reconcile Information and finishing or postponing.

Menu Item	Description
Reconcile Information...	Opens the Reconciling Information Window.
Finish (**Ctrl+F**)	Complete the reconciliation of this account.
Postpone (**Ctrl+P**)	Postpone the reconciliation of this account.
Cancel	Cancel the reconciliation of this account.

Table 4.24. Account Menu - Access to account operations.

Menu Item	Description
Open Account	Opens a transaction register for the accounts
Edit Account	Modify name or characteristic of selected account. the section called "Editing an Account"
Transfer... (**Ctrl+T**)	Opens a Transfer assistant for entering a transfer transaction between any two accounts.
Check & Repair	Verify and repair this account if necessary.

Table 4.25. Transaction Menu - Access to transaction editing operations.

Menu Item	Description
New	Add a new transaction to the account.
Balance	Opens the account's register window with a pre-compiled balancing transaction.
Edit	Edit the currently selected transaction.
Delete	Remove the currently selected transaction.

Table 4.26. Help Menu - Access to help.

Menu Item	Description
Help	Open this Help text file.

Toolbar Buttons

The Reconcile window has a *Toolbar* to quickly access some common functions used with reconciliation.

Table 4.27. Reconcile Window *Toolbar*

Toolbar Button	Description
New	Add a new transaction to the account.
Balance	Opens the account's register window with a pre-compiled balancing transaction.
Edit	Edit the currently selected transaction.
Delete	Remove the currently selected transaction.
Open	Open an Account transaction window.

Toolbar Button	Description
Finish	Complete the reconciliation of this account. **Note** This button is not active (grayed out) until the Difference value in the balance pane (lower right) is 0.
Postpone	Postpone the reconciliation of this account.
Cancel	Cancel the reconciliation of this account.

Schedule Transaction Window

To simplify navigation the following are the topics covered in this section; the section called "Scheduled Menu", the section called "Scheduled Transactions *Toolbar* Buttons", the section called "Scheduled Transactions Window". the section called "Edit Scheduled Transaction Window",

The detailed explanation of scheduling transactions is described in the section called "Scheduling Transactions".

Scheduled Transactions Main Display Window

This window is shown when Actions → Scheduled Transactions → Scheduled Transactions Editor is selected from the *Menubar*. This will open a new tab window with the Scheduled Transactions displayed.

Scheduled Transaction Main Window Components

Table 4.28. Components of the Schedule Transactions Window.

Component	Description
Menubar	Contains the Menus used in the Schedule Transactions Window. It provides the standard list of *Menubar* options and an additional option, Scheduled, which presents options; New, Edit or Delete. If no transaction is highlighted Edit and Delete will be "grayed out".
Toolbar (Icons and/or Text)	Contains buttons used to access Schedule Transitions tasks.
Tabs	Tabs to switch between open displays.
Transactions	The Transactions pane contains a list of transactions scheduled and related characteristics.
Upcoming	The Upcoming pane contains a calendar of the next months In this calendar the days in which one or more transactions are scheduled, are highlighted with a circle. You can change the time interval displayed in the calendar by selecting a different period from the View: drop down list on the right.

Component	Description
	Tip Click on a date in the pane and the details about the scheduled transactions on that date will be displayed.

Scheduled Menu

The following table describe the Scheduled menu options available in the *Menubar* when you are in the Scheduled Transaction window.

Table 4.29. Scheduled Menu - Access to scheduled transaction editing operations.

Menu Item	Description
New	Add a new scheduled transaction.
Edit	Edit the currently selected transaction.
Delete	Remove the currently selected transaction.

Scheduled Transactions *Toolbar* Buttons

The Scheduled Transactions window has a *Toolbar* to quickly access some common functions used with scheduling.

Table 4.30. Scheduled Transactions Window *Toolbar*

Toolbar Button	Description
Save (**Ctrl+S**)	Save the current schedule of transactions.
Close (**Ctrl+W**)	Close the Scheduled Transactions window.
New	Add a new scheduled transaction.
Edit	Edit the currently selected transaction.
Delete	Remove the currently selected transaction.

Budget Window

Actions → Budget → Open Budget will open the default budget or offer you a choice if there is more than one budget. A new tab will open with the budget displayed.

Budget Window Menus

Here are some menu items that are particularly useful to working with budgets.

Budget Window - Edit menu

Table 4.31. Edit Menu - Special items for the budget window.

Menu Item	Description
Estimate Budget	Estimate a budget value for the selected accounts from past transactions.

Menu Item	Description
Delete Budget	Delete this budget.
Budget Options	Edit this budget's options.

Budget Window - Actions menu

Table 4.32. Actions Menu - Items in the standard menu that relate to budgets.

Menu Item	Description	
Budget →	Opens the Budget sub-menu to select budget actions.	
	New Budget	Create a new budget and open it in a new tab.
	Open Budget	If no budget exists, create a new budget and open it. If only one budget exists, open it; otherwise user selects one to open.
	Copy Budget	If no budgets exist yet, just open a new budget. If only one budget exists, create a copy of it; otherwise user selects one to copy. If a copy is made, then the copy is opened in a new tab.

Budget Window - Reports menu

Using more than one budget

When there is more than one budget, the reports will use the budget selected in book options by default. See the section called "Book Options" and the section called "Budgeting Book Options Tab" for more details. After the report is displayed, the budget it uses can be changed in the report options General tab.

Table 4.33. Reports Menu - Items in the standard menu that relate to budgets.

Menu Item	Description	
Budget →	Opens the Budget sub-menu to select a budget report.	
	Budget Balance Sheet	
	Budget Barchart	
	Budget Flow	This report includes information from one budget period at a time. The left column of numbers shows the budgeted amounts, and the right column of numbers shows the actual amounts. It only shows certain accounts, those that have no sub-accounts.
	Budget Income Statement	

Menu Item	Description	
	Budget Profit & Loss	This report is identical to the Budget Income Statement report.
	Budget Report	The budget report shows all accounts and all periods. For each period it gives the budgeted amount and the actual amount. There is an option to add another column showing the difference (budgeted - actual).

Budget Window Toolbar Buttons

The Budget window has a *Toolbar* to quickly access common functions used with budgeting.

Table 4.34. Budget Window *Toolbar*

Toolbar Button	Description
Save (**Ctrl+S**)	Save the current budget.
Close (**Ctrl+W**)	Close the Budget window.
Options	Edit this budget's options.
Estimate	Estimate a budget value for the selected accounts from past transactions.
Delete	Delete this budget.

Budget Window Main Display

The budget window contains a list of accounts down the left hand side, and a set of columns down the right hand side that represent budget values. Each column corresponds to a budget *period*. The number of periods for a budget can be changed using the Budget Options dialog.

Procedure 4.1. Entering a budget value

1. *Click* the row corresponding to the account you wish to budget

2. Choose the period this value is for, and *click* in the cell corresponding to that period

3. Type the value in the cell

4. Press **Enter** to finish editing the value.

Budget Options

Table 4.35. Budget options

Option	Description
Budget Name	The budget name is used in the tab's name and also in any reports you create with the budget.

Option	Description
Notes	A description of the budget.
Budget Period	The budget period includes when the budget starts (start date) and how long each budget period lasts.
Number of Periods	The number of periods in the budget.

Business Windows

Customers Overview

To open the Customers Overview window, click Business → Customer → Customers Overview.

Table 4.36. Customers Overview - Toolbar Buttons

Toolbar Buttons	Description
New	Create a new customer
Edit	Edit the selected customer
New Invoice	Create a new invoice (by default it is for the selected customer)
Customer Listing	Show customer aging overview for all customers

Table 4.37. Customer context menu

Context menu item	Description
Rename Page	
Edit Customer	Edit the selected customer
New Invoice	Create a new invoice
Customer Report	Show customer report

Note

The customer context menu appears if you right click on a customer in the list.

Vendors Overview

To open the Vendors Overview window, click Business → Vendor → Vendors Overview.

Table 4.38. Vendors Overview - Toolbar Buttons

Toolbar Buttons	Description
New	Create a new vendor
Edit	Edit the selected vendor
New Bill	Create a new bill (by default it is for the selected vendor)
Vendor Listing	Show vendor aging overview for all vendors

Table 4.39. Vendor context menu

Context menu item	Description
Rename Page	
Edit Vendor	Edit the selected vendor
New Bill	Create a new bill
Vendor Report	Show vendor report

Note

The vendor context menu appears if you right click on a vendor in the list.

Employees Overview

To open the Employees Overview window, click Business → Employee → Employees Overview.

Table 4.40. Employees Overview - Toolbar Buttons

Toolbar Buttons	Description
New	Create a new employee
Edit	Edit the selected employee
New Voucher	Create a new voucher (by default it is for the selected employee)

Table 4.41. Employee context menu

Context menu item	Description
Rename Page	
Edit Employee	Edit the selected employee
New Voucher	Create a new voucher
Employee Report	Show employee report

Note

The employee context menu appears if you right click on an employee in the list.

Chapter 5. Setting Up, Editing & Working with Accounts

This section describes the process of setting up, editing and working with GnuCash Accounts. In GnuCash an Account is used as the basic tool to organize the recording of where money comes from and goes to. GnuCash also extends the concept of real world accounts such as a bank account or loan account to grouping income and expense accounts. This allows you to quickly see where you spent your money and what your major income and expenses are. GnuCash sets Account Types (as described in the next section) to help in organizing and grouping accounts. Account Types can be used to create a Chart of Accounts.

Types of GnuCash Accounts

GnuCash supports a number of different account types. It is recommended to choose an appropriate account type based on the list of account types described below.

Warning

The Accounts Payable and Accounts Receivable types are used internally by GnuCash's business features. Transactions involving these accounts should not be added, changed or deleted in any way other than by using

- post/unpost bill/invoice/voucher or

- process payment

Table 5.1. Types of GnuCash Accounts.

Account Type	Description
Accounts Payable	Accounts Payable are used by businesses to record amounts that must be paid. Example: The business has bought something, but the business has not paid the bill until later. **Note** Previous versions of this help defined A/P and A/R the other way round.
Accounts Receivable	Accounts Receivable records amounts for which money has not yet been received. Example: A business has sold something and issued a bill, but the client has not payed until later. **Note** Previous versions of this help defined A/P and A/R the other way round.
Asset	Asset accounts are used for tracking things that are of value and can be used or sold to pay debts. (Normally a placeholder account)

Account Type	Description
Bank	The Bank account type denotes savings or checking accounts held at a bank or other financial institution. Some of these accounts may bear interest. This is also the appropriate account type for check (debit) cards, which directly withdraw payments from a checking account.
Cash	The Cash account type is used to denote the cash that you store in your wallet, shoe box, piggyback, or mattress.
Credit Card	The Credit Card account type is used to denote credit card accounts, both for cards that allow floating lines of credit (e.g. VISA, MasterCard, or Discover) and with cards that do not permit continuing balances (e.g. American Express)
Currency	Currency Accounts were used for trading currencies, but have been replaced by the Currency Transfer pane on the Transfer Funds Window (the section called "Transfer Funds Dialog Box").
Equity	Equity accounts are used to store the opening balances when you first start using GnuCash or start a new accounting period.
Expense	Any expense such as food, clothing, taxes, etc. This type is called a category in Quicken.
Income	Any income received from sources such as salary, interest, dividends, etc. This type is called a category in Quicken.
Liability	Liability accounts are used for tracking debts or financial obligations. (Normally a placeholder account)
Mutual Fund	A professionally managed portfolio of stocks and bonds or other investments divided up into shares.
Stock	A share of ownership in a corporation, which entitles its owner to all the risks and rewards that go with it.

The **New Account Hierarchy Setup** assistant described in the first section of this help is a convenient way of setting up a set of accounts to use as a framework of account types.

When new accounts are created the available choices of account types are grayed out according to what type the parent account is. The following list contains the possible choices.

- Accounts Payable: All accounts except Equity, Expense and Income can be child accounts.

- Accounts Receivable: All accounts except Equity, Expense and Income can be child accounts.

- Asset: All accounts except Equity, Expense and Income can be child accounts.

- Bank: All accounts except Equity, Expense and Income can be child accounts.

- Cash: All accounts except Equity, Expense and Income can be child accounts.

- Credit Card: All accounts except Equity, Expense and Income can be child accounts.

- Currency: All accounts except Equity, Expense and Income can be child accounts.

- Equity: Only Equity accounts can be child accounts.

- Expense: Only Expense or Income accounts can be child accounts.

- Income: Only Expense or Income accounts can be child accounts.

- Liability: All accounts except Equity, Expense and Income can be child accounts.

- Mutual Fund: All accounts except Equity, Expense and Income can be child accounts.

- Stock: All accounts except Equity, Expense and Income can be child accounts.

Creating a Chart of Accounts

The Chart of Accounts is like a table of contents for your finances. The best way to conceptualize a chart of accounts is as a tree. The main branches represent entire categories or groups, while the leaves of the tree denote individual bank accounts or expense categories. When a summary report is requested, typically only the main branches are shown in the report, rather than the individual accounts. For example, a chart of accounts might look like the following:

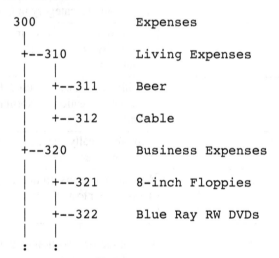

```
300              Expenses
 |
 +--310          Living Expenses
 |   |
 |   +--311      Beer
 |   |
 |   +--312      Cable
 |
 +--320          Business Expenses
 |   |
 |   +--321      8-inch Floppies
 |   |
 |   +--322      Blue Ray RW DVDs
 |   |
 :   :
```

Accounts codes

Note that accounts not only have names; they may have codes, to order the accounts. When a report is generated, the sort order is determined by the numbering. It's customary to have the leaf accounts end in non-zero digits, while parent nodes have increasing numbers of zeros.

Warning

GnuCash does not prevent duplicate numbering, although we would encourage you to avoid this. Account codes are treated as numbers in base-36, thus, if you run out of numbers, you can use the letters, a through z.

Editing a Chart of Accounts

Editing the Chart of Accounts is done within the Parent Account pane of the Edit Account dialog. It is possible to move an account to any part of the Chart of Accounts. It is recommended to keep accounts generally under the related types of accounts as described in the section called "Types of GnuCash Accounts". This helps to preserve the Chart of Accounts structure.

To move the selected account to a different parent account just select the account in the Parent Account pane. If New top level account is selected then the account will be moved to the top level.

Creating a New Account

To create a new account go to Actions → New Account... or click the New *Toolbar* icon in the Account Tree Window. The New Account dialog will be opened.

The New Account properties dialog consists of two tabs, the General tab and the Opening Balance tab.

Creating a New Account involves planning in advance several details that are used in the New Account dialog.

- What type of account is needed.

- Where it fits in the structure of the Chart of Accounts.

- If there is an Opening Balance.

- If there is a Commodity (security/currency) needed for the account.

- If on-line updating of the commodity price is needed.

These details are described below.

General Information Tab

The General tab is used to access the basic information about the account. It provides a way of connecting the account to stock information if it is one of the currency, mutual fund or stock account types. It can also be flagged as a Placeholder account. It displays if it is flagged as a Tax Related account (which is set through the Edit → Tax Report Options dialog).

There are seven fields in the Identification section of this tab.

1. Account Name: The name for the account such as First Bank Checking.

2. Account Code: The optional number code as described in Accounts codes.

3. Description: Optional description for the account.

4. Security/Currency:

Note

The Type field in the Select Security is determined by the selection of Account Type panel in the New Account screen.

- For accounts other than *Stock* or *Mutual Fund* this should be the default currency, USD (US Dollar) or your local currency symbol. If this account is for a foreign currency then use the Select... button to choose a different currency from the currencies pull-down list.

- For Accounts containing a *Stock* and *Mutual Fund*; first select stock or mutual fund in the Account Type panel, then the Parent Account, then use the Select... button, to choose the Type (usually the exchange the security is traded on) and security from the Select Security window.

  If the required security/fund is not on the list, and you have the correct Type you will need to create the security/fund. To create a commodity for mutual fund and stock accounts select the New... button in the Select Security screen, to bring up the New Security: screen. The options are described in detail in the Security Editor the section called "Security Editor" section. Fill in a name, symbol and type and Close to create the security. After the security is created select the Type: (usually the exchange the security is traded on) and the name in the Currency/security: drop down list and Close the screen.

5. Smallest Fraction: The smallest fraction that will be tracked.

6. Account Color: The color to assign to the account's register tab. Click on the color button to open the Pick a Color screen. To reset the account color click the Default button.

7. Notes: This is a free form text box that can be used for any additional notes about the account.

Below the panes are 3 check-boxes: one to show if the account is Tax Related, one to mark the account as a Placeholder, and one to mark an account Hidden.

The Tax Related check-box means that an account has been flagged to be included in the Tax Schedule Report. This flag is only displayed on the Edit Account dialog and is set in the Income Tax Information dialog (Edit → Tax Report Options). See the Tax Schedule Report and TXF Export section in Reports Chapter (the section called "General Reports").

The Placeholder check-box sets an account to read-only status and prevents the addition of transaction data to the account.

Note

Setting an account to Placeholder will also hide that account in the pop-up account list in a register. Sub-accounts to the placeholder account will still display in the pop-up, however.

The Hidden check box hides an account (and any sub-accounts) in the account tree. To reset this option, you will first need to open the View → Filter By... dialog for the account tree and check the Show hidden accounts option. Doing so will allow you to select the account and reopen this dialog.

Note

Hidden accounts still appear in the pop-up account list in a register. To remove an account from this pop-up account list as well, check the Placeholder check box.

Below these checkboxes is a pane that contains a list of Account Types. Select a type from the descriptions in the section called "Types of GnuCash Accounts".

The next pane contains an account tree to choose a Parent Account. To create a new account tree select New top level account.

Note

The available choices in the Account Type pane depends on the selected account in the Parent Account pane. For example if the Parent Account is *Assets* you will see only *Equity* in the Account Type pane. This is to help maintain a proper account structure for the Chart of Accounts.

Steps to enable On-line price updating

- GnuCash relies on an external tool to retrieve online quotes. This tool is a Perl module named "Finance::Quote" and has to be installed on your computer independently from GnuCash. The first step in enabling online price updating should thus be to ensure Finance::Quote is properly installed.

  To determine if the Perl module Finance::Quote is already installed on your system, type "perldoc Finance::Quote" in a terminal window and check to see if there is any documentation available. If you see the documentation, then the module is installed, if you do not see the documentation, then it has not been installed.

  Installing Finance::Quote differs from one operating system to another. For the various supported systems, you can follow these guidelines:

  - Linux: Most linux distributions (like Fedora, openSuse, Mandriva, Ubuntu, and so on) have a package in their software repositories for the Finance::Quote perl module. So in most cases, you can simply use your preferred package manager (yum, apt, rpm, synaptics, yast,...) to install the module. The name of the package may vary from one distribution to another. It's often called something like "perl-Finance-Quote".

  - Windows: Finance::Quote on Windows requires perl to be installed already. If you haven't done so, you should first install ActivePerl, or more recently, Strawberry Perl.

    The Windows installer from the GnuCash home page comes with a small helper program to install Finance::Quote for you. You can find it in the Start Menu under the GnuCash group and is called "Install Online Price Retrieval".

  - Mac OS X: If you have installed GnuCash from the installer found on the GnuCash home page, Finance::Quote is already installed for you.

  - If none of the above applies to your setup, you can try these alternative, more generic instructions:

    1. Close any GnuCash applications you have running.

    2. Locate the folder where GnuCash is installed by searching for "gnc-fq-update" (without the quotes).

    3. Change to that directory, open a root shell and run the command "gnc-fq-update" (without the quotation marks). This will launch a Perl CPAN update session that will go out onto the Internet and install the Finance::Quote module on your system. The gnc-fq-update program is interactive, however, with most systems you should be able to answer "no" to the first question: "Are you ready for manual configuration? [yes]" and the update will continue automatically from that point.

  After installation is complete, you should run the "gnc-fq-dump" test program, in the same directory, distributed with GnuCash to test if Finance::Quote is installed and working properly.

Note

If you feel uncomfortable about performing any of these steps, please either email the Gnu-Cash-user mailing list (`<gnucash-user@gnucash.org>`) for help or come to the Gnu-Cash IRC channel on irc.gnome.org. More information is available on the GnuCash Wiki FAQ for example http://wiki.gnucash.org/wiki/FAQ#Q:_How_do_I_fix_a_.22system_error.22_or_.22unknown_error.22_when_getting_stock_quotes.3F You can also leave out this step and manually update your stock prices.

• Create the Account for the mutual fund or stock with it listed in the Security/Currency field, as described above.

Tip

When creating these accounts it is a good time to create income accounts to track dividends, capital gains (long and short) and expense account(s) for tracking commissions and losses (if you track losses as expenses).

• Create the mutual fund or stock with either the Security Editor for existing stock/funds or the New Security/Currency dialog for a new stock/fund.

Select Get On-line Quotes:, Type of Quote Source and Timezone.

Online currency quotes require that the check-box for Online quotes and the timezone be selected in the Security screen and the Security Editor check-box for "get quote" box is checked for those currencies that are to be downloaded.

• Get On-line Quotes: This check-box is to enable this security/fund to have quotes downloaded from an on-line source.

• Type of Quote Source use the radio buttons to select the type of source for the Online quotes. Multiple: quote sources like "Europe" should be used if fail-over to multiple sites are desirable. Single: selections will only return information from the specified source.

After selecting the type of source for price quotes, select a quote source from the pull-down menu. Currently among the supported quote sources are; Yahoo, Yahoo Europe, Fidelity Investments, T. Rowe Price, the Vanguard Group, the Australian Stock Exchange (ASX) and TIAA-CREF.

Note

Note that Yahoo will provide price quotes for many mutual funds including Fidelity, T.Rowe Price and Vanguard, and that the quoted prices at Yahoo should be identical to those that may be found at the source sites.

If you are outside the US and use one of the different Yahoo sources or multiple sources containing Yahoo, you should append the market code for the security such as PA for Paris, BE for Berlin, etc. Example: 12150.PA (a Peugeot security in the Paris market). Table A.4, "Yahoo Codes for Exchanges and Markets" below lists suffixes for various markets around the world.

Pseudo-symbols for TIAA-CREF funds are listed in table Table A.5, "Pseudo-symbols that can be used for TIAA-CREF quotes".

- Timezone for these quotes: Select the timezone for the source of the on-line quotes you are receiving. For example, Yahoo normally quotes Eastern timezone, so choose America/New York if you use that quote source.

- Select a commodity to the Price Editor.

- Select Get Quotes in the Price Editor.

- Check the latest price for the selected security.

If you wish to update price quotes from the command line, you can do so by the following command:

```
gnucash --add-price-quotes <gnucash-file-name>
```

The command **gnucash --add-price-quotes <gnucash-file-name>** can be used to fetch the current prices of your stocks. The file specified "<gnucash-file-name>" will depend on the name and location of your data file. This can be determined by the name displayed in the top frame of the GnuCash window, before the "-". The file name can also be found under File in the list of recently opened file; the first item, numbered 1, is the name of the currently open file.

This can be automated in Mac OSX by creating a crontab entry. For example, to update your file every Friday evening (18:00) after markets close (modify the time accordingly for your time zone), you could add the following to your personal crontab:

```
0 18 * * 5 /path/to/gnucash --add-price-quotes /path/to/gnucash-filename
> /dev/null 2>&1'
```

For Linux, which needs dbus, usually started by the desktop manager, to communicate with dconf or gconf:

```
0 18 * * 5 env `dbus-launch` sh -c 'trap "kill $DBUS_SESSION_BUS_PID"
EXIT; /path/to/gnucash --add-price-quotes /path/to/gnucash-filename > /
dev/null 2>&1'
```

Remember that Mutual Fund "prices" are really "Net Asset Value" and require several hours after the exchange closes before being available. If NAVs are downloaded before the current days NAVs are determined, yesterday's NAVs are retrieved.

Opening Balance tab

The Opening Balance tab is visible only when creating a new account, and is disabled for Stock and Mutual Fund accounts. In the latter case, opening balances must be created by hand. Please see Section 8.5.1 in the *Tutorial and Concepts Guide* for instructions if you need to create an opening balance in a Stock or Mutual Fund account. It is used to record the beginning balance for an account. This allows it to be used for two different scenarios. If using GnuCash for the first time to record transactions, it can be used as a beginning balance. If the accounts in use are closed at the end of a period and new accounts are created, it is used to close and carry balances forward.

There are three panes in this tab. The top pane contains the Balance Information.

- Balance: The balance to start the account with.

- Date: The date the opening balance should be recorded.

The next pane is the Transfer Type pane.

- Use Opening Balances Equity account: This transfers the opening balance for the account from a standard Equity account called Opening Balances.

- Select Transfer Account: This enables the pane below so a different account can be used to transfer the opening balance.

The last pane is the Transfer Account pane. Select the account to use for opening balances from the list of accounts in this pane.

Editing an Account

The Edit Account dialog consists of just the General tab. This tab has the same information that was described in the section called "Creating a New Account". To access the Edit Account dialog go to Edit → Edit Account (menu shortcut **Ctrl+E**) or click the Edit *Toolbar* icon in the Account Tree Window.

Renumbering Subaccounts

Use Renumber Subaccounts to rewrite the account codes for all children of the current account. For example, you have the following account structure:

Table 5.2. Starting account numbers.

Code	Name
10	Colors
10-1	Red
10-2	Orange
10-3	Yellow.
10-4	Blue
10-5	Violet

You now need to add the "Green" account, but you want it to sort between the Yellow and Blue accounts. Instead of having to manually renumber all the accounts starting with Blue, you can use the Renumber subaccount command on the Colors account. In the pop-up dialog the prefix value should default to "10", the account code for the colors account. If you set an interval value of "5" and click Renumber you will end up with the following account structure:

Table 5.3. Renumbered account numbers

Code	Name
10	Colors
10-05	Red
10-10	Orange
10-15	Yellow.
10-20	Blue
10-25	Violet

Now you have room in the account code numbering space to add the Green account with an account code to force the proper ordering.

Table 5.4. Final account numbers.

Code	Name
10	Colors
10-05	Red
10-10	Orange
10-15	Yellow.
10-18	Green
10-20	Blue
10-25	Violet

Deleting an Account

Deleting an Account means removing all transaction information and information about this account from the file. This cannot be undone. You will be prompted to verify that you wish to remove the account. If the account still contains transaction information you will be warned that this account contains transactions.

A side effect of removing an account that contains transactions is that you will end up with unbalanced accounts. This will be indicated in the account by a gray check-box next to the debit and credit amounts.

You can automatically repair these unbalanced accounts by using the Actions → Check & Repair menu. This will automatically assign the unbalanced amounts to a new account named **Imbalance.**

Reconciling an Account to a Statement

Reconciliation of Accounts in GnuCash with statements from a bank or other institution is a way of double checking the accuracy of your (and your banks) transactions and the balance of your accounts. It also is useful to track uncleared checks and other outstanding transactions.

The reconciling process in GnuCash involves two dialogs: the the section called "Reconciling Information" dialog followed by the the section called "Reconcile" window. They provide access to various GnuCash functions to make it easy to enter and update account information during the reconciliation.

Tip

The Reconcile window is accessed from the account tree window or the account register window by going to Actions → Reconcile... or using the menu shortcut **Alt+A, R**.

The *Summary Bar* at the bottom of the Account Register Window indicates the amounts of Present (Balance), Future (Balance), Cleared (Transactions), Reconciled (Transactions) and Projected Minimum. On-line account information can be used to mark which transactions the bank has processed by changing the R (reconciliation status) column in the register from n (new) to c (cleared). The bank statement is then used with the Reconcile window to reconcile the account which changes the R field to y (reconciled).

Reconciling Information

The Reconcile Information dialog is used to indicate the closing Statement Date and the Starting Balance (fixed from last reconciliation) and Ending Balance from the statement. The Include Sub-accounts check-box is used if one or more subaccounts are used to track the account you are reconciling. The Enter Interest

Payment button is used to add a transfer to the accounts for an interest payment. If selected a dialog will be displayed to add the the section called "Interest Payment" to the account.

Note

The Enter Interest Payment button is shown only if you are reconciling an account of *Bank* type.

When you have entered all relevant data, press Ok to proceed to the the section called "Reconcile" dialog or Cancel to discard the reconciliation process.

Interest Payment

There are three panes in the Interest Payment dialog. At the bottom is a button called No Auto Interest Payments for this Account which will cancel the dialog. The top pane contains the Payment Information.

- Amount: Enter the amount of the interest payment.

- Date: Select the date for the interest payment.

- Num: Enter a number for the transaction (optional).

- Description: Enter an informational description for the transaction.

- Memo: Enter a note about the transaction (optional).

The Reconcile Account pane highlights in the tree the account that the interest payment will be transferred to or from.

The Payment From pane contains a list of accounts where you can select the source account.

Note

If the payment is for a credit or loan account then usually the payment would be from an *Expense* account. If the payment is for a checking or savings account then usually this would be from an *Income* account.

Tip

The Show Income/Expense check-box shows or hides the *Income* and *Expense* accounts.

Select OK to enter the interest transaction (or Cancel the payment) and return to the initial reconciliation screen.

Reconcile

Note

For a detailed description of menu items and buttons on the reconcile window, see the section called "Reconcile Window".

The Reconcile dialog is where the actual process of matching your statement to GnuCash data takes place on a per transaction basis.

The Reconcile dialog is composed of a *toolbar* and three panes; Funds In on the left, Funds out on the right and a balance pane.

Note

If you enabled the option Use formal accounting labels in the Accounts section of the GnuCash preferences, you will see Debits and Credits panes instead of Funds In and Funds Out panes.

The Funds In and Funds Out pane shows all unreconciled deposits to the account. Both panes are composed of five columns.

Tip

To order the listed transactions with a preferred criteria, click on the relevant column header. To reverse the selected order click a second time on the column header.

Date	The date of the unreconciled transaction.
Num	The number of the unreconciled transaction.
Description	The Description of the unreconciled transaction.
Amount	The Amount of the unreconciled transaction.
R	Shows a check if the transaction will be reconciled when done.

To mark a transaction as reconciled just click on it and a checkmark will appear on the relevant R column.

Tip

You can check or uncheck the reconcile status of all transactions in either pane by clicking on a transaction in the required pane then clicking **Ctrl-A** followed by **space**. This will toggle the reconcile status of all transactions in the pane to either checked or unchecked state. This procedure can be repeated to achieve the desired status for the transactions in the pane.

Note

Under each pane a Total for reconciled transactions is shown.

The balance pane shows a summary of the balances used in reconciliation.

Statement Date	The date on the statement set on the the section called "Reconciling Information".
Starting Balance	The balance at the end of the last reconciliation.
Ending Balance	The balance entered from the statement.
Reconciled Balance	The balance of selected transactions.
Difference	The difference between the Reconciled and Ending balances.

The set of unreconciled transactions in the Funds In and Funds Out panes can be changed by using the menus and *Toolbar* to access the account and transaction information. You can create a New transaction, Edit a selected transaction, add a Balance transaction (of the same amount as listed under Difference in the balance pane), and delete the selected transaction.

Tip

To modify a listed transaction, double click on it.

By pressing the Open icon the register of the account to reconcile will be opened.

If you wish to postpone the reconciliation until later use the Reconcile → Postpone menu item (menu shortcut **Ctrl+P**) or pressing the Postpone icon. If you wish to cancel the reconciliation use the Reconcile → Cancel menu item or press the Cancel icon.

All previous commands are also available in the Reconcile dialog menu.

Select each unreconciled transaction matching a transaction on the statement so a green tick appears in the R column. The Balance pane changes to reflect each selected transaction until the Ending Balance *equals* the Reconciled Balance and the Difference is *zero*. Once this is done select the Finish button or Reconcile → Finish (menu shortcut **Ctrl+F**) to finish the reconcile process.

Chapter 6. Common Transaction Operations

A *transaction* represents the movement of money from one account to another account. Whenever you spend or receive money, or transfer money between accounts, that is a transaction. In GnuCash transactions always involve at least two accounts.

GnuCash uses accounts as a way of grouping or organizing the recording of transactions. This section describes the methods GnuCash has to help enter transactions quickly into the register.

GnuCash has several methods available for entering transactions.

- Entering directly into the register window is the most common way of entering transactions.

- Using the Transfer Funds window .

- Importing transactions either from a file or via on-line banking.

Transfer Funds Dialog Box

The Transfer Funds Dialog Box, accessed via Actions → Transfer... or its shortcut or by pressing the Transfer icon from the account register tab, serves two purposes in GnuCash:

- A way to create a simple (i.e. two-split) transaction between arbitrary accounts.

- Collect exchange rate or amount information in a multi-currency transaction (see the section called "Multiple Currency/Commodity Transactions").

Note

The Basic Information and Transfer Accounts panes will be disabled in the Transfer Funds dialog when it is being used only to collect exchange rate or amount information.

Basic Information

The Basic Information section collects the entries for constructing a transaction: Date, description, amount, etc.

- Amount: The amount of the transaction in the Transfer Fromaccount's commodity.

- Date: The posting date for the transaction, i.e. the date that you want to record it in your book.

- Num: A reference number for the transaction, often a check number.

- Description: The description of the transaction, often the payer or payee.

- Memo: Additional information you might want to note about the transaction. Anything entered here will be added to the Memo fields of *both* splits.

Transfer Accounts

The Transfer From and Transfer To tree views are used to select the accounts which will participate in the transaction. They normally show only Asset and Liability accounts. If you need to use an Income or Expense account in one of them, check the Show Income/Expense checkbox below the appropriate view.

- Choose the Transfer From account.

- Choose the Transfer To account.

Currency Transfer

The Currency Transfer pane is used to collect the needed information to enter the amount of the Transfer To split. You may enter either a price or an amount and GnuCash will compute the other. If you have Online Price Retrieval installed (see the section called "Steps to enable On-line price updating") you can use the Fetch Rate button to retrieve a current quote.

The Currency Transfer pane is enabled only if the selected accounts use different commodities or the Transfer Funds dialog was launched to collect price or amount information from editing a transaction in the register.

The Currency Transfer pane is organized as a radio group with two selections, Exchange Rate and To Amount. Each consists of a radio button and a numeric entry.

If a relevant price is available in the price database (see the section called "Adding a stock price manually") the Exchange Rate will have that as a default entry.

- Select the Exchange Rate radio button if you want to enter a price or use the Fetch Rate button.

- Select the To Amount radio button if you want to enter the amount of the *To Account* split.

- Enter the price/exchange rate or the amount in the numeric entry corresponding to radio button you selected. GnuCash will calculate the other amount for you when you exit the field. If it's enabled you can use the Fetch Rate button to retrieve a current quote.

Note

If you have created a price in the Price Editor (see the section called "Adding a stock price manually") for the current date quote retrieval will not update that price. You must first delete the manually-created price in the Price Editor before clicking the Fetch Rate button.

Note

The Fetch Rate button will immediately create or replace a price in the Price Editor unless there is an existing manually-created price for today.

Finishing Up

Select OK to commit the transaction (or confirm the price/amount) or Cancel to dismiss the dialog without entering the transaction.

Note

When committing a transaction or confirming an exchange rate the price on the transaction date in the Price Editor may be updated. See the section called "Price Editor" for details.

Enter Transaction via register

When the Account Register Window for an account is opened the list of transactions for that account is shown. This window has the name of the account on its tab. The menus contain several functions that alter the display of transactions. The *Toolbar* also contains several functions that are often used when entering or manipulating transactions. These are described in the the section called "Account Register & General Journal Window" section of this document.

Entering Directly in the Register Window

The register window will look slightly different depending on the style options you have chosen. The following describes entering simple transactions in the basic ledger style. The cursor is placed in the date field by default when the register window is opened.

Note

When working on transactions in GnuCash, be aware that the **Enter** key and the **Tab** key behave differently, and perform different actions.

The **Enter** key moves to the first field of the next split, regardless of which field you are in. If there is no next split, proceeds to the next transaction. In any case, **Enter** finishes the transaction edit, and any imbalance is posted to *Imbalance-CUR*, where *CUR* is the currency of the transaction.

The **Tab** key moves to the next field in the current split. If it's the last field, moves to the next split, creating a new one if there isn't one. If the split is blank, the **Tab** key finishes the transaction and posts any imbalance to *Imbalance-CUR*, as above.

1. Selecting the small icon on the right of the date field drops down a date selection calendar. Use the arrows to select the correct month and year for the transaction then select the date. Selecting the icon once more will close the date selection calendar. It is also possible to type in the date or part of the date and let GnuCash fill the rest.

2. Press **Tab** to move to or select the Num field. Here you can enter a check or transaction number. Pressing **+** (plus) will automatically advance the number by one from the last transaction to have a number.

3. Press **Tab** to move or select the Description field. This field is used to enter either a payee or other description for the transaction. It will automatically attempt to fill the payee name as you type.

4. At this stage one of two things will happen if tab is pressed. If GnuCash matches an existing transaction the cursor will jump to one of the amount fields, automatically filling in the transfer account. Selecting any field with the mouse instead of tabbing will not automatically fill the transferring account field. If there is no matching (existing) transaction, GnuCash will move the cursor to the Transfer field with only one line of the transaction supplied.

5. Accounts may be selected either by typing them in or by pressing the small button on the right of the Transfer field, which will display a pick list of all non-placeholder accounts. Note that this pick list will still display hidden accounts. If you have hidden an account in your chart of accounts, you may want to set the account also to be a placeholder account so that it doesn't display here.

   When typing, GnuCash will fill in available accounts as you type. For example, if you have *Equity* and *Expenses* top-level accounts, typing **E** will fill in **Equity** because it sorts before **Expenses**. Continuing to type **x** will present **Expenses** the account separator (**:** by default, see the section called "Accounts"Account Preferences about changing it) will accept the currently offered account so that you can start typing the name of a child account.

6. The next field (R) is used for reconciliation. This is described in the Reconcile an Account to a Statement section. the section called "Reconciling an Account to a Statement"

7. Press the **Tab** key to move to the first of the amount fields. The names of the next two columns are different according to what type of account is opened. For example, *Bank* accounts show Deposit and Withdrawal here, *Credit Card* accounts show Payment and Charge, and *Stock* accounts show Shares, Price, Buy and Sell.

8. Enter an amount for the transaction in the correct fields. When the transaction is "balanced" pressing the **Enter** key, selecting the Enter icon or going to Transaction → Enter Transaction will finish the transaction. Selecting the Cancel icon or going to Transaction → Cancel Transaction will erase the transaction.

9. Transactions with just one transfer account will show the name of that account in the Transfer field in completed transactions. (The Transfer field is the fourth (4) from the left in the register display.)

10.To move to the blank transaction at the bottom of the register, press the Blank *Toolbar* icon or go to Actions → Blank Transaction.

Multiple Split Transactions

The register window will look slightly different depending on the style options you have chosen. The following describes entering transactions with multiple splits in the basic ledger style. GnuCash describes as a "Split" when money is transferred to or from more than two accounts in a transaction. The cursor is placed in the date field by default when the register window is opened.

The multiple account lines will not be displayed in the Basic Ledger unless the Split icon or the Action → Split Transaction option have been selected.

1. Selecting the triangle icon on the right of the date field drops down a date selection dialog. Use the arrows to select the correct month and year for the transaction then select the date. Selecting the icon once more will close the date selection calendar. It is also possible to type in the date or part of the date and let GnuCash fill the rest.

2. Press **Tab** to move to or select the Num field. Here you can enter a check or transaction number. Pressing **+** (plus) will automatically advance the number by one from the last transaction to have a number.

3. Press **Tab** to move to or select the Description field. This field is used to enter either a payee or other description for the transaction. It will automatically attempt to fill the payee name as you type.

4. At this stage one of two things will happen if tab is pressed. If GnuCash matches an existing transaction the cursor will jump to one of the amount fields, automatically filling in the transfer account. Selecting any field with the mouse instead of tabbing will not automatically fill the transferring account field. If there is no matching (existing) transaction, GnuCash will move the cursor to the Transfer field with only one line of the transaction supplied.

5. When typing in the Transfer field GnuCash will also attempt to automatically match the account. It does this alphabetically, so typing *Ex* will match the *Expenses* section of the account list. When the section is matched, it is possible to move to a child account by pressing : (colon). If after typing *Ex* you press : then the cursor will move to the first child account in the list. Typing combinations of letters and : will allow movement down the tree of accounts quickly. The small icon on the right of the Transfer field can be used as an alternate way of selecting accounts.

6. The next field is used for reconciliation. This is described in the section called "Reconciling an Account to a Statement"

7. Press **Tab** to move to the first of the amount fields. The names of the next two columns are different according to what type of account is opened. For example, Bank accounts show Deposit and Withdrawal here, Credit Card accounts show Payment and Charge, and Stock accounts show Shares, Price, Buy and Sell.

8. Enter the total amount for the transaction in the correct field. Before pressing **Tab** or **Enter** read next step.

9. To enter the additional splits, press the Split button on the *Toolbar* or select Actions → Split Transaction. Transactions with more than one split show the text *--Split Transaction--* and the Split button will need to be used to show the details.

10. The display will expand, the titles of the amount columns will be renamed and the Transfer column name will be blank. The first line contains the description and the amount of the transaction. The second line contains the currently opened account name in the Account field and the amount of the transaction. The third line contains the transfer account name in the Account field. If the amount is not balanced, GnuCash will indicate this by placing gray check-boxes in the amount columns with the unbalanced amount in a blank last row.

11. When one of the short lines is selected, the column titles will change. The very first and last (Date and Balance) columns will have blank titles. Num will change to Action, Description to Memo, the now blank Transfer column will change to Account. The last two amount columns will show the name described in step seven.

12. The Action and Memo columns are optional to fill out at this stage. Action is used to describe what kind of account transfer is involved. Memo is an additional description of the transfer.

13. Move to the missing amount field on the third line and fill in the amount. Pressing the **Enter** key, selecting the Enter icon or going to Actions → Enter will now move the cursor to the next line.

14. The Account column contains the list of transfer accounts. This column is the one that is used to add splits. The method described in step five can be used to select another account on a blank line. Add as many additional splits as needed.

15. When the transaction is balanced the gray check-boxes will disappear and the last blank line will not have an amount.

16. Pressing **Enter** as described above will jump to the next transaction. Selecting the next transaction will close the split or it can be manually closed by pressing the Split icon or selecting Actions → Split Transaction.

Multiple Currency/Commodity Transactions

Any transaction that has splits whose accounts are denominated in different commodities (currencies are a subset of commodities) requires an exchange rate to convert between the two. For more information please see Chapter 10 of the *Tutorial and Concepts Guide*.

Registers for accounts of type STOCK or FUND display four columns, Shares, Price, Buy, and Sell (the last two will be Credit and Debit respectively if you've enabled Use formal accounting labels in the Accounts tab of Preferences). Enter any two and GnuCash will calculate the other for you; if you enter 3 and the result doesn't balance GnuCash will ask which one to change to make the split balance.

Registers of other types have only Credit and Debit (the names will be different depending on the account type if you haven't enabled Use formal accounting labels) and so use the Transfer Dialog with most of the fields disabled to collect either an Exchange Rate or a To Amount (the amount in the other currency/comodity). Please see (the section called "Currency Transfer") for details of using this dialog.

Note

When committing a transaction or confirming an exchange rate the price on the transaction date in the Price Editor may be updated. See the section called "Price Editor" for details.

Editing a Transaction

Editing a transaction involves just selecting the part of the transaction that needs to be changed. Once the changes are complete pressing the **Enter** key, selecting the Enter icon or going to Transaction → Enter Transaction will now move the cursor to the next line or transaction.

To see a more detailed view of a transaction for editing in Basic Ledger, press the Split button on the *Toolbar* or select Actions → Split Transaction.

Deleting a Transaction

If a transaction needs to be removed from the register, select the transaction and press either the Delete icon on the *Toolbar* or go to Transaction → Delete Transaction. A window will appear to confirm the delete, unless the preference has been changed. The window presents two options; "Remember and don't ask again", and "Remember and don't ask again this session". The response will be set according to the selected checkbox. The preference can also be reset via Actions → Reset Warnings. the section called "Reset Warnings...".

Parts of a transaction can also be removed by pressing the Split button on the *Toolbar* or selecting Actions → Split Transaction. The part of the transaction that needs to be deleted can be then selected for deletion.

Add Reversing Transaction

In formal accounting, transactions should never be deleted or altered. Instead, when a mistake is made, the original transaction remains in the ledger, and a reversing transaction is added to the ledger. This *reversing transaction* restores the ledger to its state before the error, allowing the user to enter the transaction again correctly.

While a user can certainly enter reversing transactions manually, GnuCash includes a menu option (Transaction → Add Reversing Transaction) that can quickly create the reversing transaction for you. This option only appears when you are in an account register. When you are in the transaction that needs to be reversed, all you need to do is select this menu item, and a duplicate transaction that reverses the active transaction is immediately created.

Note

Once you choose the menu item, a reversing transaction is immediately created in the account using the current date. You may wish to locate the new transaction at the end of the register, and add explanatory notes to it.

Removing Transaction Splits

Removing Transaction Splits involves erasing all splits except the one for the account that is opened. This is a useful way of reusing a previous transaction that has multiple splits that need to be changed. (Note this can be done without opening the split, but doing so makes the effect more visible)

1. If in Basic Ledger, press the Split button on the *Toolbar* or select Actions → Split Transaction to open the transaction. If in other modes select transaction.

2. Select Transaction → Remove Transaction Splits.

   A window will appear to confirm the delete, unless the preference has been changed. The window presents two options; "Remember and don't ask again", and "Remember and don't ask again this session". The response will be set according to the selected checkbox. The preference can also be reset via Actions → Reset Warnings. the section called "Reset Warnings...".

3. All Accounts and their related details will be removed except for the currently opened account.

4. The amount is not balanced and GnuCash will indicate this by placing gray check-boxes in the amount columns with the unbalanced amount in the blank last row.

5. Edit the transaction to fill in the new details.

Copying a Transaction

Copying Transactions is available from the Transaction menu. The Transaction menu has Cut Transaction, Copy Transaction and Paste Transaction which allows a whole transaction to be cut or copied and pasted to a new transaction line. This way of copying a transaction will use the date showing in the new transaction blank line.

The Transaction → Duplicate Transaction... or the *Toolbar* Duplicate which, unlike the Copy method, allows for choosing a different date.

- Select the transaction to duplicate.

- Go to Transaction → Duplicate Transaction...

- A dialog called **Duplicate Transaction** will prompt for a new Date and Num for the transaction.

- Press OK to add the transaction to the register.

Setting the reconcile status (R field) of a transaction

In the GnuCash register there is a column named R. This field indicates the status of a transaction. Possible values are:

n Default status when a transaction is created

c Cleared. Status may be assigned either manually or by an import process.

y Status assigned solely by the reconciliation process (see the section called "Reconciling an Account to a Statement"). Places limits optionally requiring confirmation on editing fields in that line of a transaction.

f Frozen. Not implemented at this time

v Voided. Status is assigned or released manually through the transaction menu (the section called "Account Register - Transaction Menu") to a transaction and applies to every line in the transaction. It hides most of the transaction details but does not delete them. When a transaction is voided a reason entry is required that appears to the right of the description.

Jump to another Account Register

When using the Account Register Window it is frequently useful to be able to view another account and also the transfer account at the same time. GnuCash allows you to do this quickly by using the Jump button available in the *Toolbar* or the Actions → Jump menu item in the Account Register Window.

Select the transaction in the Account Register Window and either click the Jump icon or select Actions → Jump to open the Account Register Window target. If the transaction is split between more than one transfer account then you will need to show all the split transfer accounts first and select the transfer account to jump to.

Scheduling Transactions

Scheduled Transactions provide the ability to have reminders scheduled or transactions scheduled to be entered at a specified date. This is combined with the **Since Last Run** assistant (the section called "Since Last Run Assistant") to review and enter the transactions. The Mortgage & Loan Repayment assistant (the section called "Mortgage & Loan Repayment Assistant") is used to setup a scheduled transaction to repay a compounding interest loan. The Scheduled Transaction Editor (the section called "Edit Scheduled Transaction Window") is used to create and edit transactions that are to be added to the register in an automated way.

The easiest way to setup a scheduled transaction is to use an existing transaction in an account register as a template. Select the transaction you wish to use as a template and then either select the Schedule icon on the *Toolbar* or go to Actions → Schedule.... This will bring up the **Make Scheduled Transaction** dialog.

- Name: Enter a name to use for the scheduled transaction. This will be used in the Description field of the transaction.

- Frequency: Choose the time period you want between scheduled entries. The dates that the transactions will be entered will show in the mini calendar pane to the right.

- Start Date: Choose a date for the scheduled transaction to start.

- Never End: This scheduled transaction has no finish date.

- End Date: Choose a date for the scheduled transaction to end.

- Number of Occurrences: Enter the number of times you wish the scheduled transaction to be added to the register.

The Advanced... button brings up the Scheduled Transaction Editor's dialog to Edit the Scheduled Transaction. This is described in the section Scheduled Transaction Editor. the section called "Edit Scheduled Transaction Window"

Scheduled Transactions Window

The Scheduled Transactions Window is used to access the list of scheduled transactions and create, edit or remove them. It also provides a calendar which displays upcoming scheduled transactions. Clicking on the calendar view and hovering over any date will pop up a small dialog that shows the transactions scheduled for that day. The yellow highlight in the calendar indicates which days have scheduled transactions. To dismiss the hover dialog click once more.

The top pane of the Scheduled Transaction Window contains the list of scheduled transactions that are currently setup. This window lists the Name of the transaction, if the transaction is enabled for scheduling, the Frequency (month and day) that the transaction is to be entered, the last time the transaction was entered and the next time the transaction will be entered.

The right side of this pane contains a down arrow button that when clicked will pull-down a window to allow selection of the characteristics displayed in the list. Unchecking the appropriate box will remove the characteristic from the display.

The *Toolbar* of this window contains three buttons to create, delete and edit scheduled transactions. New and Edit buttons opens the Edit Scheduled Transaction dialog. Delete removes the selected scheduled transaction. The same options are available thru Schedule → New/Edit/Delete, from the Scheduled Transaction Tab.

Below the list of scheduled transactions is the Upcoming calendar. This calendar displays up to the next year and highlights the dates that the scheduled transactions are scheduled to occur so it is easy to see when the transactions are scheduled. Clicking on a date in the calendar brings up a list of scheduled transactions for that date. Moving the mouse over other dates changes to the list of transactions on those dates. Clicking once more on the calendar removes the transaction list.

The Scheduled Transaction Window is activated from the Account tab or the Transaction Register via Actions → Scheduled Transaction → Scheduled Transaction Editor....

Edit Scheduled Transaction Window

The Edit Scheduled Transaction Window is divided into a Name area, Options area, Occurrences area, Recurrence Frequency area, mini calendar and Template Transaction pane.

The **Name** field is used to enter the name for the scheduled transaction. This will be used in the Description of the transaction.

The **Options** area contains check-boxes to set if the transaction is automatically created and how many days in advance the transaction is created and/or a reminder posted.

The **Occurrences** area contains selections to set for dates limits on transactions to be entered or the number of transactions to be entered.

The **Recurrence Frequency** area contains selections to set how often the transaction is scheduled to be added and on what dates this occurs.

The mini calendar provides a visual indication of what transactions are already scheduled.

The **Template Transaction** pane allows you to setup the transaction as you would like it to be entered into the register.

These options are described in more detail in the section called "Scheduling Transactions"

- From the Scheduled Transaction tab selecting a transaction from the list and pressing the Edit or New buttons will bring up the Edit Scheduled Transaction Editor.

Printing Checks

Checks are printed in GnuCash from the account register. GnuCash provides the ability to print to several standard Quicken Checks (including US Letter) or to make a custom check format. Check position and Date formats are also customizable.

To print a single check in GnuCash, select the transaction to print a check for and go to File → Print Checks. This will open the Print Checks properties dialog to print the selected transaction.

To print multiple checks in GnuCash execute a search to find the transactions you wish to print. With the search results window as the front window go to File → Print Checks. This will open the Print Checks properties dialog to print all the transactions in the search results window.

The Print Checks dialog has two tabs. The first tab, Options, is used to setup the most common options to print a check. The second tab, Custom format, is used to setup the position of various fields on the check. It is useful to print a test check to a plain piece of paper first and use that to make any adjustments needed.

The default selection in Options is for Quicken/Quickbooks (tm) US-Letter checks.

- Check format: Test with Quicken first then use custom if the position is incorrect.

- Check position: This sets if the Top, Middle or Bottom check is printed. Custom is used if the position of the checks on the page is incorrect.

- Date format: The default here is set in the Preferences International section. Choose a date format. This can also be adjusted by the Use of the Months: and Years: lines. Custom allows the date format to be set in the Format: box (%m means month, %d means day, %Y means year) A Sample of the format chosen is displayed below.

- Address: This sets the address of the Payee, if the check format includes a space for it and you are printing a single check.

The Custom format tab has two sections. The top half of the window (above the dividing line) allows you to position the fields in each check. It contains two columns to enter in the X and Y co-ordinates of the field position on the check. Positions in the Custom Check Format entry area are specified with x = 0 at the left edge of the check with x increasing to the right, and y = 0 at the top edge of the check with y increasing as you travel down. (If you are using a version of GTK prior to 2.10, then y = 0 is at the bottom of the page and y increases as you travel up.)

- Payee:

- Date:

- Amount (words):

- Amount (numbers):

- Address:

- Notes:

- Memo:

- Splits Amount:

- Splits Memo:

- Splits Account:

The part of the custom format tab below the dividing line contains fields to position the entire check correctly on the page. The Translation field is the distance from the top left corner and the Rotation field rotates the check clockwise by the indicated amount.

The Units field in the bottom half of the window specifies the units used in all the fields in both halves of the window.

Once OK is pressed on the Print Check dialog the Print GnuCash Document dialog is presented. Press OK to print the check.

Online Actions ...

Note

This section is "under construction - any input will be welcome !!".

Get Balance

Get Transactions ...

Issue Transaction

Direct Debit

General Journal

The General Journal is an advanced register used to enter transactions without needing to open individual accounts. The General Journal shows the transaction entries for all accounts on one register.

Entering transactions in the General Journal is more complicated than entering them in the individual account registers. The advantage is the General Journal provides a more comprehensive view of the transactions you have entered in all your accounts.

The General Journal defaults to showing only the previous month of transactions. This is changeable by using the "Filter By..." on the View menu.

Chapter 7. Business Features

The accounting needs of a business are quite different from that of a person. Businesses have customers that owe money, vendors which are owed money, employee payroll, more complex tax laws, etc. GnuCash offers business oriented features to facilitate these needs.

Accounts Receivable (A/R) are used by businesses to record sales for which they are not immediately paid. Accounts Payable (A/P) record bills that they have received, but might not pay until later. These types of accounts are used primarily when you have a lot of bills and receipts flowing in and out, and do not want to lose track of them just because you do not pay or get paid right away. For most home users, A/R and A/P are too complicated to be worth the effort.

Accounts Receivable (or A/R) refers to products or services provided by your company for which payment has not yet been received. This is represented on the balance sheet as an asset, because the expectation is that you will receive payment soon.

Accounts Payable (or A/P) refers to products or services bought by your company for which payment has not yet been sent. This is represented on the balance sheet as a liability because you will have to pay for them.

Initial Setup

To set up GnuCash to handle accounts receivable and accounts payable for a company the following preliminary steps must be done.

Account Setup

There are many different ways to set up a business account hierarchy. You can start with the Business Accounts setup which is available from the New Account Hierarchy assistant, or you could build one manually. To access the prebuilt Business Accounts, start GnuCash and click on File → New File and proceed until you see the list of available accounts, select *Business Accounts*.

Note

The prebuilt Business Account hierarchy will not meet your needs exactly. You will need to make adjustments for the hierarchy to function well with your particular situation. It should be close enough that it is recommended you begin with it.

Tax Tables

Tax Tables can used to determine the tax for customer invoices (or vendor bills).

A tax table can be assigned to an invoice line or bill line.

The default invoice line tax table can be assigned to each customer and the default bill line tax table can be assigned to each vendor.

The default tax table for new customers or new vendors can be specified in the *Book Options* window which can be accessed by File → Properties → Business tab.

Tax Tables are maintained using the *Sales Tax Table* editor which is accessed via menu Business → Sales Tax Table. The following fields should be entered:

- Name This is the tax table name.

- Type Either Percent % or Value $.

- Value This is the percentage or value depending on Type.

- Account This is the account to which tax will be posted. For tax collected from customers, this should probably be a Liability account as it must be payed to the government. For tax paid to vendors, if tax laws allow tax paid to vendors to offset tax collected from customers, this should probably also be a Liability account (even though it will usually have a debit balance) so that the net tax owed to the government can be easily observed.

  If you set up Tax on Purchases and Tax on Sales as subaccounts of Liabilities:Tax then the net tax will be rolled up and can be seen in the GnuCash Accounts tab.

  If unsure about tax law requirements, get professional advice.

Company Registration

After you have built the account structure and defined your tax tables, register the GnuCash file as belonging to your company by filling in the data requested in the the section called "Business Book Options Tab" accessible from the File → Properties menu item.

Counters

Define the format and last used numbers of codes such as customer, invoice, vendor, bill, employee, expense voucher, job number and order. See the section called "Counters Book Options Tab".

Business Preferences

Set options on the Business tab of the GnuCash preferences, which is accessed via Edit → Preferences (GnuCash → Preferences on Mac OS X). See the section called "Business".

Billing Terms

Billing Terms can be used to determine the payment due date and be a guide for determining discount for early payment of invoices (or vendor bills).

Note

As of GnuCash 2.6.7, Billing terms are only partially supported. Date due is calculated but discount amount is not.

Discount for early invoice payment is not implemented. There are 2 ways this may be done, although neither is recommended, and professional advice should be used to confirm that regulations are being complied with:

- After creating and posting a payment which pays the invoice in full, manually edit the payment transaction (usually strongly discouraged) and split the payment to reduce it by the amount of the discount and a create a compensating split in an income (discount) account.

- Alternatively, after creating and posting a payment for the discounted amount, create a credit note for the discount using a specific negative sales income (discount) account for the transfer account.

You can specify the billing terms on each invoice/bill. Invoice billing terms will default from the customer billing terms. Bill billing terms will default from the vendor billing terms.

Billing Terms are maintained using the Billing Terms Editor which is accessed via menu Business → Billing Terms Editor. The following fields should be entered:

• Name The internal name of the billing term. For some examples of billing term names and descriptions see http://wiki.gnucash.org/wiki/Terms

• Description The description of the billing term, printed on invoices

• There are 2 types of billing terms, with different information to be entered

   • Type Days

      • Due Days The invoice or bill is due to be paid within this number of days after the post date

      • Discount Days The number of days after the post date during which a discount will be applied for early payment

      • Discount % The percentage discount applied for early payment

   • Type Proximo

      • Due Day The day of the month bills are due

      • Discount Day The last day of the month for the early payment discount

      • Discount % The discount percentage applied if paid early

      • Cutoff Day The cutoff day for applying bills to the next month. After the cutoff, bills are applied to the following month. Negative values count backwards from the end of the month.

Accounts Receivable

GnuCash has an integrated accounts receivable system.

To use GnuCash's integrated accounts receivable system, you must first set up *Accounts Receivable* accounts of type *A/Receivable* under *Assets* to accrue income you're owed. It is within this account that the integrated A/R system will place transactions, debiting it when you post bills and crediting it when you receive payments.

Basic A/R Account Hierarchy:

-Assets
 -Accounts Receivable
 -Checking
-Income
 -Sales
-Liabilities
 -Tax
  -Tax on Purchases
  -Tax on Sales

Note

You need to add additional asset, expense, and income accounts to this hierarchy for it to be useful. The important aspects of this hierarchy are the use of an income account and the *Accounts Receivable* asset account, with account type set to *A/Receivable*.

If you deal with customers in more than one currency you will need a separate *Accounts Receivable* account for each currency.

The transactions generated by the A/R system are recorded within the *Accounts Receivable* account. You generally do not work directly with this account. You generally work with the four integrated GnuCash A/R application components available through the Business → Customer sub-menu. These four components are:

the section called "Customers"	People or companies to whom you sell products or services on credit.
the section called "Invoices"	The physical invoice you send to a customer to request payment. This invoice contains an itemized list of things you sold.
the section called "Customer Jobs"	Is where you register Customer Jobs. Jobs are a mechanism by which you can group multiple invoices to a particular customer.
the section called "Process Payment"	Used to register payments you received from a customer.

The following sections introduce the individual components in more detail.

Customers

Customers are people or companies to whom you sell goods or services. They must be registered within the A/R system.

New

To register a new customer, enter the menu Business → Customer → New Customer. Fill in customer information, such as Company Name, Address, Phone, Fax, etc. Below is a list of the other options:

- Identification - Customer Number - can be any number by which you would like to refer to this customer. You may leave it blank and a number will be chosen automatically. See the section called "Counters Book Options Tab" for more info.

- Identification - Active - differentiates active customers from inactive ones. This is useful when you have many past customers, and you want to see only those marked active.

- Billing Address - Name - is the contact name of the person to receive the invoices.

- Notes - records any additional comments about the customer.

- Billing Information - Currency - specifies the billing currency for this customer. It will default to the default currency set in Preferences

  ### Note

  All invoices will be denominated in this currency and GnuCash will require an Accounts Receivable account in this currency.

- Billing Information - Terms - specifies the default billing terms for this customer. Billing terms must be preregistered using Business → Billing Terms Editor.

- Billing Information - Discount - gives the customer a default percentage based discount at the time of invoice creation. Enter a value from 0 to 100. You can override the default discount when you create an invoice.

- Billing Information - Credit Limit - stores the maximum credit you are willing to extend to the customer. This field is for your reference purposes only. GnuCash does not use the value.

- Billing Information - Tax Included - this specifies whether nor not tax is included in invoice amounts by default. You can choose Yes, No, or Use Global.

  - Yes means that the tax is already included in amounts on invoices.

  - No means tax is not included.

  - Use Global means to use the setting made in the global preferences accessible through Edit → Preferences (Gnucash → Preferences on Mac OS X).

- Billing Information - Tax Table - specifies a default tax table to apply to invoice line items. Tax tables must be registered from the Business → Tax Table Editor menu item.

- Shipping Address - records the customer's shipping address if it is different from the billing address. The shipping address is for your reference. GnuCash does not use the value.

Find and Edit

To search for an existing customer, use the Business → Customer → Find Customer window. You select a customer to View/Edit from the results of the search. This window is also used to look up customers when creating invoices and processing payments.

If many customers match the search criteria you provide, the search can be refined by running an additional search within the current results. The current result set is searched when the Refine Current Search radio button is selected. In fact, GnuCash selects this option for you after you run the initial search.

If the customer you are searching for does not match the supplied search criteria, change the search criteria, click the New Search radio button and then the Find button. The relevant step is the New Search selection. If the customer is not in the result of the original search, and you only search within this set, the customer cannot be found, regardless of new search criteria.

Note

To return a list of all registered active customers, set the search criterion to matches regex, and place a single dot "." in the text field area. Make sure Search only active data is checked, then click Find. The regular expression "." means to match anything.

Invoices

An invoice is the paperwork you send to a customer to request payment for products or services rendered. GnuCash can generate and track invoices.

A credit note is the paperwork you send to a customer to correct products or services rendered that were incorrectly invoiced. GnuCash can generate and track credit notes via the same menu entries as invoices.

Note

This section applies to both invoices and credit notes. In order to avoid repeating everything twice and to keep the text easier to read it will refer only to invoices. You can apply it equally to credit notes. Only where the behaviour of credit notes differs from invoices this will be explicitly mentioned. Credit notes were introduced starting with GnuCash stable release 2.6.0.

New

To send an invoice to a customer you must first create a new invoice. To create an invoice use Business → Customer → New Invoice. The New Invoice window must be filled in appropriately:

- Invoice Information - Type - the type of customer document to create - either an invoice or a credit note.

- Invoice Information - Invoice ID - the identification number of this invoice. This is your internal number for this invoice. If you leave it blank, an invoice number will be generated automatically. See the section called "Counters Book Options Tab" for more info

- Invoice Information - Date Opened - the date this invoice was created.

- Billing Information - Customer - the customer who is to receive this invoice. If you remember the *company name* you entered in the New Customer window for this customer, start to type it in this field and GnuCash will try auto complete it for you. Else, press the Select... button to access the Find Customer window described in the section called "Find and Edit". Highlight the customer you are looking for with a click in the search results, then press the Select button.

- Billing Information - Job (optional) - associates the new invoice with a customer job (see the section called "Customer Jobs"). If you remember the *job name* you entered in the New Job window for this job, start to type it in this field and GnuCash will try auto complete it for you. Else, press the Select... button to access the Find Job window. This window is the same to the one described in the section called "Find and Edit". Highlight the job you are looking for with a click in the search results, then press the Select button.

- Billing Information - Billing ID - this is the customer's PO Number or other "customer reference number". You should use it to identify your invoices to this customer (and job, if you have one).

- Billing Information - Terms - the payback terms agreement for this invoice. A list of registered terms is available within the pop up menu. If you specified a default value for the selected customer, this field is initialized with the default.

When you click the OK button, the Edit Invoice window opens.

Edit

From the Edit Invoice window you can enter an itemized list of goods and services you sold on this invoice in a manner similar to how the account register works. For credit notes you enter an itemized list of goods and services you refunded instead.

There are 15 columns in the Invoice Entries area:

- Date - The date this item was sold.

- Invoiced? - X means the item is attached to this invoice, an empty box means the item is not attached to this invoice. The item is attached for you when you proceed to the next line item.

- Description (optional) - is what the item or service is called.

- Action (optional) - is a user defined field. You can place Cost Center information here, or use one of the 3 predefined actions, Hours, Material, or Project.

- Income Account - selects which income account is credited with this income.

- Quantity - tracks how many of the items you sold.

- Unit Price - is the unit price of the item.

- Discount Type - is the type of discount:

  - $ means Discount is a monetary value

  - % means Discount is a percentage.

  You can click the field to toggle between the discount types.

- Discount How - the discount can be computed as follows:

  - > means the discount applies after tax.

  - < means the discount applies before tax.

  - = means both discount and tax are applied to the pretax value.

  You can click the field to change the setting.

- Discount (optional) - is the total discount, in monetary units or percentage, depending on Discount Type. You can leave it blank for no discount. Any default discount you specified for the customer will be automatically entered for each new item.

- Taxable? - is this item taxable? X means yes, a blank field means no. You can click the field to toggle the setting.

- Tax Included? - has the tax already been included in the unit price? X means yes, a blank field means no. For example, if there is 1 item of $100 with a tax of 5% then:

  - If Tax Included is empty, then subtotal = $100 and tax = $5.

  - If Tax included is set (X), then subtotal = $95.23 and tax = $4.77. The computation is: Subtotal = Total / (1+taxrate) and Tax = Total - Subtotal = Total - (Total / (1+taxrate)).

- Tax Table (optional) - this is a pop up menu of all the available tax tables. If you make the item taxable, then this table is used to compute the amount of tax. The tax table determines tax percentages and the accounts to which tax is charged.

- Subtotal (uneditable) - is the computed subtotal for this item (less tax).

- Tax (uneditable) - is the computed tax for this item.

When you have finished entering all the items, you can Post and print the invoice.

Post

When you finish editing an invoice and are ready to print, you must Post the invoice. The invoice does not have to be posted immediately. In fact, you should only post an invoice when you are ready to print it. Posting an invoice places the transactions in an accounts receivable account.

The Post Invoice window appears and asks you to enter the following information:

- Post Date - specifies the date for the transactions entered into the accounts receivable account. By default this is the invoice's Date Opened (see the section called "New" for information about that date).

- Due Date - is the date on which payment for the invoice is expected.

  - If you specified payment terms when you created the invoice, the date is calculated according to selected terms, and the entry field is insensitive.

  - If you did not specify payment terms, enter the expected payment due date here.

- Description - is an arbitrary description. When invoice transactions are placed in the accounts receivable account, this description is entered in the memo field of those transactions.

- Post To Account - selects the accounts receivable account in which invoice transactions are posted. You can select the account from a list of existing A/Receivable accounts.

- Accumulate Splits - determines if invoice items which transfer to the same account are combined into a single split for that account or entered individually. For the sample invoice which sold Nails and a Hammer, the setting affects post results as follows:

  - Checked (splits are accumulated) - a single transfer of $575.00 from the *Income:Sales* account is recorded.

  - Not checked - the transaction created in the A/Receivable account, shows two transfers from *Income:Sales* account $100.00 and $475.00. The memo fields in the splits indicate the sale of Nails and the Hammer (the item descriptions entered on the invoice) respectively.

Find

To find an existing invoice, use the Business → Customer → Find Invoice menu item. From the results of the search, you can select an invoice to edit or view.

Note

Before you can edit a posted invoice, you will need to Unpost it.

One of the design goals in GnuCash's Account Receivable system was to allow different processes to get to the same state, so you can reach an invoice from different directions based on the way you think about the problem:

- You can search for the customer first, then list their invoices.

- You can search for invoices by number or by company name.

- You can list invoices associated with a customer job.

Print

After you post an invoice, you should print it and send it to your customer. To print an invoice use File → Print Invoice menu item.

Tip

You can modify the appearance of the invoice, IE: add a company logo, etc. To do so, see the the section called "Changing the Invoice Appearance".

Invoices can also be printed from the main window by selecting Reports → Business Reports → Printable Invoice from the main menu. The resulting report window states that no valid invoice is selected. To select the invoice to print:

1. Use the Options *Toolbar* button or select Edit → Report Options from the main menu.

2. Select the General tab of the report options dialog.

3. Click the Select button next to the Invoice Number field.

4. Search for the invoice as usual.

You can also print invoices from within the Process Payment dialog. See the the section called "Process Payment" for instructions on how to do so.

Assign Starting Invoice Number

By default, GnuCash starts with invoice number 1 and increments from there. You can manually type an invoice number into the text box each time you create an invoice, but this gets tiring and sooner or later leads to duplicate numbers.

You can change the starting invoice number if it is important you. Use File → Properties, access the Counters tab, change the Invoice number value to be one less than your desired starting invoice number and click the OK button or the Apply button.

Customer Jobs

Customer Jobs are used to group multiple invoices and credit notes to the same customer. Use of the Customer Jobs feature is optional. The feature is useful when you have multiple jobs for the same customer, and would like to view all the invoices and credit notes related to a single job.

To use customer jobs, you must create them using the Business → Customer → New Job menu item. You will see the New Job window. The editable fields are:

* Job Info - Job Number (optional) - enter the number for this job. If left blank, a number will be chosen for you. See the section called "Counters Book Options Tab" for more info.

* Job Info - Job Name - the name you want to assign to the new job.

* Owner Info - Customer - the customer for whom the job is created. If you remember the *company name* you entered in the New Customer window for this customer, start to type it in this field and GnuCash will try auto complete it for you. Else, press the Select... button to access the Find Customer window

described in the section called "Find and Edit". Highlight the customer you are looking for with a click in the search results, then press the Select button.

- Owner Info - Billing ID - the customer's reference to this job (e.g. their PO Number). This is the "Billing Identification" that they require to correlated your invoices with their order. The Billing ID you enter is used to set the billing id for new invoices associated with this job.

- Job Active - toggles this job being active or not. This is useful when you have many inactive jobs, since it is easier to search only among jobs that are marked active.

To edit an existing customer job, use the Business → Customer → Find Job menu item. Select the desired job in the search results, and click the View/Edit Job button.

To select from the invoices and credit notes associated with a given job, use Business → Customer → Find Job menu item. Select the desired job in the search results and click the View Invoices button. A window listing invoices and credit notes associated with this job appears. Select an invoice or credit note and click the View Invoice button to open an invoice editor in the main application window.

Process Payment

Eventually, you will receive payment from your customers for outstanding invoices. To register these payments, use the Process Payment application found in Business → Customer → Process Payment.

Tip

There is an alternative way of assigning a payment to (one or more) invoices where the payment transaction already exists, say in the case where transactions have been imported from a bank. There is no way to assign a payment to an invoice during the import process, so this must be done after transactions have been imported.

This can best be done starting from the asset account register holding the imported payment transaction (like your bank account). In that account, select the payment, right-click (control-click for Mac OS X) and choose Assign as payment.... The payment window will pop-up, partly filled in with the information from the transaction. Fill in the missing information like the proper customer and invoice to complete the payment.

One caveat: the logic behind Assign as payment... won't properly detect credit note reimbursements and will wrongfully interpret such a transaction as a vendor bill.

The Process Payment application consists of:

- Payment Information - Customer - the customer who paid you. If you remember the *company name* you entered in the New Customer window for this customer, start to type it in this field and GnuCash will try auto complete it for you. Else, press the Select... button to access the Find Customer window described in the section called "Find and Edit". Highlight the customer you are looking for with a click in the search results, then press the Select button.

- Payment Information - Invoice - the invoice for which payment was received. If you remember the *invoice ID*, start to type it in this field and GnuCash will try auto complete it for you. Else, press the Select... button to access the Find Invoice window described in the section called "Find". Highlight the invoice you are looking for with a click in the search results, then press the Select button.

- Payment Information - Date - the date you you received payment.

- Payment Information - Amount - the amount of money received.

- Payment Information - Num - the check number.

- Payment Information - Memo - any comments about this payment.

- Post To - the A/Receivable account to which to post this transaction.

- Transfer Account - the account where the money will be deposited (a checking account for example).

Over Payments or Pre-Payments

If a customer overpays an invoice or pays for goods or services before they have been invoiced, Process Payment for the total amount received. GnuCash will then keep track of the over-payment (or pre-payment) in the A/R account and you can use the residual when paying the next invoice.

Partial Payments

Partial payments are possible too. Select the invoice to pay. GnuCash will automatically suggest that invoice's remaining balance as payment amount. Simply adjust that amount to what you want to pay.

Writing Off a Bad Debt

Note

Please check with your accountant to ensure the following is acceptable in your region.

The usual way to do this is to process a payment for the invoice to a *BadDebt* account. Such an account would be an expense account. However, in GnuCash, you can't process a payment for an invoice directly to an expense account, so it takes two steps:

- Pay the invoice to an asset or liability account, such as your checking account.

- Change the asset or liability account, in the *non* Accounts Receivable split of the payment transaction, to the BadDebt expense account.

Specifically

- Remove all transactions from the A/R account related to the invoice, except for the invoice's transaction itself. This includes any payment transactions, and transactions between your BadDebt and A/R account.

  In case the payment has associated lot link transactions (1), remove those as well.

  If all is well, your Process Payment window for this customer should list the invoice the customer won't pay, and no prepayments.

- Pay your invoice to an arbitrary asset or liability account. It can be your checking account. We will fix that in the next step.

- Open the account register for your A/R account. For this invoice there should now be one payment transaction. If you are using GnuCash 2.6.0 - 2.6.4 there will also be one lot link transaction (1).

- Select the payment transaction and change the transfer account to your *BadDebt* account. Make sure to leave the transaction (eg by clicking on another transaction) to save the changes.

If all is well, your Process Payment window should still be clean: no pre-payments, and the bad debt invoice gone.

Note

(1): GnuCash versions 2.6.0 to 2.6.4 created lot link transactions which show in the A/R account register. This came with its own set of subtle issues. It is recommended to upgrade to the latest (or at least 2.6.6) version, which fixes a lot of small problems. Version 2.6.5 had a flaw in the logic cleaning up the lot links. Once upgraded, please run Actions → Check & Repair on your A/R and A/P accounts to clean up most of the lot link legacy. Don't forget to make a backup first just in case.

Lots are used internally for relating payments to invoices. Lots themselves are invisible in the account registers. To see them you need to open the lot viewer, which can be found in Actions → View lots while in any A/R or A/P account register. Select a lot to see the *Splits in lot*.

Lot links are *transactions* which you can see in your A/R and A/P accounts. They are unusual in the sense that all their splits are in one account (A/R or A/P). Each split in a lot link transaction is *linked* (hence the name) to an invoice or payment transaction by means of a lot.

See http://wiki.gnucash.org/wiki/Business_Features_Issues for more information.

Changing the Invoice Appearance

The default Invoice style, as shown in the section called "Print", is fairly barren. The default invoice style leaves the top part of the form blank, so you can print on company letterhead paper. There are some things you can do to change invoice appearance.

Use File → Properties to enter your Company information in the Business tab of the Book Options window. Some of the entered information is printed on the right side of invoices.

To add a customized background, heading banner or logo to invoices, modify the invoice style sheets. To do this, go to Edit → Style Sheets and select the New button in the Select HTML Style Sheet window that will appear.

Give a Name to the new style sheet (e.g. Custom Invoice) and select the Fancy Template. When you click the OK button, the HTML Style Sheet Properties window is displayed. This window presents you five sections listed in the left pane: Colors, Fonts, General, Images, and Tables. The Colors section allows you to change the colors of various items of the invoice. The Fonts section lets you set font type and dimensions. The General section allows you to set the Preparer and Prepared for information, and to Enable Links. The Images section allows you to import graphics into the style sheet. The Tables section allows you to adjust the spacing around the tables which make up the invoice.

To include a company logo, banner heading and background image, use your favorite graphics application such as The Gimp or OpenOffice Draw to save the images in either GIF or PNG format. Then import them into the style sheet using the Images section described above.

Note

The images are placed in the invoice as follows. The Background Tile is tiled to become the background image, the Heading Banner goes above the invoice text, and the Logo is placed in the upper left corner of the invoice to the left of the Heading Banner. You will probably have to try a few different sized images until you get the invoices to print nicely. Some sizing suggestions are that the Logo should be 1 square cm (~0.5 inch), and the Heading Banner should be 15 cm (~6 inches) wide and 1 cm (~0.5 inch) tall.

With the style sheet configured, when you print the invoice, you select the style sheet to use from the Options menu.

Accounts Payable

GnuCash has an integrated accounts payable system. As with *Accounts Receivable* you must have an *Accounts Payable* account set up under *Liabilities* for each currency in which you will issue invoices. The *Accounts Payable* accounts accrue the amounts you owe to others, so bills credit these accounts and payments and credit memos debit these accounts. Generally you do not directly work with this account but use the four integrated GnuCash A/P application components. The A/P components are available from the Business → Vendor sub-menu.

These A/P components are:

- Vendors are people or companies from which you buy products or services on credit.

- Bills represent the physical bills vendors send to request payment from you. A bill contains an itemized list of things you purchased.

- Jobs (optional) is where you register Vendor Jobs. Jobs are a mechanism by which you can group multiple bills from a particular vendor.

- Process Payments is where you register payments to a vendor to whom you owe money.

The following sections introduce the individual Accounts Payable application components.

Vendors

A vendor is a company or person from whom you purchase goods or services. Vendors must be registered within the A/P system.

New

To register a new vendor, select the Business → Vendor → New Vendor menu item. Fill in general information about the vendor, such as Company Name, Address, Phone, Fax, etc. Below is a list of the other options:

- Identification - Vendor Number - can be any number by which you would like to refer to this vendor. You may leave it blank and a number will be chosen automatically. See the section called "Counters Book Options Tab" for more info

- Identification - Active - differentiates active vendors from inactive ones. This is useful when you have many past vendors, and you want to see only those marked active.

- Payment Address - Name - is the contact name of the person to receive payments you make.

- Notes - records any additional comments about the vendor. Use it to track names of contact people within the vendor's company, for example.

- Payment Information - Currency - specifies the payment currency for this vendor. It will default to the default currency set in Preferences

  ### Note

  All Bills and Credit Notes will be denominated in this currency and GnuCash will require an Accounts Payable account in this currency.

- Payment Information - Terms - specifies the default payment terms for this vendor. Payment terms must be preregistered using Business → Billing Terms.

- Payment Information - Tax Included - specifies if tax is included in bills from this vendor. You can choose Yes, No, or Use Global.

  - Yes means that tax is already included in amounts on bills.

  - No means tax is not included.

  - Use Global means to use the setting made in the global preferences accessible through Edit → Preferences (Gnucash → Preferences on Mac OS X).

- Payment Information - Tax Table - specifies a default tax table to apply to bills from this vendor. Tax tables must be registered using the Business → Tax Table menu item.

Find and Edit

To search for an existing vendor, use the Business → Vendor → Find Vendor window. You select a vendor to View/Edit from the results of the search. This window is also used to look up a vendor when entering bills and processing payments.

If many vendors match the search criteria you provide, the search can be refined by running an additional search within the current results. The current result set is searched when the Refine Current Search radio button is selected. In fact, GnuCash selects this option for you after you run the initial search.

If the vendor you are searching for does not match the supplied search criteria, change the search criteria, click the New Search radio button and then the Find button. The relevant step is the New Search selection. If the vendor is not in the result of the original search, and you only search within this set, the vendor cannot be found, regardless of new search criteria.

Tip

To return a list of all registered active vendors, set the search criterion to matches regex, and place a single dot "." in the text field area. Make sure Search only active data is checked, then click Find. The regular expression "." means to match anything.

Bills

A bill is a request for payment you receive from a vendor. GnuCash can track bills.

A credit note is the document you receive from a vendor to correct products or services rendered that you were incorrectly charged for on a bill. GnuCash can generate and track credit notes via the same menu entries as bills.

Note

This section applies to both bills and credit notes. In order to avoid repeating everything twice and to keep the text easier to read it will refer only to bills. You can apply it equally to credit notes. Only where the behaviour of credit notes differs from bills this will be explicitly mentioned.

New

When you receive a bill from a vendor and want to enter it into GnuCash, you must create a new bill. To create a new bill use the Business → Vendor → New Bill menu item, and fill in the resulting window appropriately.

- Invoice Information - Type - the type of vendor document to create - either a bill or a credit note.

- Invoice Info - Invoice ID (optional) - the identification number of the invoice as emitted by the vendor (IE: the vendor's internal number for this invoice).

- Invoice Info - Date Opened - the date the Invoice was emitted by the vendor.

- Billing Info - Vendor - the issuing vendor. If you remember the *company name* you entered in the New Vendor window for this vendor, start to type it in this field and GnuCash will try auto complete it for you. Else, press the Select... button to access the Find Vendor window described in the section called "Find and Edit". Highlight the vendor you are looking for with a click in the search results, then press the Select button.

- Billing Info - Job (optional) - associates a vendor job (see the section called "Vendor Jobs") with this bill. If you remember the *job name* you entered in the New Job window for this job, start to type it in this field and GnuCash will try auto complete it for you. Else, press the Select... button to access the Find Job window. This window is very similar to the one described in the section called "Find and Edit". Highlight the job you are looking for with a click in the search results, then press the Select button.

- Billing Info - Billing ID (optional) - the vendor's ID for the bill (e.g.: their invoice #).

- Billing Info - Terms - the pay back terms agreement for this bill. A list of registered terms is available within the pop up menu. If you specified a default value for the selected vendor, this field is initialized with the default.

- Chargeback Project - Customer (optional) - the customer to associate with this bill. This is used to charge your customer later.

- Chargeback Project - Job (optional) - the customer job to associate with this bill.

When you click the OK the Edit Bill window opens.

Edit

From the Edit Bill window you can enter an itemized list of goods and services you purchased, in a manner similar to how the account register works. For credit notes you enter an itemized list of goods and services the vendor refunded instead.

There are 12 columns in the Invoice Entries area:

- Date - The date this item was sold.

- Invoiced? - X means the item is attached to this invoice, an empty box means the item is not attached to this invoice. If the box is empty you can attach the item to the invoice by first selecting the item row and then clicking in this box.

- Description (optional) - is what the item or service is called.

- Action (optional) - is a user defined field. You can place Cost Center information here, or use one of the 3 predefined actions, Hours, Material, or Project.

- Expense Account - selects the expense account to charge for this item.

- Quantity - tracks how many of the items you bought.

- Unit Price - is the unit price of the item.

- Taxable? - is this item taxable? X means yes, a blank field means no. You can click the field to toggle the setting.

- Tax Included? - has the tax already been included in the unit price? X means yes, a blank field means no.

- Tax Table (optional) - this is a pop up menu of all the available tax tables. If the item is taxable and tax has not been included in the unit price, then this tax table is used to compute the amount of tax.

- Subtotal (uneditable) - computed subtotal for this item (less tax)

- Billable - is this item billable to the chargeback customer/job?

When you have finished entering all the items, Post the bill.

Post

When you finish editing a bill, you should Post the bill. You do not have to post the bill, you can close it and return to it later. You have to post the bill eventually. Posting a bill places its transactions into an accounts payable account. The Post Bill window appears and asks you to enter information:

- Post Date - specifies the date for the transactions entered into the accounts payable account.

- Due Date - is the date on which payment for the bill is expected.

    - If you specified payment terms when you created the bill, the date is calculated according to selected terms, and the entry field is insensitive.

    - If you did not specify payment terms, enter the expected payment due date here.

- Description - is an arbitrary description. When bill transactions are placed in the accounts payable account, this description is entered in the memo field of those transactions.

- Post To Account - selects the accounts payable account in which bill transactions are posted. You can select the account from a list of existing A/Payable accounts.

- Accumulate Splits - determines if bill items which transfer to the same account are combined into a single split for that account or entered individually. For the sample bill for Letterhead and Envelopes, the setting affects post results as follows:

    - Checked (splits are accumulated) - a single transfer of $100.00 to the *Expenses:Office Supplies* account is recorded.

    - Not checked - the transaction created in the A/Payable account, shows two transfers to *Expenses:Office Supplies* account $75.00 and $25.00. The memo fields in the splits indicate the purchase of Letterhead and Envelopes (the item descriptions entered on the bill) respectively.

Find

To find an existing bill, use the Business → Vendor → Find Bill menu item. From the results of the search, you can select a bill to edit, or view.

Note

Before you can edit a posted bill, you will need to Unpost it.

Note

There are other ways to access an existing bill. These are similar to accessing invoices for your customers. See the section called "Find" for more information.

Vendor Jobs

Vendor Jobs are used to group multiple bills and credit notes from a single vendor. Use of the vendor jobs feature is optional. The feature is useful when you have multiple jobs for the same vendor, and would like to view all the bills and credit notes for a single job.

To use vendor jobs, you must create them using the Business → Vendor → New Job menu item. You will see the New Job window. The editable fields are:

- Job Info - Job Number (optional) - enter the number for this job. If left blank, a number will be chosen for you.

- Job Info - Job Name - the name you want to assign to the new job.

- Owner Info - Vendor - the vendor for whom the job is created.

- Owner Info - Billing ID - the vendor's reference to this job (e.g. their PO Number).

- Job Active - toggles this job being active or not. This is useful when you have many inactive jobs, since it is easier to search only among jobs that are marked active.

To edit an existing vendor job, use the Business → Vendor → Find Job menu item. Select the desired job in the search results, and click the View/Edit Job button.

To select from the bills and credit notes associated with a given job, use the Business → Vendor → Find Job menu item. Select the desired job in the search results and click the View Invoices button. A window listing bills and credit notes associated with this job appears. Select a bill or credit note and click the View Invoice button to open a bill editor in the main application window.

Process Payment

Eventually, you need to pay your bills. To do so, use the Process Payment application found in Business → Vendor → Process Payment.

Tip

There is an alternative way of assigning a payment to (one or more) bills where the payment transaction already exists, say in the case where transactions are imported from a bank.

This can best be done starting from the asset account register holding the imported payment transaction (like your bank account). In that account, select the payment, right-click (control-click for Mac OS X) and choose Assign as payment.... The payment window will pop-up, partly filled in with the information from the transaction. Fill in the missing information like the proper vendor and bill to complete the payment.

One caveat: the logic behind Assign as payment... won't properly detect credit note reimbursements and will wrongfully interpret such a transaction as a customer invoice.

The Process Payment application consists of:

- Payment Information - Vendor - the vendor you wish to pay. If you remember the *company name* you entered in the New Vendor window for this vendor, start to type it in this field and GnuCash will try auto complete it for you. Else, press the Select... button to access the Find Vendor window described in the section called "Find and Edit". Highlight the vendor you are looking for with a click in the search results, then press the Select button.

- Payment Information - Bill - the bill you wish to pay. If you remember the *bill ID*, start to type it in this field and GnuCash will try auto complete it for you. Else, press the Select... button to access the Find Bill window described in the section called "Find". Highlight the bill you are looking for with a click in the search results, then press the Select button in the search window.

- Payment Information - Date - the date you wish to make the payment, normally the current date.

- Payment Information - Amount - the amount of money to transfer in this payment.

- Payment Information - Num - the check number.

- Payment Information - Memo - any comments about this payment.

- Post To - the A/Payable account to post this transaction.

- Transfer Account - the account from which money for the payments comes from, such as a checking account.

Over Payments or Pre-Payments

If you wish to overpay an invoice or pay for goods or services before they have been invoiced, Process Payment for the total amount payed. GnuCash will then keep track of the over-payment (or pre-payment) in the A/P account and you can use the residual in the future.

Partial Payments

You may wish to partially pay a bill. Select the bill to pay. GnuCash will automatically suggest that bill's remaining balance as payment amount. Simply adjust that amount to what you want to pay.

Employees

GnuCash can help your company by tracking employees. You can register a the section called "New Employee", the section called "Find and Edit" existing employees, create the section called "New Expense Voucher/Credit Note" and the section called "Find and Edit Expense Voucher/Credit Note".

Expense vouchers are used to reimburse employees for authorized expenses (f.e. travel, parking, food etc...). Employee credit notes are the opposite of expense vouchers.

New Employee

To register a new employee, select the Business → Employee → New Employee menu item. The New Employee window will open with two tabs:

- Employee tab

- Access Control tab

Employee tab

- Identification - Employee Number - can be any number by which you would like to refer to this employee. You may leave it blank and a number will be chosen automatically. See the section called "Counters Book Options Tab" for more info.

- Identification - Username (Mandatory) - a unique username to identify the employee.

- Identification - Active (Optional) - differentiates active employees from inactive ones. This is useful when you have many past employees, and you want to see only those marked Active.

- Payment Address - Name (Mandatory) - the full name of the employee.

- Payment Address - Address (Mandatory) - the address of the employee.

- Payment Address - Phone, Fax, Email (Optional)- other optional contact information for the employee.

- Interface - Language (Optional) -

- Payment Information - Terms (Optional) - specifies the default payment terms for this employee. Payment terms must be preregistered using Business → Billing Terms.

- Billing - Default Hours per Day (Optional) -

- Billing - Default Rate (Optional) -

- Billing - Currency - specifies the billing currency for this employee. It will default to the default currency set in Preferences

Note

All expense vouchers and credit notes for this employee will be denominated in this currency and GnuCash will require an Accounts Payable account in this currency.

- Billing - Credit Account (Optional) -

Access Control tab

- Access Control List

Find and Edit

To search for an existing employee, use the Business → Employee → Find Employee... menu. You select an employee to View/Edit from the results of the search. This window is also used to look up an employee when entering voucher and processing payments.

If many employees match the search criteria you provide, the search can be refined by running an additional search within the current results. The current result set is searched when the Refine Current Search radio button is selected. In fact, GnuCash selects this option for you after you run the initial search.

Note

If the employee you are searching for does not match the supplied search criteria, change the search criteria, click the New Search radio button and then the Find button. The relevant step is the New Search selection. If the employee is not in the result of the original search, and you only search within this set, the employee cannot be found, regardless of new search criteria.

Tip

To return a list of all registered active employees, set the search criterion to matches regex, and place a single dot "." in the text field area. Make sure Search only active data is checked, then click Find. The regular expression "." means to match anything.

New Expense Voucher/Credit Note

To register a new expense voucher/ Credit Note, select the Business → Employee → New Expense Voucher... menu item. The New Expense Voucher window will open. You can enter the following data:

- Voucher information - Type (Optional) - select if you are entering a Voucher or a credit note.

- Voucher information - Voucher ID (Optional) - can be any number by which you would like to refer to this voucher. You may leave it blank and a number will be chosen automatically. See the section called "Counters Book Options Tab" for more info.

- Voucher information - Date opened - the date of the voucher. Click on the button on the right of the date to open a calendar.

- Billing information - Employee (Mandatory) - the employee to which the voucher refers.

Tip

The field supports auto-completion so if you start typing GnuCash will try to complete the text automatically using existing employees name. You can also press the button Select... to open the Find Employee window.

- Billing information - Billing ID (Optional) - the identification number of the document (f.e. the bill number for a dinner).

- Billing information - Terms (Optional) - the pay back terms agreement for this bill. A list of registered terms is available within the pop up menu.

- Default chargeback project - Customer (Optional) - the Customer to which the voucher refers.

Tip

The field supports auto-completion so if you start typing GnuCash will try to complete the text automatically using an existing Customer name. You can also press the button Select... to open the Find Customer window.

- Default chargeback project - Job (Optional) - the Customer Job to which the voucher refers.

Note

you can type in this field only if there are one or more jobs registered in GnuCash belonging to the selected Customer.

Tip

The field supports auto-completion so if you start typing GnuCash will try to complete the text automatically using an existing Customer name. You can also press the button Select... to open the Find Customer window.

• Notes - records any additional comments about the voucher/credit note.

Find and Edit Expense Voucher/Credit Note

To search for an existing Expense Voucher, use the Business → Employee → Find Expense Voucher... menu item. You select an Expense Voucher to View/Edit from the results of the search. This window is also used to look up an expense voucher when entering vouchers and processing payments.

If many expense vouchers match the search criteria you provide, the search can be refined by running an additional search within the current results. The current result set is searched when the Refine Current Search radio button is selected. In fact, GnuCash selects this option for you after you run the initial search.

Note

If the expense voucher you are searching for does not match the supplied search criteria, change the search criteria, click the New Search radio button and then the Find button. The relevant step is the New Search selection. If the expense voucher is not in the result of the original search, and you only search within this set, the voucher cannot be found, regardless of new search criteria.

Tip

To return a list of all expense vouchers, set the search criterion to matches regex, and place a single dot "." in the text field area. Make sure Search only active data is checked, then click Find. The regular expression "." means to match anything.

Chapter 8. Tools & Assistants

There are many specialized Tools used in GnuCash. These tools enable access to the enhanced functionality in GnuCash. These tools are accessed via the Tools option from any window that displays a Tools menu. Several of these tools may not be displayed depending on if your software was not configured to support Online banking, or the tools appropriate for the current window.

Find

The GnuCash *Find* assistant can be used to find transactions or to perform business related research on your data file.

Find Transaction

Find Transaction is used to search for transactions in GnuCash and display the results in a register window. To open the Find Transaction dialog in Split Search mode, you can type the keyboard shortcut **Ctrl+f**.

Exactly which transactions are searched depends on where you invoke the tool from. If you start from the main accounts hierarchy page, all transactions will be searched. If you start from an individual account register, only transactions in that account will be searched. And if you filter the transactions in a register using View → Filter By... , then only transactions in that account and shown by the filter will be searched.

Note

The first row of the Find Transaction dialog indicates that you are performing a Split Search.

There are two panes in the Find Transaction dialog. The top pane contains the Search Criteria buttons and the bottom pane contains the Type of Search selection.

There are two buttons in the top of the Search Criteria pane. The left button allows you to Add another criteria row to search for multiple criteria. The existing criteria row needs to be completed before adding a new row. The right button is used to Search for items where all criteria are met or Search for items where any criteria are met. The all criteria are met search requires all of the criteria rows to have at least one match. The any criteria are met search requires only one of the criteria rows to be matched.

The criteria row in the Search Criteria pane is used to combine different criteria buttons (see table Table 8.1, "Search criteria buttons - Split Search" for a comprehensive list of combinations)

In the Type of Search pane there are five selections. The first option is always enabled, the following three are available when you invoke the Find... option from a register window or after performing the first Find if the Find... command was invoked from any other window. The last option is available only for Business search.

New Search	Perform a new transaction search
Refine current search	Search within the results of the previous search
Add results to current search	Search based on the first set of criteria or the new criteria
Delete results from current search	Discard any results that match the previous search results

Search only active data   Search only if data are marked as active. This selector is greyed out for the Split Search as it is meaningful only for business related search

Note

When selecting search criteria keep in mind that criteria are applied to individual splits or fields in transactions, and that the entire transaction is included in the results. There is no visual indication in the results to indicate which split or field met the search criteria.

When search criteria are selected, you can press the Find button. You will be presented with the search results in a new register tab. A report of the search results may created and printed using Reports → Account Report. The Account Report has limited formatting options but, like all GnuCash reports, being in html format, can be copied and pasted into a spreadsheet for further formatting. Alternatively, the Account Report can be exported to an html file, and the html file may be opened in a spreadsheet.

Note

Press the Close button to close the Find Transaction dialog.

Table 8.1. Search criteria buttons - Split Search

Button 1	Button 2	Button 3	Button 4	Button 5	Button 6	Button 7	Button 8
Description[a]	contains	Criteria entry field	Is entry Case Insensitive?	Remove row			
	matches regex[b]						
	does not match regex[b]						
Memo[a]	contains	Criteria entry field	Is entry Case Insensitive?	Remove row			
	matches regex[b]						
	does not match regex[b]						
Number[a]	contains	Criteria entry field	Is entry Case Insensitive?	Remove row			
	matches regex[b]						
	does not match regex[b]						
Action	contains	Criteria entry field	Is entry Case Insensitive?	Remove row			
	matches regex[b]						
	does not match regex[b]						
Notes	contains	Criteria entry field	Is entry Case Insensitive?	Remove row			

Button 1	Button 2	Button 3	Button 4	Button 5	Button 6	Button 7	Button 8
	matches regex[b]						
	does not match regex[b]						
Date Posted	is before	Date selection field	Remove row				
	is before or on						
	is on						
	is not on						
	is after						
	is on or after						
Value	has credits or debits	less than	Amount entry field	Remove row			
		less than or equal to					
		equal to					
		not equal to					
		greater than					
		greater than or equal to					
	has credits	less than					
		less than or equal to					
		equal to					
		not equal to					
		greater than					
		greater than or equal to					
	has debits	less than					
		less than or equal to					
		equal to					
		not equal to					
		greater than					
		greater than or equal to					
Shares	is less than	Amount entry field	Remove row				
	is less than or equal to						
	equals						

Button 1	Button 2	Button 3	Button 4	Button 5	Button 6	Button 7	Button 8
	does not equal to						
	is greater than						
	is greater than or equal to						
Share Price	is less than	Amount entry field	Remove row				
	is less than or equal to						
	equals						
	is not equal to						
	is greater than						
	is greater than or equal to						
Reconcile[c]	is / is not	Not Cleared	Cleared	Reconciled	Frozen	Voided	Remove row
Balanced	is / is not	set true	Remove row				
Account[d]	matches any account / matches no accounts	Choose Accounts	Remove row				
All Accounts[e]	matches all accounts	Choose Accounts	Remove row				

[a]The Description, Memo, Number are common to all lines in a transaction.

[b]*regex* means regular expression text search as used in various computer programs such as Perl

[c]The Reconcile option applies the selected criteria to each line of a transaction individually. Each transaction line may have only one of the indicated values, but there is often a mix of values within a complete transaction, so companion lines may not meet the selected criteria. See separate note defining status values. For a detailed description of transaction statuses see the section called "Setting the reconcile status (R field) of a transaction"

[d]The Account option performs a search where the accounts selected in the Choose Accounts dialog will both be searched individually for results. This means that a match in any of the selected accounts will either be displayed (matches any account) or discarded (matches no account).

[e]The All Accounts option performs a search where accounts selected in the Choose Accounts dialog will only return results that match in both accounts.

Explanations of the Criteria

The Reconcile criterion deserves some more explanation. Think of the selected reconciliation status buttons (Not Cleared, Cleared, and so on) as a single group, joined with a logical "or". In other words, the selection "is " or "is not" applies to the "or" of the selected status buttons. The buttons which are left unselected are simply ignored. (It's not the same as saying the reconciliation status *must not* be one of these.)

For example: if you select Reconcile is Cleared Reconciled, that means you're saying "I want all transactions which contain cleared splits OR reconciled splits" (imagine an invisible "OR" between all the selected status buttons). It's the same as selecting Reconcile is Cleared, then adding another search criterion with the Add button, then on the new line selecting Reconcile is Reconciled, and finally selecting Search for items where any criteria are met. In either case, GnuCash will show you exactly the same set of transactions.

Find Customer, Invoice, Job, Vendor, Bill, Employee, Expense Voucher

The business find assistant is used to search for business related items (Customer, Invoice, Job, Vendor, Bill, Employee, Expense Voucher). To open the business search dialog select the desired item to Find from the Business → Customer/Vendor/Employee submenus.

Tip

The titlebar and the first row of the assistant dialog reports the item type you are searching for: Customer, Invoice, Job, Vendor, Bill, Employee, Expense Voucher.

There are two panes in the Find dialog. The top pane contains the Search Criteria buttons and the bottom pane contains the Type of Search selection.

Search Criteria section

There are two buttons in the top of the Search Criteria pane. The left button allows you to Add another criteria row to search for multiple criteria.

Note

The existing criteria row needs to be completed before adding a new row.

The right button is used to Search for items where all criteria are met or Search for items where any criteria are met. The all criteria are met search requires all of the criteria rows to have at least one match. The any criteria are met search requires only one of the criteria rows to be matched.

The criteria row in the Search Criteria pane is used to combine different criteria buttons (see tables Table 8.2, "Search criteria buttons - Customer Search", Table 8.3, "Search criteria buttons - Invoice Search", Table 8.4, "Search criteria buttons - Job Search", Table 8.5, "Search criteria buttons - Vendor Search", Table 8.6, "Search criteria buttons - Bill Search", Table 8.7, "Search criteria buttons - Employee Search" Table 8.8, "Search criteria buttons - Expense Voucher Search" for a comprehensive list of combinations)

Type of Search section

In the Type of Search pane there are five selections. The first and alst options are always selectable while the following three are available only when you perform the first search by setting some search criteria and pressing the Find button.

New Search	Perform a new search
Refine current search	Search within the results of the previous search
Add results to current search	Search based on the first set of criteria or the new criteria

| Delete results from current search | Discard any results that match the previous search results |
| Search only active data | Search only if data are marked as active. |

The rest of the search dialog

When search criteria are selected, you can press the Find button. You will be presented with the list of search results in the same Find dialog.

Tip

Aside from the results, GnuCash gives you some buttons to manage the highlighted result.

Tip

In the bottom right of the Find dialog there is a button that allows you to create a New business item.

Note

Press the Close button to close the Find assistant dialog.

List of search criteria buttons

Table 8.2. Search criteria buttons - Customer Search

Button 1	Button 2	Button 3	Button 4	Button 5	Button 6	Button 7	Button 8
Company Name	contains matches regex[b] does not match regex[b]	Criteria entry field	Is entry Case Insensitive?	Remove row			
Customer ID	contains matches regex[b] does not match regex[b]	Criteria entry field	Is entry Case Insensitive?	Remove row			
Billing Contact	contains matches regex[b] does not match regex[b]	Criteria entry field	Is entry Case Insensitive?	Remove row			
Shipping Contact	contains	Criteria entry field	Is entry Case Insensitive?	Remove row			

Button 1	Button 2	Button 3	Button 4	Button 5	Button 6	Button 7	Button 8
	matches regex[b]						
	does not match regex[b]						

Table 8.3. Search criteria buttons - Invoice Search

Button 1	Button 2	Button 3	Button 4	Button 5	Button 6	Button 7	Button 8
Invoice ID	contains / matches regex[b] / does not match regex[b]	Criteria entry field	Is entry Case Insensitive?	Remove row			
Company Name	contains / matches regex[b] / does not match regex[b]	Criteria entry field	Is entry Case Insensitive?	Remove row			
Date Opened	is before / is before or on / is on / is not on / is after / is on or after	Date selection field	Remove row				
Is Posted?	is / is not	set true	Remove row				
Date Posted	is before / is before or on / is on / is not on / is after / is on or after	Date selection field	Remove row				
Is Paid?	is / is not	set true	Remove row				
Billing ID	contains	Criteria entry field		Remove row			

Button 1	Button 2	Button 3	Button 4	Button 5	Button 6	Button 7	Button 8
	matches regex[b]		Is entry Case Insensitive?				
	does not match regex[b]						
Invoice Notes	contains	Criteria entry field	Is entry Case Insensitive?	Remove row			
	matches regex[b]						
	does not match regex[b]						
Invoice Owner	is	Customer	Criteria entry field	Select...	Remove row		
		Vendor					
		Employee					
		Job					
	is not	Customer					
		Vendor					
		Employee					
		Job					

Table 8.4. Search criteria buttons - Job Search

Button 1	Button 2	Button 3	Button 4	Button 5	Button 6	Button 7	Button 8
Job Name	contains	Criteria entry field	Is entry Case Insensitive?	Remove row			
	matches regex[b]						
	does not match regex[b]						
Job Number	contains	Criteria entry field	Is entry Case Insensitive?	Remove row			
	matches regex[b]						
	does not match regex[b]						
Billing ID	contains	Criteria entry field	Is entry Case Insensitive?	Remove row			
	matches regex[b]						
	does not match regex[b]						
Only Active?	is	set true	Remove row				
	is not						

Button 1	Button 2	Button 3	Button 4	Button 5	Button 6	Button 7	Button 8
Owner's Name	contains matches regex[b] does not match regex[b]	Criteria entry field	Is entry Case Insensitive?	Remove row			

Table 8.5. Search criteria buttons - Vendor Search

Button 1	Button 2	Button 3	Button 4	Button 5	Button 6	Button 7	Button 8
Company Name	contains matches regex[b] does not match regex[b]	Criteria entry field	Is entry Case Insensitive?	Remove row			
Vendor ID	contains matches regex[b] does not match regex[b]	Criteria entry field	Is entry Case Insensitive?	Remove row			
Billing Contact	contains matches regex[b] does not match regex[b]	Criteria entry field	Is entry Case Insensitive?	Remove row			

Table 8.6. Search criteria buttons - Bill Search

Button 1	Button 2	Button 3	Button 4	Button 5	Button 6	Button 7	Button 8
Bill ID	contains matches regex[b] does not match regex[b]	Criteria entry field	Is entry Case Insensitive?	Remove row			
Company Name	contains matches regex[b] does not match regex[b]	Criteria entry field	Is entry Case Insensitive?	Remove row			
Due Date	is before	Date selection field	Remove row				

Button 1	Button 2	Button 3	Button 4	Button 5	Button 6	Button 7	Button 8
	is before or on						
	is on						
	is not on						
	is after						
	is on or after						
Date Opened	is before	Date selection field	Remove row				
	is before or on						
	is on						
	is not on						
	is after						
	is on or after						
Is Posted?	is	set true	Remove row				
	is not						
Date Posted	is before	Date selection field	Remove row				
	is before or on						
	is on						
	is not on						
	is after						
	is on or after						
Is Paid?	is	set true	Remove row				
	is not						
Billing ID	contains	Criteria entry field	Is entry Case Insensitive?	Remove row			
	matches regex[b]						
	does not match regex[b]						
Bill Notes	contains	Criteria entry field	Is entry Case Insensitive?	Remove row			
	matches regex[b]						
	does not match regex[b]						
Bill Owner	is	Customer	Criteria entry field	Select...	Remove row		
		Vendor					

Button 1	Button 2	Button 3	Button 4	Button 5	Button 6	Button 7	Button 8
		Employee					
		Job					
	is not	Customer					
		Vendor					
		Employee					
		Job					

Table 8.7. Search criteria buttons - Employee Search

Button 1	Button 2	Button 3	Button 4	Button 5	Button 6	Button 7	Button 8
Employee Name	contains	Criteria entry field	Is entry Case Insensitive?	Remove row			
	matches regex[b]						
	does not match regex[b]						
Employee Username	contains	Criteria entry field	Is entry Case Insensitive?	Remove row			
	matches regex[b]						
	does not match regex[b]						
Employee ID	contains	Criteria entry field	Is entry Case Insensitive?	Remove row			
	matches regex[b]						
	does not match regex[b]						

Table 8.8. Search criteria buttons - Expense Voucher Search

Button 1	Button 2	Button 3	Button 4	Button 5	Button 6	Button 7	Button 8
Voucher ID	contains	Criteria entry field	Is entry Case Insensitive?	Remove row			
	matches regex[b]						
	does not match regex[b]						
Employee Name	contains	Criteria entry field	Is entry Case Insensitive?	Remove row			
	matches regex[b]						
	does not match regex[b]						

Button 1	Button 2	Button 3	Button 4	Button 5	Button 6	Button 7	Button 8
Due Date	is before	Date selection field	Remove row				
	is before or on						
	is on						
	is not on						
	is after						
	is on or after						
Date Opened	is before	Date selection field	Remove row				
	is before or on						
	is on						
	is not on						
	is after						
	is on or after						
Is Posted?	is	set true	Remove row				
	is not						
Date Posted	is before	Date selection field	Remove row				
	is before or on						
	is on						
	is not on						
	is after						
	is on or after						
Is Paid?	is	set true	Remove row				
	is not						
Billing ID	contains	Criteria entry field	Is entry Case Insensitive?	Remove row			
	matches regex[b]						
	does not match regex[b]						
Voucher Notes	contains	Criteria entry field	Is entry Case Insensitive?	Remove row			
	matches regex[b]						
	does not match regex[b]						

Button 1	Button 2	Button 3	Button 4	Button 5	Button 6	Button 7	Button 8
Voucher Owner	is	Customer	Criteria entry field	Select...	Remove row		
		Vendor					
		Employee					
		Job					
	is not	Customer					
		Vendor					
		Employee					
		Job					

Since Last Run Assistant

The Since Last Run assistant is run automatically when GnuCash is started. It is used to enter into the register any transactions that are due to be automatically entered (see the section called "Scheduling Transactions"). The run on GnuCash start can be altered in the Scheduled Transactions tab of the GnuCash Preferences. To run the Since Last Run assistant manually, go to Actions → Scheduled Transactions → Since Last Run...

In the Since Last Run assistant window you can see three columns:

Transaction   The name assigned in the Scheduled Transaction Editor that identifies the scheduled transaction.

State   The state column of the scheduled transaction can be one of the following:

> ## Tip
>
> Click on the state field in the row of a transaction to change its state (this option is available only if the state field is not *empty*)

Ignored   If a scheduled transaction is being displayed, either to be created or as a reminder, the user can set the status to Ignored to skip this event. The scheduled transaction will not be entered in the register and the next reminder for this scheduled transaction will be the next occurrence. For instance, if you have a scheduled transaction set up with a reminder to transfer $500 at the end of the month to your *savings* account but you bought yourself a computer this month and don't have the money for this month's transfer then you would set the status to Ignored.

Postponed   If a scheduled transaction has been listed with a status To-create but you want to hold it and not have it entered to your register yet, then you can set it to Postponed. When at some later time you change it back to To-create it will be created with the original posted-date. If you want to change that you must edit the transaction after it's created.

Reminder   You are *n* days from the scheduled transaction due date. The number of days *n* to remind in advance, is set either in the GnuCash Preferences Scheduled Transactions tab or in the Overview tab of the Scheduled Transaction Editor.

To-create	This scheduled transaction will be automatically created when you press OK.
Empty	An empty field means that no operations are pending for the scheduled transaction.

At the bottom of the window there are two buttons:

- The Cancel button is used to exit the Since Last Run window without creating the transactions scheduled to be entered.

- The Ok button closes the Since Last Run window and applies the pending operations.

At the bottom right of the Since Last Run window there is also an option that allows to Review created transactions. If this option is enabled when there are one or more transactions To-create, pressing OK will open a register window in which are shown the details of the scheduled transactions splits entered automatically by GnuCash.

Mortgage & Loan Repayment Assistant

This assistant creates a loan repayment scheduled transaction. When used to setup a scheduled transaction, the assistant creates a variable formula so that the compounding interest is correctly calculated. To start this assistant manually go to Actions → Scheduled Transactions → Mortgage and Loan Repayment....

It does not support zero-interest loans, but one doesn't really need an assistant for that: Just create a scheduled transaction for the principal divided by the number of payments that lasts for the number of payments. For example, if one has borrowed $1200 for a year at no interest and promised to pay it back in monthly installments, the repayment schedule is $100 monthly for twelve months.

The Mortgage and Loan Repayment assistant opens with a screen that briefly describes what this assistant does. The three buttons at the very bottom of the screen will not change while using the assistant.

- The Cancel button is used to exit the assistant and cancel creating the scheduled transaction. Any selections you have made in this assistant up to this point will be lost.

- The Back button will bring up the previous screen so you can change a selection made on that screen.

- The Forward button will bring up the next screen so you can continue though the assistant.

The next screen allows you to enter the basic loan information. This is usually the information provided by the bank when loan and disclosure documents are given to the borrower. Here you can also setup an account that the scheduled transaction will use to enter the payment transaction.

- Loan Account: Choose an account for the loan payment transactions or use New... to setup a new account for the transactions.

- Loan Amount: Enter the amount of the loan.

- Interest Rate: Enter the loan interest rate in percent per compounding period. The Assistant supports rates between .001% and 100%.

- Type: Choose the type of loan. If an adjustable rate is used the frequency screen is enabled.

- Interest Rate Change Frequency: Choose the frequency for the rate change and the start date of the rate change.

- Start Date: Choose the date the loan is starting on.

- Length: Enter the length of the loan with the number and period, e.g. 60 months or 5 years.

- Months Remaining: This tells the Assistant how many months remain on the loan. The default value assumes that the loan is paid up through today. For example, if a 5-year loan started on 1 January 2012 and today is 12 July 2015, the default months remaining is 18. If you want to create past payment transactions you'll set the months remaining accordingly: In our example, if you wanted to create all of the payments you'd set "months remaining" to 60; if you wanted to start tracking the payments at the beginning of 2015 you'd enter 24.

The next screen is used to set escrow, insurance and tax options for the loan. It is mainly used for mortgage payments. When each of the options here is set, this enables additional pages in the assistant to setup those portions of the payments. All of the pages will be described here, even though some may not show if that option is not chosen.

- ... utilize an escrow account for payments?: This selection enables the use of an account setup for tracking escrow payments. If the mortgage or loan uses an escrow account to pay taxes, insurance, etc then setup an account here.

- ... pay "Taxes"?: adds an additional page to setup a scheduled transaction to pay taxes.

- ... pay "Insurance"?: adds an additional page to setup a scheduled transaction to pay insurance payments.

- ... pay "PMI"?: adds an additional page to setup a scheduled transaction to pay PMI payments.

- ... pay "Other Expense"?: adds an additional page to setup a scheduled transaction to pay other expenses.

The next screen is used to setup the details of the scheduled transaction for the Loan Repayment.

- Transaction Memo: The name entered here will be used as the name for the scheduled transaction, the description of the scheduled transaction and the memo.

- Payment Amount: Shows the variable used to calculate the payment amount.

- Payment From: Choose an account to pay the loan amount from.

- Principal To: Choose an account to transfer the principal part of the loan to.

- Interest To: Choose an account to transfer the interest part of the loan to.

- Repayment Frequency: Select the Frequency and start date for loan repayments. Note that the start date will be the posted date of the first scheduled transaction. This is not taken into account for calculating the remaining duration of the loan, see Months Remaining:. Make sure that you set both to reflect your intentions or you may get surprising results.

The next screen is used to setup the details of the scheduled transaction for the Tax payment.

- Transaction Memo: The name entered here will be used as the name for the scheduled transaction, the description of the scheduled transaction and the memo.

- Amount: Enter the payment amount.

- Payment From: Choose an account to pay the tax amount from.

- Payment To: Choose an account to transfer the tax payment to.

- Repayment Frequency: Select the Frequency and start date for tax payments.

The next screen is used to setup the details of the scheduled transaction for the Insurance payment.

- Transaction Memo: The name entered here will be used as the name for the scheduled transaction, the description of the scheduled transaction and the memo.

- Amount: Enter the payment amount.

- Payment From: Choose an account to pay the insurance amount from.

- Payment To: Choose an account to transfer the insurance payment to.

- Repayment Frequency: Select the Frequency and start date for insurance payments.

The next screen is used to setup the details of the scheduled transaction for the PMI payment.

- Transaction Memo: The name entered here will be used as the name for the scheduled transaction, the description of the scheduled transaction and the memo.

- Amount: Enter the payment amount.

- Payment From: Choose an account to pay the PMI amount from.

- Payment To: Choose an account to transfer the PMI payment to.

- Repayment Frequency: Select the Frequency and start date for PMI payments.

The next screen is used to setup the details of the scheduled transaction for the Other Expense payment.

- Transaction Memo: The name entered here will be used as the name for the scheduled transaction, the description of the scheduled transaction and the memo.

- Amount: Enter the payment amount.

- Payment From: Choose an account to pay the other expense amount from.

- Payment To: Choose an account to transfer the other expense payment to.

- Repayment Frequency: Select the Frequency and start date for other expense payments.

The last screen gives you a list of three choices to finish the assistant.

- The Cancel button is used to exit the assistant and cancel creating a new loan scheduled transaction. Any selections you have made in this assistant up to this point will be lost.

- The Back button will bring up the previous screen so you can change a selection made on that screen.

- The Finish button creates the scheduled transaction.

You should now have the Mortgage or Loan Repayment scheduled transaction setup.

Recording a Stock Split

Stock splits commonly occur when a company decides its stock price is too expensive for individual investors to buy the stock. Splits have the effect of lowering the price of a single share while keeping the value of shares owned by investors who have already purchased shares.

Stock Split Assistant

GnuCash uses the Stock Split assistant to record stock splits. This provides a way of entering the details of the stock split and also any change in stock price or cash disbursement as a result of the stock split.

The Stock Split assistant is accessed by going to Actions → Stock Split....

The Stock Split assistant opens with a screen that briefly describes what this assistant does. The three buttons at the very bottom of the screen will not change while using the assistant.

- The Cancel button is used to exit the assistant and cancel entering the stock split information. Any selections you have made in this assistant up to this point will be lost.

- The Back button will bring up the previous screen so you can change a selection made on that screen.

- The Forward button will bring up the next screen so you can continue though the assistant.

The next screen allows you to select a Stock Account. Select an account from the list to record a stock split or merger.

- Account: Lists the GnuCash account name for the stock.

- Symbol: The stock symbol for the stock associated with this account.

- Shares: The amount of shares that have been purchased in the account.

The next screen lets you set the Stock Split Details. The top part of the screen contains details used in creating the stock split transaction.

- Date: Choose the date of the stock split.

- Share Distribution: Enter the amount of shares gained from the stock split. For a stock merger enter a negative number.

- Description: Enter a description or leave as the default.

The bottom part of the screen contains details used to record a price for the split (optional).

- New Price: Enter the price of the shares on the day of the stock split.

- Currency: Choose the currency of the shares.

The next screen lets you enter a transaction for a cash disbursement (Cash In Lieu) as a result of the stock split (optional).

- Cash Amount: Enter the amount of the Cash disbursement.

- Memo: Enter a memo or leave as the default.

- Income Account: Choose an Income Account for the disbursement.

- Asset Account: Choose an Asset Account for the disbursement.

The last screen gives you a list of three choices to finish the assistant.

- The Cancel button is used to exit the assistant and cancel creating the Stock Split transactions. Any selections you have made in this assistant up to this point will be lost.

- The Back button will bring up the previous screen so you can change a selection made on that screen.

- The Finish button creates the transactions for the Stock Split.

You should now have successfully entered the Stock Split or Merger.

HBCI (Online Banking) Setup Assistant

Note

This section is "under construction - any input will be welcome !!".

The HBCI Assistant is used to create and edit data to enable access to Online banking transactions. Currently the best instruction for this process are in the GnuCash wiki at Setting up OFXDirectConnect in GnuCash 2 [http://wiki.gnucash.org/wiki/Setting_up_OFXDirectConnect_in_GnuCash_2]. If HBCI Setup does not appear in your Tools menu, verify that you are in an Account Tree or Register tab.

Price Editor

Note

GnuCash uses the term *commodity* to mean anything that it counts: Currencies, securities (i.e intangible assets like stock or mutual fund shares and bonds), or tangible assets like trucks and computers. When valuing one commodity in terms of another it uses the term *Exchange Rate* between two currencies and *Price* between a non-currency commodity and a currency commodity. For the rest of this section we'll use "price" to mean both price and exchange rate and "commodity" to mean any sort of commodity except where currency behavior is different.

The Price Editor is used to list and edit the price of one commodity in another commodity. New prices can be added, existing prices can be edited, and prices can be retrieved from a variety of sources on the World-Wide Web when the commodity is properly configured.

Each commodity pair can have one price per day. An existing price will be overwritten by a newer one if the newer one has the same or a more preferred source. The order of source preference (1 is most preferred) is:

1. user:price-editor: Prices created manually in the Price Editor

2. Finance::Quote: Online quotes

3. user:price: Prices entered explicitly in the Exchange Rateentry of the Transfer Funds dialog box or in the Price column of a register for an account of types STOCK or MUTUAL

4. user:xfer-dialog: Prices calculated from an entry in the To Amount entry of the Transfer Funds dialog box.

5. user:split-register: Prices calculated from the Shares and Debit or Credit columns of a register for an account of types STOCK or MUTUAL

6. user:stock-split: Prices entered in the Stock Split Assistant

Note

Prices created manually in the Price Editor are preferred over prices retrieved via Finance::Quote so Finance::Quote will fail to update such manually-created prices.

The Price Editor displays existing prices as follows:

- **Security:** The Security/commodity being priced. The display is sorted by the Namespace that the individual securities are listed on. The list is expanded by clicking on the caret on the left of the name.

- **Currency:** The currency the price is recorded in.

- **Date:** The date the price was recorded.

- **Source:** The source of the commodities price quote, listed above.

- **Type:** There are several different types of stock price quotes.

    - **Bid:** Indicates what a specialist dealer is prepared to pay for a stock.

    - **Ask:** Indicates at what price the dealers are prepared to sell a stock.

    - **Last:** Indicate the price at which the last trade in that stock/security occurred at. This is the price most commonly quoted in the media.

    - **Net Asset Value:** Are typically used for mutual funds. They are calculated on the net value of the fund's assets each day around the time of the market close and are in effect until the next recalculation.

    - **Unknown:** Use this if the type of price quoted is not known.

- **Price:** The actual price of the commodity.

Adding a stock price manually

To add a new price, click on Add, and enter the details of the security and price into the dialog box. To edit an existing price, select the price in the price list, click the Edit button, and edit the figures.

To remove just one price, select the price and click the Remove button. If you want to remove all prices older than a certain date, click on the Remove Old button and enter the details in the dialog box.

A pop-up will display with the message **"Delete all stock prices based upon the criteria below:"**. Enter the date of the last price you wish to delete.

Two check-boxes are below the date field;

- Delete manually entered prices - If checked, delete manually entered stock prices dated earlier than the specified date. Otherwise only stock prices added by Finance::Quote will be deleted.

- Delete last price for a stock - If checked, delete all prices before the specified date. Otherwise the last stock price dated before the date will be kept and all earlier quotes deleted.

Configuring for use of the Get Quotes button

To support on-line quotations for a particular stock or mutual fund account, you must first enable on-line price quoting and select a price source in the Security. This is described in detail in the section called "Configuring Securities/Currencies for On-Line Retrieval of Prices". Once on-line quotes are enabled, and Finance::Quote is installed, you can update prices for your stocks and mutual funds manually by clicking the Get Quotes button.

Security Editor

The Security Editor is used to create and edit commodities that are used by mutual fund and stock type accounts. It also shows the details of National Currencies that are used by GnuCash.

To show the details for National Currencies click the Show National Currencies check-box at the bottom of the screen.

Each entry in the editor shows the details used by the security/currency:

- **Type:** Categories for organizing securities. GnuCash has the following built in:

  - CURRENCY or ISO4317: These are used for national currencies and are not editable with the Security Editor.

  - FUND: Ordinarily used for open-ended mutual funds, i.e., those that one purchases from and sells to only the issuing company and that are priced daily at their net asset value.

  - AMEX, ASX, EUREX, NASDAQ, and NYSE: These represent a few of the exchanges on which stocks, closed-end mutual funds, and exchange-traded funds are traded.

  - Template: This is a reserved word. It will not normally appear in the Security Editor unless you type it in, and if you do it will cause problems. Don't use it.

  If your investment doesn't fit into one of these categories, for example if you trade stocks on the DAX or LSE, you can easily create your own type simply by typing it into the field. The type of security has no meaning to Gnucash (except Template, don't use that!), it's there only to make it easier for you to find the security from the selection lists.

- **Symbol:** Indicates the symbol or abbreviation for the commodity. This is usually the ticker symbol (for stocks) or other unique abbreviation for the commodity. If the commodity is traded on any public exchange, it is important to use the same identifier used on that exchange. For national currencies the symbol is the ISO-4217 currency code.

- **Name:** The full name of the commodity is a recognizable name such as *US Dollars* or *IBM Common Stock*.

- **Code:** This is any numeric or alphanumeric code that is used to identify the commodity. The CUSIP code is a unique identifying numeric string that is associated with every stock, bond or mutual fund, and most kinds of traded options, futures and commodities. This code is not required.

- **Fraction:** This is the smallest traded unit of the commodity, expressed as a fraction of a single nominal unit. This unit is used by GnuCash accounts as the default fraction for trades in the commodity.

Adding or Editing a Commodity

To add a new commodity (stock, or mutual fund), click on Add, and enter the details of the commodity into the **New Security** dialog box. To edit an existing commodity, select the commodity from the Commodities list, click the Edit button, and edit the **Edit Security** dialog box. To remove a commodity, select the commodity and click the Remove button.

The fields in the New/Edit Security screens are the same as defined for the Security Editor the section called "Security Editor". Below these fields are the options for Online Quotes.

Configuring Securities/Currencies for On-Line Retrieval of Prices

To support on-line quotations for a particular stock or mutual fund account, you must first enable on-line price quoting and select a price source in the Security Editor. Online currency quotes require only that the check-box for Online quotes and the timezone be selected, and that the "Get Quotes" box be checked in the Security Editor.

Detailed instructions are in the section on Creating New Accounts. the section called "Steps to enable On-line price updating"

Loan Repayment Calculator

The Loan Repayment Calculator is used to calculate compound interest. It provides a way of entering four of the five parameters of a compound interest calculation and then calculating the remaining figure.

The calculator is split into two panes. The left pane has five fields with a Calculate button and a Clear button. The Calculate button is used to select the figure to calculate. The Clear button is used to clear any amount in the field.

- **Payment Periods:** This field is used to select the number of payments you wish to use in the calculation.

- **Interest Rate:** This field is used for the interest rate percentage.

- **Present Value:** This field usually contains the amount you have borrowed. It is the base amount you wish to compound.

- **Periodic Payment:** This field contains the amount that is the payment for the period selected (IE month-ly, weekly, etc). If it is for repaying a loan it should be a negative number.

- **Future Value:** This field contains the final value at the end of the periods above. If we are repaying a loan in full it would be *0*.

The right pane contains buttons to select what sort of payments and compounding is used for the left pane calculations.

- Compounding: This button allows you to select the interval used if the Discrete Compounding button is selected.

- Payments: This button allows you to select the interval used for the Payment Periods field.

- End of Period Payments: Use this button if the payment is at the end of the period.

- Beginning of Period Payments: Use this button if the payment is at the beginning of the period.

- Discrete Compounding: This button is used where interest is charged at a discrete interval defined by the Compounding button above.

- Continuous Compounding: This button is used when the interest is charged continuously.

- Payment Total: This field shows the total amount paid.

Examples of using the Loan Repayment Calculator are given in the Tutorial and Concepts Guide. GnuCash Tutorial and Concepts Guide's Chapter on Loans [http://svn.gnucash.org/docs/guide/loans_calcs1.html]

Close Book

The Close Book dialog box is used for "closing the books,"--an accounting process that resets the balances of the income and expense accounts. In this process, income account balances are transferred into an income equity account, while expense account balances are transferred into an expense equity account.

You must specify both these accounts, which may be the same. You must also specify the date for the closing transfer.

Dialog Box Details

The dialog box has the following parts:

- Closing Date: Specify the date for the closing transfer. You can type in a date or choose one from the drop-down.

- Income Total: Specify the account into which the total balance of all income accounts will be transferred. Optionally you can create a new account to receive the transfer using the New button.

- Expense Total: Specify the account into which the total balance of all expense accounts will be transferred. Again, you can optionally create a new account to receive the transfer using the New button.

- Description: Specify the description that will be entered in the closing entry.

How It Works

GnuCash closes books by creating one transaction per currency for income accounts, and one transaction per currency for expense accounts. The transactions all use the date selected by the user, and each transaction may contain any number of splits. Each split moves the balance out of one income or expense account. The last split in each closing transaction moves the total offsetting debit/credit balance into the specified equity account.

Each transaction will use the description provided by the user in the Description: entry.

The fact that GnuCash just uses transactions to close the books makes it very simple to undo a book closing: just delete the closing transactions.

What It Doesn't Do

The book closing tool does not delete any accounts or transactions; create any new files; or hide any accounts.

Necessity

Note that closing the books in GnuCash is unnecessary. You do not need to zero out your income and expense accounts at the end of each financial period. GnuCash's built-in reports automatically handle concepts like retained earnings between two different financial periods.

In fact, closing the books reduces the usefulness of the standard reports because the reports don't currently understand closing transactions. So from their point of view it simply looks like the net income or expense in each account for a given period was simply zero.

Conclusion

If you close your books, be prepared to see inaccuracies in the standard reports. On the other hand, you will see current-period income and expense figures in the chart of accounts.

Lots in Account

GnuCash uses *lots* in 2 ways:

- To link security buy transactions to sell transactions so the real cost of the sold securities can be used to calculate capital gain or loss. See the section called "Lots for Security Capital Gains".

- To link payments or credit notes to the invoices to which they apply in the Business Features. See the section called "Lots for Business Features".

Lots for Security Capital Gains

The Lots in Account SSSS window, where SSSS is the security account, is used to manually or automatically link security transaction splits to lots and create capital gain/loss transactions to account for the difference between the costs of buying a security and the value received by selling it.

To open the Lots in Account window, open the security account register, then select Actions → View Lots.

Figure 8.1. Lots in Account window for Security Capital Gains

An image of the *Lots in Account* window for a security account.

Screen Elements

Adjusting the Size of Screen Elements

As well as adjusting the size of the whole window, it is possible to adjust the proportions of the window elements both horizontally and vertically.

There are 2 bars for adjusting the window horizontally. One between the Title and the Lots in This Account panel, and the other between the Splits free panel and the >> and << buttons.

The window proportions may be adjusted vertically by dragging the vertical bar located to the right of Show only open lots.

These resizing bars can be hard to see, so move the mouse pointer until it changes to the resize pointer then click and drag the bar. The resize pointers are different depending on your operating system and theme. Here are some examples of resize pointers:

It is not possible to individually adjust the size of panel columns.

Fields

- Title: Shows the title for the highlighted (selected) lot in the Lots in This Account panel. When a new lot is created by clicking the New Lot button, it has a default title of *Lot n* where n is a number starting at 0 (for each security account) and incrementing by 1. Deleting a lot does not reset the next number to be used, but the title can be changed as required.

- Notes: Notes for the highlighted lot. Users are free to enter anything they wish and the notes can be changed as required.

Panels

The order of the items in all the panels in this window can be adjusted by clicking on the column headings.

- Lots in This Account panel

  This panel shows lots for this security account.

  If Show only open lots is checked, only lots that have not been completely sold are shown.

  Columns

  - Type: Always blank for security lots. This window is also used for business lots (which link payments to invoices) when coming from an Accounts Payable or Receivable account and in that case, Type will be *I* for invoice. Credit Notes are also Type I.

  - Opened: *Open* if there are no splits in the lot, otherwise the date of the earliest split in this lot.

  - Closed: *Open* if the lot is not fully sold, otherwise the date of the last sell split.

  - Title: Lot Title.

  - Balance: Number of unsold securities in this lot.

  - Gains: Calculated gains or losses for this lot.

- Splits free panel

  This panel shows buy and sell splits for this security account which are not linked to a lot. Capital Gains splits (Shares and Price are 0) are not shown.

  Columns

  - Date: Transaction Date Posted.

  - Num: Transaction Num.

  - Description: Transaction Description.

  - Amount: Number of shares bought or sold from the transaction split. Positive for buys, negative for sells. If the security transaction split has been split into multiple subsplits (because a split may only be linked to 1 lot), this amount will not be the full transaction amount, but only the amount for this split.

  - Value: Amount x split price.

  - Gain/Loss: For sell splits, shows calculated gain or loss. This will be recalculated during scrubbing.

- Balance: Cumulative number of unsold shares for free splits.

- Splits in Lot panel

This panel shows splits linked to the highlighted lot in the Lots in This Account panel. This panel will be empty until a lot is highlighted in the Lots in This Account panel. Capital Gains splits (Shares and Price are 0) are not shown.

Columns

- Date: Transaction Date Posted.

- Num: Transaction Num.

- Description: Transaction Description.

- Amount: Split number of shares bought or sold. Positive for buys, negative for sells. If the security transaction split has been split into multiple subsplits (say by scrubbing because a split may only be linked to 1 lot), this amount will not be the full transaction amount, but only the amount for this split.

- Value: Amount (No of Shares) x split price.

- Gain/Loss: For sell splits, shows calculated gain or loss. This will be recalculated during scrubbing.

- Balance: The number of unsold shares in this lot after this transaction.

Buttons

- >>: Links a free split (buy or sell) to a lot. This button is not enabled until both a lot and a free split are highlighted. The split moves from the Splits free panel to the Splits in lot panel.

  Multiple buy splits and multiple sell splits may be linked to the same lot. Refer to following section about the Scrub Account button for details of the capital gains transactions created in these situations.

- <<: Unlinks a split from a lot. The split moves from the Splits in lot panel to the Splits free panel. This button is not enabled until a split in the Splits in lot panel is highlighted. When the last split is unlinked from a lot, the lot is automatically deleted if there is no capital gain/loss transaction.

- New Lot: Creates a new lot which shows in the Lots in This Account panel. The new lot is not linked to any split.

- Scrub Account:

  - Creates a lot for each buy transaction split that is not already linked to a lot.

    A new lot is created for each unlinked buy transaction split because gains on investments, in some jurisdictions, may be taxed at different rates depending on how long they were held before being sold. As a separate capital gains transaction is created for each lot, this makes it easier to determine tax on the capital gains based on the lot opened and closed dates.

    If you know that the capital gains from a sale are all to be taxed at the same rate, you can manually link multiple buys to a lot so scrubbing will only create 1 capital gains transaction.

    It is also possible to manually link multiple sell transaction splits to a lot. In this case scrubbing creates a capital gains transaction per sell transaction split based on the average cost of securities held at the time of each sale, assuming acquisitions are allocated to sales using the security account costing method (currently only FIFO). As this makes it complicated to manually verify the costs are correct, it may be wise to limit this to specific situations, say for example if there are multiple sales on the same day.

- Links buy and sell transaction splits to lots using FIFO method.

- Calculates gain/loss and creates a separate capital gain/loss transaction for each lot that does not already have one.

Note

If gain/loss splits have been manually entered as part of a sell transaction, scrubbing does not recognize them, so if manually adding gain/loss, always separate the gain/loss splits from the transaction that reduces the No of Shares, by putting them in a separate transaction.

- Scrub: Scrub only the highlighted lot. This button is only enabled if a lot is highlighted. If no buy splits are linked to the highlighted lot, nothing is done. The Scrub button will link any free sell splits to the lot as required until the sum of the sell split amounts equals the sum of the buy split amounts. If the sum of the sell split amounts is greater than the sum of the buy split amounts, a sell split will itself be split into 2 splits, with the remaining amount in an unlinked split.

Note

For both the Scrub Account and the Scrub buttons:

The Gain/Loss for each lot is recalculated and a capital gain transaction is created if needed. The transaction has 1 split for the security account and the other with account *Orphaned Gains-CCC* where CCC is the security currency. The *Orphaned Gains-CCC* account is used because GnuCash doesn't know which capital gain or loss account should be used, so the user must change it to the required income (or expense) gain or loss account.

- Delete: Delete the highlighted lot. Any linked splits are automatically freed (unlinked). This button is only enabled if a lot is highlighted.

- Close: Close the Lots in Account SSSS window.

See Tutorial and Concepts Guide, Automatic Calculation of Capital Gain or Loss Using Lots [https://www.gnucash.org/docs/v2.6/C/gnucash-guide/invest-sellLots.html] for more details.

Lots for Business Features

Introduction

For business features, lots are used to link payments or credit notes to the invoices to which they apply. This is for both customer invoices and vendor bills.

There are 2 main uses for the Lots in Account window in relation to the business features:

1. To enquire about which payments or credit notes offset particular invoices. For each invoice and credit note, GnuCash automatically creates 1 (and only 1) lot. By selecting the lot for the invoice or credit note in the Lots in This Account panel, all the transaction splits for that lot show in the Splits in Lot panel.

Tip

Alternatively, print the invoice and check the Payments option on the Display tab in the report options. The Tax Invoice always shows payments so does not have the Payments option.

2. To correct mistakes that are hard to correct otherwise (either due to bugs in past versions of gnucash or due to unintended use of said features). Some of these use cases are found on this wiki page [https://wiki.gnucash.org/wiki/Business_Features_Issues]. In the context of the normal operation of business features , the Lots in Account window is *not* used to create, delete, link or unlink lots. Lots are usually generated and manipulated internally only by the business features programs.

To open the Lots in Account AAAA window, where AAAA is the *Accounts Receivable* (AR) or *Accounts Payable* (AP) account, open the *AR* or *AP* account register, then select Actions → View Lots.

Figure 8.2. Lots in Account window for business features

An image of the Lots in Account window for an Accounts Receivable account.

Screen Elements

The screen elements of the Lots in Account window for an AR or AP account are the same as for a security account, although the actions and data are different. As this window is only used for creating, deleting, linking or unlinking lots in *exceptional* circumstances, the differences are not described. See the section called "Screen Elements" for a description of the screen elements and what the buttons do when used with the lots of a security account.

Chapter 9. Reports And Charts

Note

This section is a "work in process". Some of the material has not been reviewed for V2.0. While it may not be strictly accurate, it is at least a "guide".

Introduction

Reports and Charts give GnuCash the ability to present an overview of financial data in various ways. This can range from a simple summary of account totals to an advanced portfolio view. This section will present an explanation of the main GnuCash reports and how to adjust them.

To run a report or chart, click on the Reports menu, then either select a report (it will open with standard options), or click on Saved Report Configuration to select a report you have previously configured and saved.

Once the report has opened, click on the Options toolbar button to configure the report as needed, for example to set the report date or select accounts.

Tip

If you intend to save a report configuration, you should choose a named report date option such as *Today* rather than enter a specific date so it is not necessary to enter a specific date again in future reports.

Tip

If you often run a report with a date as at the start or end of an accounting period, set the accounting period start and end dates in Edit → Preferences → Accounting Period then select appropriate report date options. See the section called "Accounting Period".

Tip

If you cannot find a specific report to suit your requirements, you may be able to use the Find Transaction assistant (Edit → Find) to select a set of transactions, and then report them using Reports → Account Report . Further formatting or analysis may be done by copying and pasting the report into a spreadsheet.

After you have configured a report, you can save the configuration for future use by clicking either the Save Report Configuration or Save Report Configuration As... button.

Saving a Report Configuration

To save a report configuration for future use, while the required report tab is selected, go to the report options, select the *General* tab and change the *Report Name* to a meaningful unique name. Do not confuse this with the *Report Title* which prints at the top of a report.

Click the Save Report Configuration or Save Report Configuration As... button. This will store your customized report options in a file in your home directory. E.g. Linux: *~/.gnucash/saved-reports-[versioninfo]*

The first time you save a report with a name that has not already been saved, you can use either the Save Report Configuration or the Save Report Configuration As... button. You can modify the report name before saving it.

After a report configuration for a specific name has been saved, the Save Report Configuration button will immediately update the saved report configuration without giving the opportunity to save the configuration with a new name. Use the Save Report Configuration As... button to save the current report configuration with a new name.

After your customized report has been saved, it is available for use by the Reports → Saved Report Configurations menu and it will also be listed when starting Reports → Sample & Custom → Custom Multicolumn Report .

Working with Saved Report Configurations

Selecting Reports → Saved Report Configurations will open a dialog window with a list of the *Saved Report Configurations* you have previously created. In this context *Saved Report Configurations* means the set of customized settings for standard reports.

The *Saved Report Configurations* window lists each of your previously saved report configurations, and 3 small buttons at the end of each. These buttons perform the following actions

• Load (and run) report configuration. Double clicking a report configuration also performs this action.

• Edit report configuration name. This enables a report configuration to be renamed.

• Delete report configuration.

Configuring Reports and Charts

GnuCash reports have many configuration options. First, run the original report itself. Then, access the report options with the Options button on the toolbar.

Note

Check changed Graphic Engine Options

Report Options Buttons

After modifying report options, either

• Click the OK button to apply the changes, regenerate the report and close the options window.

or

• Click the Apply button to apply the changes, regenerate the report and leave the options window open for possible further changes. In this case, both the Apply and OK buttons will be disabled, indicating changes have been applied, until further changes are made.

or

• Click the Cancel button to close the options window without applying any unapplied changes.

Common Report Options

Many reports share similar options. Some common ones include:

- Report Name: Set the title of the report. This is also used to print the report for later viewing.

- Date Options: Reports typically specify either a single date, or a date range, for the report. Dates can be specified in two ways, either directly (using the date selector), or by selecting a relative date from the menu. Relative dates allow you to specify dates like Beginning of this year or Today.

    ## Tip

    If you often run a report with a date as at the start or end of an accounting period, set the accounting period start and end dates in Edit → Preferences → Accounting Period then select appropriate report date options. See the section called "Accounting Period".

- Step Size: This option is used on bar charts to determine the interval which each bar represents. Typical values are daily, weekly, monthly, and yearly.

- Accounts: Select the appropriate accounts for the report. Note that in some reports only certain types of accounts can be selected. For example, an expense piechart only allows expense accounts to be selected.

- Show Long Account Names: This option allows displaying either short account names (for example, Power) or long account names (for example, Utilities:Power).

- Include Subaccounts?: Summary reports typically have an include all subaccounts option, which if selected ensures that all subaccounts are included if the parent account is.

- Depth: This option allows the selection of how many levels the report displays subaccounts. If the subaccounts go deeper than selected, an overall value for all the subaccounts is calculated and included in a total. To make sure every account selected is individually displayed, select All.

- Style Sheet: Select a Style Sheet. Style sheets control how reports are displayed. At the moment, there are four style sheets: Default, Easy, Footer and Technicolor. You can customize each of these from the Edit → Style Sheets... menu item. This is described in the the section called "Changing Style Sheets" section.

- Plot Dimensions: There are width and height options for most charts, which specify the displayed dimensions (in pixels).

- Report Currency: Select the report currency. Generally, values will be converted to this currency for display.

    The default Report Currency is defined in Edit → Preferences Reports tab. See the section called "Reports".

- Price Source: Select how stock and currency prices are calculated in this report. Choose between a weighted average of prices over all transactions, prices at current values, or prices at the time of the report date.

- Totals: Charts display totals in the chart legend if this option is selected.

- Maximum Slices: Controls the maximum number of slices displayed in a piechart - other accounts will be placed in a slice marked Other.

- Maximum Bars: Controls the maximum number of bars displayed in a barchart.

- Display Columns: Choose columns to show from the register.

Reports Listed By Class

GnuCash has classified the main types of reports into major classes. These are all available under the Reports menu.

General Reports

The General Reports include the Account Summary Report, the Future Scheduled Transactions Summary, the Tax Schedule Report and TXF Export, and the Transaction Report and also the reports in the Sample & Custom menu.

Account Summary

Future Scheduled Transactions Summary

Tax Schedule Report and TXF Export

The tax schedule report lists all taxable income and deductible expense amounts used in the preparation of US Income Tax returns. The purpose of the report is to provide a complete audit trail for these amounts. The report is intended to be used by a tax payer to manually prepare his or her own tax return, or alternatively, to be provided to a tax preparer for that purpose. The report can also be used to generate an export of all tax related income and expenses to a TXF (Tax eXchange Format) file (this is in addition to exporting to the HTML format that all reports allow). The TXF file can be imported into tax filing programs such as TaxCut or TurboTax. The report should be run, inspected carefully for errors or omissions, and then corrections made to transactions, report settings, currency conversion rates or the account structure as needed. This process should be repeated as often as needed until all the amounts on the report are correct before a final version is used and saved along with the tax returns.

For accounts specified in the report options (none = all) that are also flagged as Tax-related, all transactions for the time period selected (also in the report options) are included. The report sorts transactions by date within account providing subtotals by account within tax code within Form or Schedule line number. Support is also provided for multiple copies of and for sub-line items for selected Forms/Schedules. Optionally uses special date processing to include federal estimated tax payments after year end.

All totals are in USD since this is the currency required for filing US Income Tax returns. Non-USD transaction amounts are converted to USD using the transaction conversion rate to USD, if available. If not, a conversion rate from the price database is used (either the date nearest the transaction date or nearest the report date as specified in the report options; if none is available, transaction amounts are converted to zero and the report provides a comment accordingly). A complete audit trail of conversions is provided.

Note

For this to work, the user has to segregate taxable and non taxable income to different accounts, as well as deductible and non deductible expenses. The Income Tax Information dialog is used for this. To access the Income Tax Information dialog go to Edit → Tax Report Options. The user also must set the TXF category of each tax related account. The Income Tax Information dialog is described in the the section called "Setting Tax Report Options" section.

Transaction Report

This report lists transactions in selected accounts during a specified financial period. Two fields may be optionally used for sorting and totalling.

Report Options

Figure 9.1. *Transaction Report, Report Options*

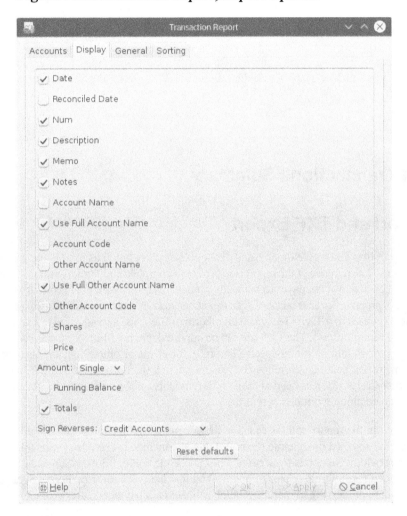

This is an image of the *Transaction Report, Report Options, Display tab*.

- *Accounts tab*

  - Accounts: Select one or more accounts to be reported.

    There are 4 buttons to aid account selection

Select All	Select all accounts
Clear All	Clear the selection and unselect all accounts
Select Children	Select all descendants of selected account
Select Default	Select the default account selection

- Show Hidden Accounts: Show accounts that have been marked hidden.

- Filter By: Optionally select accounts to be either included or excluded depending on Filter type

- Show Hidden Accounts: Show accounts that have been marked hidden in the Filter By list of accounts

- Filter Type: One of

None	Do not do any filtering
Include Transactions to/from Filter Accounts	Include Transactions to/from Filter Accounts only
Exclude Transactions to/from Filter Accounts	Exclude Transactions to/from all Filter Accounts

- Void Transactions: One of

Non-void only	Show only non-voided transactions
Void only	Show only voided transactions
Both	Show both and include voided transactions in totals

- Reset defaults button: Reset all values to their defaults

- *Display tab*

  - Date

  - Reconciled Date

  - Num

  - Description

  - Memo

  - Notes: Display the notes if the memo is unavailable

  - Account Name

  - Use Full Account Name

  - Account Code

  - Other Account Name: For multi-split transactions, this parameter should be unticked. See below for more details.

  - Use Full Other Account Name

  - Other Account Code

  - Shares: Display number of shares

  - Price: Display share prices

  - Amount: One of

None	Do not display Amount
Single	Single column display
Double	Two column display

- Running Balance

- Totals

- Sign Reverses: One of

None	Do not display signs reversed
Credit Accounts	Reverse amount display for Liability, Payable, Equity, Credit Card and Income accounts
Income and Expense	Reverse amount display for Income and Expense accounts

- Reset defaults button Reset all values to their defaults

- *General tab*

  - Report name: Enter a descriptive name for this report

  - Stylesheet: Select Default, Easy, Footer or Technicolor

  - Start Date: Enter or select a specific Start Date

    or select one of the following named start date options which will be used to determine the start date each time the report is run

Today	The current date
Start of this month	First day of the current month
Start of previous month	First day of the previous month
Start of current quarter	First day of the current quarterly accounting period
Start of previous quarter	First day of the previous quarterly accounting period
Start of this year	First day of the current calendar year
Start of previous year	First day of the previous calendar year
Start of accounting period	First day of the accounting period as defined in the global preferences

  - End Date: Enter or select a specific End Date,

    or select one of the following named end date options which will be used to determine the end date each time the report is run

Today	The current date
End of this month	Last day of the current month
End of previous month	Last day of the previous month

End of current quarter	Last day of the current quarterly accounting period
End of previous quarter	Last day of the previous quarterly accounting period
End of this year	Last day of the current calendar year
End of previous year	Last day of the previous calendar year
End of accounting period	Last day of the accounting period as defined in the global preferences

- Style: One of

Single	Display 1 line
Multi-Line	Display N lines

Note

In stable version 2.8.0, the *Style* option will be renamed to *Detail Level* and moved to the Display tab.

- Common Currency: Convert all transactions into a common currency

- Report's currency: Select the currency to display values

- Table for Exporting: Formats the table for cut & paste exporting with extra cells

- Reset defaults button: Reset all values to their defaults

- *Sorting tab*

  - Primary Key: Primary Sort Key. One of

None	Do not sort
Account Name	Sort and subtotal by account name
Account Code	Sort and subtotal by account code
Date	Sort by date
Exact Time	Sort by exact time
Reconciled Date	Sort by the reconciled date
Register Order	Sort as within the register
Other Account Name	Sort by account transferred from/to's name
Other Account Code	Sort by account transferred from/to's code
Amount	Sort by amount
Description	Sort by description
Number	Sort by check/transaction number
Memo	Sort by memo

- Show Full Account Name: Show the full account name for subtotals and subtitles

- Show Account Code: Show the account code for subtotals and subtitles

- Primary Subtotal: Subtotal according to the primary key

- Primary Subtotal for Date Key: Do a date subtotal. Only configurable if primary key is date, exact time or register order. One of None, weekly, monthly, quarterly or yearly

- Primary Sort Order: One of

Ascending	Smallest to largest, earliest to latest
Descending	Largest to smallest, latest to earliest

- Secondary Key: Secondary Sort Key. Same options as Primary Key

- Secondary Subtotal: Subtotal according to the secondary key

- Secondary Subtotal for Date Key: Do a date subtotal. Only configurable if primary key is date, exact time or register order. One of None, weekly, monthly, quarterly or yearly

- Secondary Sort Order: One of

Ascending	Smallest to largest, earliest to latest
Descending	Largest to smallest, latest to earliest

- Reset defaults button: Reset all values to their defaults

Displaying Split Account Details

This is controled by the *Style* option on the General tab.

Note

In stable version 2.8.0 this option will be renamed to *Detail Level* on the Display tab.

In *Single* line mode, there's only one line per transaction. So you can have the account name on one side of the equation and

a. the other account name if there's only one other split in the transaction

or

b. "Split" if there are multiple other splits in the transaction. You can't display multiple "other" account names in one line. There's just no room for it.

In the case of *Multi-Line* mode, this report uses a completely different concept. For each transaction, every split (both the split in this account and the split(s) in the other account(s) !) is printed on a separate line. And every split really means every split: both the split which belongs in the account being reported and the split(s) in the other account(s) that balance the transaction. So even the most basic transaction, with only two splits (this account and other account) will print two lines in multiline mode.

For a simple transaction like this

Description	Account	Debit	Credit
Cheques Received			
"multiple payers"	IncomeAccount		£30.00
	BankAccount	£30.00	

then on a Transaction Report for the bank account the details appear pretty much as above.

For clarity of the accounts, you might enter transactions with multiple splits referring to the same account. For example, the above transaction might well be entered like this

Description	Account	Debit	Credit
Cheques Received			
"FirstPayer"	IncomeAccount		£10.00
"SecondPayer"	IncomeAccount		£20.00
	BankAccount	£30.00	

When this transaction is printed on the bank account's Transaction Report in *Single* line mode, then under *other account* it simply prints the word *split* instead of the account name.

To display the additional split detail, you need to set *Single/Multi-Line* to *Multi-Line* and then tick *Display -> Account Name*. Do NOT tick *Display -> Other Account Name*.

You can choose whether or not to turn off the full account name using *Display -> Use Full Account Name*.

Use Full Other Account Name has no effect in *Multi-Line* mode.

Assets & Liabilities

The Assets & Liabilities reports includes the Balance Sheet report, Investment reports and the Net Worth report.

- Advanced Portfolio:

Columns

- Account: Stock Account

- Symbol: Ticker Symbol/Abbreviation as defined in the Security Editor. A report option can suppress this column.

- Listing: Type as defined in the Security Editor. A report option can suppress this column.

- Shares: Number of shares (quantity). A report option sets how many decimal places to show. A report option can suppress this column.

- Price: Unit market price as at report date. A report option can suppress this column.

- Basis: Cost of all shares acquired by any means, including brokerage fees if the option to include them is checked. Report option *Basis calculation method* can be set to Average, LIFO or FIFO.

- Value: Number of shares * Unit market price as at report date

- Money In: Sum of the cost of stock purchased, excluding stock acquired as part of a Dividend Reinvestment Plan. I.e. External money used to purchase shares.

- Money Out: Money from selling shares or a spin off transaction.

- Realized Gain: Money received for selling shares minus basis for shares sold, minus brokerage fees for the sale if the option to include them in basis is checked.

- Unrealized Gain: Value less Basis for unsold shares

- Total Gain: Realized Gain + Unrealized Gain

- Rate of Gain: Total Gain / Money In * 100 (from GnuCash 2.6.1 onwards)

- Income: Total of all income transactions associated with a stock account.

Note

To include income from dividends which are not reinvested (if there is no split to the stock account in the income transaction, the report has no way of associating the income with a particular stock) :

Ensure there is a dummy transaction split to the stock account with quantity 0, price 1 and value 0 in the dividend transaction. Enter the dummy stock split with no values in the dividend account and it will create the transaction with price 1 even though you cannot see the Price column in that register.

In GnuCash 2.6.6, this report was modified to simplify the recording of dividend and interest payments. With this change it may not be necessary to include the dummy stock split in the transaction. The report will find income (and expense) transactions that are in the parent account of the stock account being reported on. This is done by looking in the parent account for transactions that have exactly two splits (not counting trading account splits) where the other split is to an income or expense account with the same name as the stock's account.

For example given an account structure like

```
        Assets (type ASSET)
          Broker (type ASSET)
            Widget Stock (type STOCK)
        Income (type INCOME)
          Dividends (type INCOME)
            Widget Stock (type INCOME)
```

A transaction that debits the "Assets:Broker" account and credits the "Income:Dividends:Widget Stock" account will count as income even though it doesn't have a split with account "Assets:Broker:Widget Stock".

This only works if the parent account ("Assets:Broker" in this case) is a Bank or Asset account and the Income/Expense account has the same name as the stock account. It won't double count transactions that have a dummy split since they won't have exactly two split transactions.

It will not work if the income or expense account split is to a subaccount of the account with the same name as the stock account i.e. "Income:Dividends:Widget Stock:Franked"

- Brokerage Fees: Brokerage Fees

- Total Return: Total Gain + Income

- Rate of Return: Total Return / Money In * 100

Common report options are described in the section called "Configuring Reports and Charts"

Report Specific Options

- Accounts Tab

  - Include accounts with no shares: Unchecked (default) or checked.

- Display Tab

  - Show ticker symbols: Checked (default) or unchecked. If unchecked, Symbol column will be omitted.

  - Show listings: Checked (default) or unchecked. If unchecked, Listing column (source of shares price quotes) will be omitted.

  - Show number of shares: Checked (default) or unchecked. If unchecked, Shares column will be omitted.

  - Share decimal places: The number of decimal places to show in the number of shares. Default is 2.

  - Show prices: Checked (default) or unchecked. If unchecked, Price column will be omitted.

- General Tab

  - Price Source: Nearest in time (default) or Most Recent.

  - Basis calculation method: Average (default), FIFO or LIFO.

  - Set preference for price list data: Checked (default): Use price list data. If there is no relevant price list data, transaction prices will be used and there will be a warning. Unchecked: Get prices from stock transactions.

  - How to report brokerage fees: Include in basis (default), Include in gain or Ignore.

- Asset Barchart:

  The Asset Barchart report displays bars that present the value of all assets in a GnuCash file over time. By default, the report shows all accounts in *Accounts Receivable*, *Current Assets*, *Fixed Assets*, *Investments* and Special Accounts (if they exist) and it displays monthly bars for the current financial period. This report provides a graphic view of the assets in the file over time.

  ## Tip

  Like all the generic reports, the user can assign a title and save the report with it's selected options for re-use later.

  The display is in the form of either a stacked barchart or simple barchart with an option to display a table of the values.

  This report calculates and displays a default of 8 bars or up to 24 separate asset accounts value at the end of the day on several dates through a specified time period. The report automatically selects the most significant accounts to display with all other selected accounts summed as *Other*.

  The report exploits the outline structure of the chart of accounts to allow the user to select top level accounts and sub-accounts down to a user-selectable depth. Selected sub-accounts below the selected depth are automatically *summed up* into the next level when it is also selected. The default number of sub-account levels is 2, giving a summary view. Increasing the number of sub-levels increases the detail available to display. It is possible to un-select a higher level account and leave sub-accounts selected to force greater detail to appear in the report.

By default the report includes all *asset* accounts and sub-accounts, as well as *Imbalance* and *Orphan* Special accounts in whatever currencies or commodities may be present. The report's base currency is the default currency of the GnuCash file but if the file has data for multiple currencies, then it can be changed to another currency.

Since each account may be individually selected, the report can be designed to focus on a small subset of data such as current assets or investments.

The overall interval of the report defaults to start at the start of the current accounting period and to end at the end of the current accounting period. Numerous other starting choices and ending choices are available.

The first bar shows the selected values at the end of the day on the first date chosen. There are a number of choices for step size from *day* to *year* with the default being *month*. Note that if any step date would fall on the 29th, 30th or 31st in a month that does not have such a date the next interval will be 31 days later. For that step only the date will *slip* up to 3 days into the following month. This is true for releases at least through 2.4.13. Bug 639049 is open in Bugzilla to modify this behavior.

Currently, there is no option to start the report on the last day of any period. There is also no option to show *beginning* balances or *end of previous step* balances. This makes it difficult to correlate this report to business quarterly reports, for example.

The Net Worth linechart report, Liability barchart report and Net Worth barchart report are similar except for the graphic type and default account groups selected.

Other features are customizable in a manner similar to other standard reports.

- Asset Piechart:

- Average Balance:

- Balance Sheet: This report summarizes assets, liabilities, and equity. When properly maintained, assets should equal the sum of liabilities and equity. If that is not the case, there is some kind of internal imbalance in the accounts.

- Balance Sheet using eguile-gnc:

- General Journal:

- General Ledger:

- Investment Portfolio: This report summarizes the value of the stocks in the current portfolio.

- Liability Barchart:

- Liability Piechart:

- Net Worth Barchart: Net worth is the difference between the value of assets or liabilities.

- Net Worth Linechart: Net worth plotted over time. Net worth is the difference between the value of assets or liabilities.

- Price Scatterplot:

Business Reports

The Business Reports includes Customer and Vendor Reports and Printable Invoices as well as Aging reports.

Customer Report

Customer Summary

Easy Invoice

Employee Report

Fancy Invoice

Job Report

Payable Aging

This report provides a listing of vendors and their aged outstanding balances. Vendors may be included if they have posted business transactions (e.g. invoices) for the selected accounts payable account. It shows their current balance, and how much they have due from invoices over time periods 0-30 days, 31-60 days, 61-90 days, and over 90 days. The report also contains links to each vendor and to their current vendor report.

Optionally, vendor address details may be also shown.

Tip

To export vendor address details, say in order to do a mail merge, select the optional vendor address details in the report options display tab, apply the options to regenerate the report, then copy and paste the report into a spreadsheet. Alternatively, the report can be exported to a .html file, then read into a spreadsheet.

Report Options

Note

See *Common Report Options* in the *Configuring Reports and Charts* section of this help manual for more details of the common options.

- *General tab*

  - Report name: Enter a descriptive name for this report - see common report options.

  - Stylesheet: Select a style sheet for this report - see common report options.

  - To: Select a date to report on or a named date. Transactions up to and including the selected date will be used to calculate the outstanding aged balances. See common report options.

- Report's currency: Select the currency to display the values in - see common report options.

- Price Source: Select the source of price information used for currency conversion if needed. One of

Average Cost	The volume-weighted average cost of purchases
Weighted Average (default)	The weighted average of all currency transactions in the past
Most recent	The most recent recorded price
Nearest in time	The price recorded nearest in time to the report date

- Show Multi-currency Totals: If not selected, all totals are shown in the report currency.

- Sort By: Sort companies by one of

Name (default)	Company name
Total Owed	Total amount owed to company
Bracket Total Owed	Amount owed in oldest bracket. If same, use next oldest

- Sort Order: One of

Increasing (default)	
Decreasing	

- Show zero balance items: Show companies even if they have a zero outstanding balance.

- Due or Post Date: Leading date. Which date to use to determine aging. One of

Due Date (default)	
Post Date	

- Payable Account: The accounts payable account used to select vendors to be reported. Vendors are included if they have a posted business transaction (usually an invoice) on or before the report date and also meet the *Show zero balance items* criteria.

- *Display tab*

  - Address Name: Display vendor address name. This, and other fields, may be useful if copying this report to a spreadsheet for use in a mail merge.

  - Address 1: Display address line 1.

  - Address 2: Display address line 2.

  - Address 3: Display address line 3.

  - Address 4: Display address line 4.

  - Phone: Display address phone number. 130

  - Fax: Display address fax number.

- Email: Display email address.

- Active: Display vendor active status.

Printable Invoice

Receivable Aging

This report provides a listing of customers and their aged outstanding balances. Customers may be included if they have posted business transactions (e.g. invoices) for the selected accounts receivable account. It shows their current balance, and how much they have outstanding from invoices over time periods 0-30 days, 31-60 days, 61-90 days, and over 90 days. The report also contains links to each customer and to their current customer report.

Optionally, customer address details may be also shown.

Tip

To export customer address details, say in order to do a mail merge, select the optional customer address details in the report options display tab, apply the options to regenerate the report, then copy and paste the report into a spreadsheet. Alternatively, the report can be exported to a .html file, then read into a spreadsheet.

Report Options

Note

See *Common Report Options* in the *Configuring Reports and Charts* section of this help manual for more details of the common options.

- *General tab*

  - Report name: Enter a descriptive name for this report - see common report options.

  - Stylesheet: Select a style sheet for this report - see common report options.

  - To: Select a date to report on or a named date. Transactions up to and including the selected date will be used to calculate the outstanding aged balances. See common report options.

  - Report's currency: Select the currency to display the values in - see common report options.

  - Price Source: Select the source of price information used for currency conversion if needed. One of

Average Cost	The volume-weighted average cost of purchases
Weighted Average (default)	The weighted average of all currency transactions in the past
Most recent	The most recent recorded price
Nearest in time	The price recorded nearest in time to the report date

- Show Multi-currency Totals: If not selected, all totals are shown in the report currency.

- Sort By: Sort companies by one of

Name (default)	Company name
Total Owed	Total amount owed by company
Bracket Total Owed	Amount owed in oldest bracket. If same, use next oldest

- Sort Order: One of

Increasing (default)	
Decreasing	

- Show zero balance items: Show companies even if they have a zero outstanding balance.

- Due or Post Date: Leading date. Which date to use to determine aging. One of

Due Date (default)	
Post Date	

- Receivables Account: The accounts receivable account used to select customers to be reported. Customers are included if they have a posted business transaction (usually an invoice) on or before the report date and also meet the *Show zero balance items* criteria.

- *Display tab*

  - Address Source: Which customer address fields to display. One of

Billing (default)	Address fields from billing address.
Shipping	Address fields from shipping address.

  - Address Name: Display customer address name. This, and other fields, may be useful if copying this report to a spreadsheet for use in a mail merge.

  - Address 1: Display address line 1.

  - Address 2: Display address line 2.

  - Address 3: Display address line 3.

  - Address 4: Display address line 4.

  - Phone: Display address phone number.

  - Fax: Display address fax number.

  - Email: Display email address.

  - Active: Display vendor active status.

Tax Invoice

Vendor Report

Income & Expense

The Income & Expense reports includes the Cash Flow and Income Statement reports.

- Cash Flow:

- Equity Statement:

- Expense Barchart:

- Expense Piechart:

- Expense vs Day of Week:

- Income & Expense Chart:

- Income Barchart:

- Income Piechart:

- Income Statement: This report summarizes sources of income and expenditure. (This report was called Profit & Loss in gnucash-1.8.)

- Income vs Day of Week:

- Profit & Loss: This is the same report as the Income Statement but with a different title.

- Trial Balance: This report summarizes sources of income and expenditure.

Sample & Custom

Welcome Sample Report

Custom Multicolumn Report

This report is used to place multiple reports into a single report window to examine a set of financial information at a glance.

Sample Report with Examples

Budget

Budget Balance Sheet

Budget Barchart

Budget Flow

Budget Income Statement

Budget Profit & Loss

Budget Report

This report is used to compare budgeted and real amounts for selected accounts. It allows you to review how well you follow the budget.

The report is generated as a table in which each row represents an account and each set of columns shows the *budgeted amount*, the *real amount*, and the *difference* between them for each report period.

Each entry in the *real amount* column is the sum of all the splits in the row's account over the column's period. For example, if the report is set up for monthly periods, the column is for May, and the row is for Expenses:Groceries, then the value will be the sum of all Expenses:Groceries splits for that May.

The report supports selecting a range of periods instead all of them. Periods that are out of range can be included in the report as the consolidated columns around the selected range. This allows you to focus on particular periods, for example the current one, and is especially useful for budgets with many periods. For example, if you have a 12 period budget you can make a 3 column report with the format "(all periods before columns set) (current period columns set) (all periods after columns set)" that is easily fits on the screen and allows you to match values with account names.

Budget report options

Note

Here we describe only options that are specific for the Budget Report. You can find information about standard parameters in the section called "Configuring Reports and Charts".

- *Show budget* - include the budgeted values for the period

- *Show actual* - include the real values for the period

- *Show difference* - include the difference between budgeted and real values for the period. Enabling this option does not force including budgeted and actual values in the report

- *Show Column with totals* - Adds a final column set containing budgeted, real value, and difference columns summing those values across all periods of the report.

- *Rollup budget amounts to parent* - not used in the report, can be deleted or should be fixed

- *Include accounts with zero total balances and budget values* - enables display of accounts with no budget or splits in any period.

- *Budget* - Select the budget to use for report generation

- *Report for range of budget periods* - Enables reporting on a subset of the budget by selecting a beginning and an ending period.

- *Range start* - a combobox with a list of options to select the start period:

  1. *First* - select first budget period

  2. *Previous* - select previous period.

3. *Current* - select current period.

4. *Next* - select next period.

5. *Last* - select last budget period

6. *Manual* - enables spinbox where you can select exact period

Note

The *current*, *previous*, and *next* options select the period based on the date on which the report is run, with *current* being the period in which the date falls, *previous* being the one before that, and *next* the period after. If the current date falls outside the date range covered by the budget, the *first* or *last* period will be used as appropriate.

- *Exact start period* - options for select exact start period, enabled only if the range start option is set to *Manual*

- *Range end* - a combobox with a list of options to select the end period. Values are the same as in *Range start* options

- *Exact end period* - the same as *Exact start period* but for the end of range

- *Include collapsed periods before selected* - if on, then includes in the report all budget periods, that are before selected period range, as a single consolidated column set

- *Include collapsed periods after selected* - if on, then includes in the report all budget periods, that are after selected period range, as a single consolidated column set.

Printing or Exporting Reports and Charts

Note

Verify !!! How customize printing with Gnome?

GnuCash is able to print reports and to export the reports to HTML (web) pages. The Print GnuCash Document dialog is accessed from the Print button on the *Toolbar* or go to File → Print in the menu. To Export a report to a web page (HTML) select the Export button on the *Toolbar* and type in a file name.

Most reports, being presented in HTML, can also be copied and pasted into a spreadsheet.

The Print GnuCash Document dialog is used to select which Printer to send the print job to or to print to a File. It also contains a Preview button to view the document before printing. Press Print to send the job to the selected printer or Cancel to dismiss the Print dialog.

Printing from an open register prints the Account Report, which is also called the Register Report. This lists transactions in the account with a total. Other reports print as viewed in the Report screen.

Creating Reports and Charts

Note

This section may need updating !!!

It is possible to write reports if the current ones are not suitable. To do this you will need to know Scheme (a LISP-like programming language), and it is an excellent idea to have a copy of the GnuCash source code available.

The reporting interface is documented in the source code file `src/report/report-system/doc/report-html.txt`. The file `src/report/utility-reports/hello-world.scm` in the GnuCash source distribution provides a good example of how reports are developed.

Accessing the GnuCash API

It is also necessary to access data from the engine to get information for your report. This is *since version 2.1.x* performed by a set of Scheme wrapper functions that are documented in the file `src/engine/swig-engine.c`. *Up to version 2.0.5* it was `src/g-wrap/gnc.html`. Examine some of the other reports in src/scm/report for an indication of how they are used.

Some users started a table in the GnuCash wiki Custom Reports#The GnuCash API [http://wiki.gnucash.org/wiki/Custom_Reports#The_GnuCash_API].

Because the above file only contains the syntax of the function you can use the Doxygen source documentation either local after running

```
./configure --enable-doxygen --enable-html-docs
make doc
```

on your sources or online http://code.gnucash.org/docs/MAINT/ or http://code.gnucash.org/docs/MASTER/ to get more information about the functions.

Report Rendering

At present, reports are produced by calling a HTML-generation API, which outputs a dialect of HTML and rendering this with a HTML widget. This has limitations, particularly when trying to align objects precisely, as might be necessary for printing onto pre-printed invoices for example.

Chapter 10. Customizing GnuCash

Account Display Options

The View → Filter By ... is used to set or modify the view of the account tree window. The Accounts tab of this form allows the selection of the types of accounts to display. These selections effect the view on each specific open window of the account tree.

The Other tab allows enabling/disabling of the options; Show Hidden accounts, Show zero total accounts.

The account tree window, by default, only shows the quantity of each commodity that you own, under the column heading Total. Often, however, you may want to display other values. This is easily accomplished by clicking on the Options button (the small down pointing arrow on the right side of the main account window *Titlebar*), and selecting the option(s) to display. These selections set the view on all open windows of the account tree.

Setting Preferences

The GnuCash Preferences window allows you to customize your GnuCash session by setting several options. From the GnuCash menu select Edit → Preferences (GnuCash → Preferences on Mac OS X). The GnuCash Preferences window will open. Using the tabs on the left make your desired changes. The settings in this dialog are set per user and not stored with the file. This is in contrast to the settings described in the section called "Book Options", which are kept with, and are part of, the file (or Book), and as such are common to all users. So GnuCash Preferences settings are individual to each user who uses a given file and any changes made by one user will not affect other users of that file. Also, a given user's preferences will be common to all files that that user opens with GnuCash.

Tip

Pausing the cursor for a couple of seconds over options in these windows will display a tooltip with in-depth information on the choice.

Note

The changes you make will be applied at once.

To close the GnuCash Preferences window press the Close button.

Each tab in the GnuCash Preferences window is discussed in its own section below. For a listing of the tabs, see Chapter 10, *Customizing GnuCash*.

Accounting Period

Figure 10.1. The Preferences window, Accounting Period tab

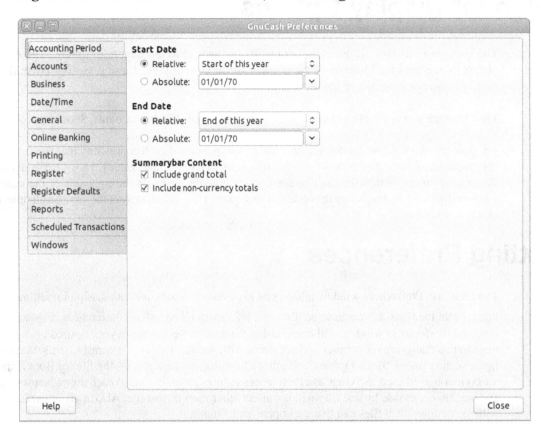

- Start Date: This item sets the accounting period's start date.

  - Relative: Use the specified relative starting date for profit/loss calculations. Also use this date for net assets calculations. Relative defines start by today or start of current/previous year, quarter, month.

  - Absolute: Use the specified absolute starting date for profit/loss calculations. Also use this date for net assets calculations.

- End Date: This item sets the accounting period's end date.

  - Relative: Use the specified relative ending date for profit/loss calculations. Also use this date for net assets calculations.

  - Absolute: Use the specified absolute ending date for profit/loss calculations. Also use this date for net assets calculations.

- Summarybar content

  - Include grand total: If checked, show in the *Summarybar* a grand total of all accounts converted to the default currency.

  - Include non-currency totals: if this option is selected, GnuCash will include in the *Summarybar* a total for non-currency items (for instance number of shares).

Accounts

Figure 10.2. The Preferences window, Accounts tab

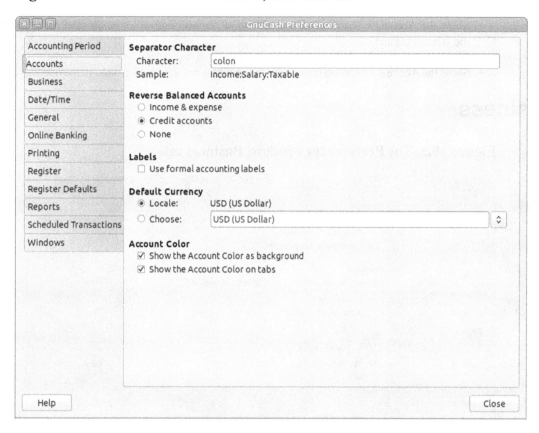

- Separator Character: The account separator is the character that separates a parent account from its sub-account, for example Utilities:Electric. The default is a : (Colon), but you can also select / (Slash), \ (Backslash), - (Dash) or . (Period), or any Unicode character that isn't a letter or a number.

- Reverse Balanced accounts: This option lets you determine whether account balances will display as positive or negative numbers:

  - Income & Expense assigns a positive credit balance to income account balances and a negative debit balance to expense account balances. See the section called "Types of GnuCash Accounts" for more information on these account types.

  - Credit accounts (default) displays a positive balance for account types that would normally carry a credit balance (income, credit, liability, equity). See the section called "Types of GnuCash Accounts" for more information on these account types.

  - None shows all credit balances as negative and all debit balances as positive.

- Labels: Select this option if you want column headings in the register to refer to debits and credits instead of the default informal headings such as withdrawal and deposit.

- Default Currency: This item determines which currency will be selected by default when creating new accounts.

  - Locale: Use the system locale currency for all newly created accounts.

- Choose: specify the currency to use, independent of your system settings.

- Account Color: This option lets you manage the display of the account color set in the Edit Account window:

  - Show the Account Colors as background: show the accounts color as account name background in the Accounts Page.

  - Show the Account Colors on tabs: show the accounts color as background in the account register tabs.

Business

Figure 10.3. The Preferences window, Business tab

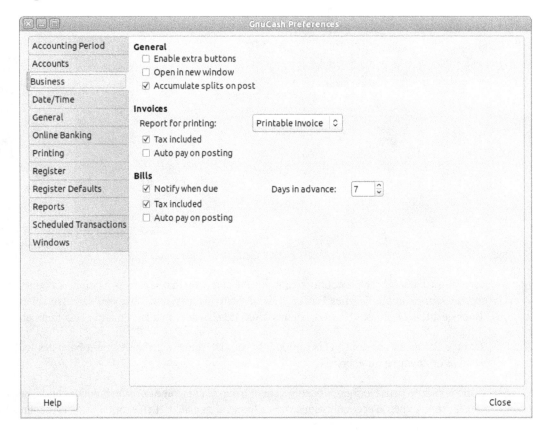

- General

  - Enable extra buttons: If checked, extra toolbar buttons for common business functions are shown.

  - Open in new window: If checked, each invoice will be opened in its own top level window. If clear, the invoice will be opened in the current window.

  - Accumulate splits on post: Whether multiple entries in an invoice which transfer to the same account should be accumulated into a single split by default.

- Invoices

  - Report for printing: Allows to select the invoice report to be used for printing.

- Tax Included: Whether tax is included by default in entries on invoices. This setting is inherited by new customers and vendors.

- Auto pay on posting: If enabled, at post time automatically attempt to pay customer documents with outstanding pre-payments and counter documents.

    ## Note

    Counter documents are documents with opposite sign. For example for an invoice, customer credit notes and negative invoices are considered counter documents.

    The pre-payments and documents obviously have to be against the same customer.

- Bills

    - Notify when due: Lets you set whether you want to be notified at GnuCash startup of when a bill is soon to be due.

    - Days in advance: How many days before the due date to warn about bills coming due.

    - Tax Included: Whether tax is included by default in entries on bills. This setting is inherited by new customers and vendors.

    - Process payments on posting: If enabled, at post time automatically attempt to pay vendor documents with outstanding pre-payments and counter documents.

        ## Note

        Counter documents are documents with opposite sign. For example for a bill, vendor credit notes and negative bills are considered counter documents.

        The pre-payments and documents obviously have to be against the same vendor.

Date/Time

Figure 10.4. The Preferences window, Date/Time tab

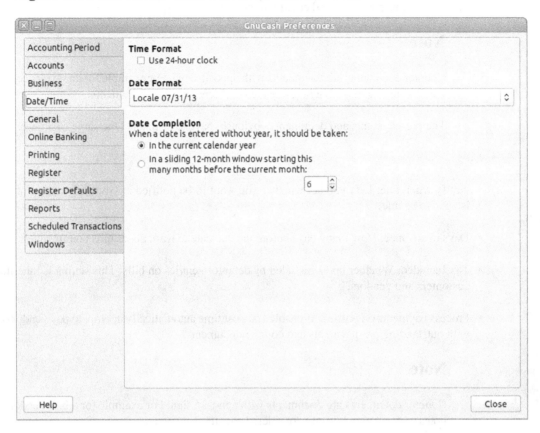

- Time Format

  - Use 24-hour clock: Lets you specify if you want to use 24 or 12 hours time format. That is if 11 o'clock at night should be represented as 11PM or 23:00.

- Date Format: This option controls the appearance of the date (you can see a preview of the date beside each of the choices). The available choices are:

  - US: Use the date format common in the United States.

  - UK: Use the date format common in the United Kingdom.

  - Europe: Use the date format common in continental Europe.

  - ISO: Use the date format specified by the ISO-8601 standard.

  - Locale: Use the date format specified by the system locale.

- Date completion: This option lets you manage the case when a date is entered without a year:

  - In the current calendar year: (Default) Dates will be completed so that they are within the current calendar year.

- In a sliding 12-month window starting a configurable number of months before the current month: Dates will be completed so that they are close to the current date. You can enter the maximum number of months to go backwards in time when completing dates.

General

Figure 10.5. The Preferences window, General tab

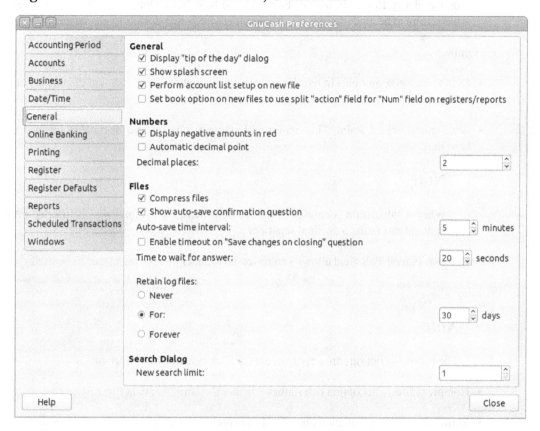

- General

  - Display "Tip of the Day" dialog: This option displays or hides the Tip of the Day screen when Gnu-Cash is started.

  - Show splash screen: With this option you can enable or disable the visualization of the startup screen while GnuCash is starting up.

  - Perform account list setup on new file: This option turns off the display of the New Account Hierarchy Setup assistant when the entry File → New File is selected from the GnuCash menu.

  - Set book option on new files to use split "action" field for "Num" field on registers/reports: If selected, the displayed setting on the New Book Options dialog for the Use Split Action Field for Number setting will be selected and, if saved, the book option for the new file will be set so that the "Num" field on registers shows/updates the split-action field and the transaction-num field is shown on the second line in double line mode (and is not visible in single line mode). Otherwise, the displayed setting on the dialog will not be selected and, if saved, the book option for the new file will be set so that the "Num" field on registers shows/updates the transaction-num field. See the discussion in the section called "Book Options" about how to set book options including the option for the section called "Use

Split Action Field for Number". Regardless of the setting of this preference, the user can modify the initially displayed setting for this option on the New Book Options dialog before saving the options.

Note

If the New Book Options dialog appears in situations where a new book is being set up, the settings from this preference will determine the default setting for the corresponding check box on the dialog. However, the OK button on the New Book Options dialog must be pressed for the setting to be made for the new book; otherwise it will default to *not selected*.

- Numbers

  - Display negative amounts in red: If you turn off this option, GnuCash will display negative numbers in black.

  - Automatic Decimal Point: This option will automatically insert a decimal point into numbers you type in.

    ### Note

    When a calculation is entered in the Amount field, the decimal sign is inserted into *every* operand that omits a decimal separator.

  - Decimal Places: This field allows you to set the number of decimal places to be used.

- Files

  ### Note

  The following options are only relevant for files saved in XML format.

  - Compress files: This option determines whether the GnuCash data file will be compressed or not.

  - Show auto-save confirmation question: If this option is enabled, GnuCash will show you a confirmation screen each time the auto-save process is started.

  - Auto-save time interval: This field sets the number of minutes between each automatic saving of the file. Set to 0 to disable the auto-save feature.

  - Enable timout on "Save changes on closing" question: If enabled, the Save changes on closing question will only wait a limited number of seconds for an answer. If the user didn't answer within that time, the changes will be saved automatically and the question window closed. You can set the number of seconds in the Time to wait for answer field.

  - Retain log files: In this section you can set your preferences about the log files using the provided radio buttons.

    - Never: Disable the creation of log files.

    - For: Enter a specific number of days for which keep the files.

    - Forever: Disable the auto deletion of log files; retains the log files forever.

- Search Dialog

  - New search limit: Defaults to "new search" if fewer than this number of items is returned.

Online Banking

Figure 10.6. The Preferences window, Online Banking tab

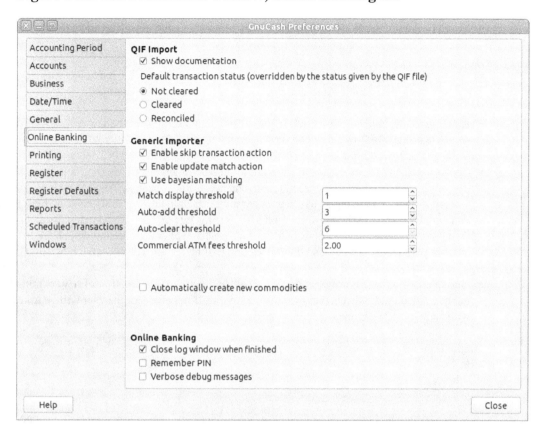

- QIF Import

    - Show documentation: The first time you use the QIF importer you may notice that the importer has detailed instructions on how to import a file. Once you have become familiar with using the importer, you might want to turn off this option. Turning off the option gives you less detail in the importer screens.

    - Default transaction status (overridden by the status given by the QIF file): In this section you can set the default status for imported transactions using the provided self-explainingradio buttons:

        - Not cleared (Default)

        - Cleared

        - Reconciled

- Generic Importer

    - Enable skip transaction action: Enable the SKIP action in the transaction matcher. If enabled, a transaction whose best match's score is in the yellow zone (above the Auto-ADD threshold but below the Auto-CLEAR threshold) will be skipped by default.

    - Enable update match action: Enable the UPDATE AND RECONCILE action in the transaction matcher. If enabled, a transaction whose best match's score is above the Auto-CLEAR threshold and has a different date or amount than the matching existing transaction will cause the existing transaction to be updated and cleared by default.

- Use Bayesian matching: Use Bayesian algorithms to match new transactions with existing accounts.

- Match display threshold: The minimal score a potential match must have to be displayed in the match list.

- Auto-add threshold: A transaction whose best match's score is in the red zone (above display threshold, but below or equal to Auto-add threshold) will be added by default.

- Auto-clear threshold: A transaction whose best match's score is in the green zone (above or equal to Auto-clear threshold) will be cleared by default.

- Commercial ATM fees threshold: In some places commercial ATMs (not belonging to a financial institution) are installed in places like convenience stores. These ATMs add their fee directly to the amount instead of showing up as a separate transaction or in your monthly banking fees. For example, you withdraw $100, and you are charged $101.50 plus Interac fees. If you manually entered that $100, the amounts won't match. You should set this to whatever is the maximum such fee in your area (in units of your local currency), so the transaction will be recognized as a match by GnuCash.

- Automatically create new commodities: Enables the automatic creation of new commodities if any unknown commodity is encountered during import. If not enabled, the user will be asked what to do with each unknown commodity.

- Online Banking

Note

This section is shown only if GnuCash is compiled with Aqbanking and HBCI support.

- Close log window when finished: Close the log window when the operation is completed.

- Remember PIN: Enable this option if you want GnuCash to remember the PIN you enter for online banking authentication.

- Verbose debug messages: Enable this option if you want GnuCash to show more information about the online banking operations.

Printing

Figure 10.7. The Preferences window, Printing tab

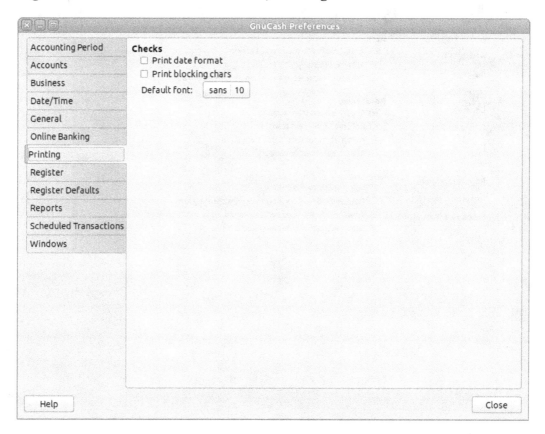

The Printing tab allows you to set some options that affect the printing of checks on paper.

- Print date format: Enable this option if you want to print on the check, below the actual date, its format in 8 point type.

- Print blocking chars: Enable this option to print a series of three asterisks before and after each text field in the check.

- Default font: Click the button on the left to open a Pick a Font screen in which you can customize the font that will be used to print checks.

Register

Figure 10.8. The Preferences window, Register tab

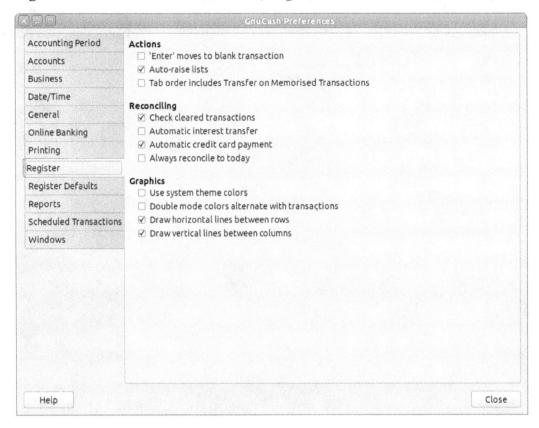

- Actions

  - 'Enter' moves to blank transaction: If selected, move the cursor to the blank transaction at the end of the register after the user presses the **Enter** key. Otherwise the cursor will be moved down one row.

  - Auto-raise lists: If selected, all lists will automatically be expanded when input focus is in the list field.

  - Tab order includes Transfer on Memorised Transaction: If selected, when the transaction is auto filled, pressing the **Tab** key in the register the cursor's jump will include the Transfer field.

- Reconciling

  - Check cleared transactions: If selected, automatically check off cleared transactions when reconciling.

  - Automatic interest transfer: If selected, prior to reconciling an account which charges or pays interest, prompt the user to enter a transaction for the interest charge or payment. Currently only enabled for Bank, Credit, Mutual, Asset, Receivable, Payable, and Liability accounts.

  - Automatic credit card payment: If selected, after reconciling a credit card statement, prompt the user to enter a credit card payment.

  - Always reconcile to today: If selected, always open the reconcile screen with today's date for statement date, regardless of previous reconciliation.

- Graphics

- Don't use GnuCash built-in colors: If selected, the system color theme will be applied to register windows. Otherwise the original GnuCash register color will be used.

- Double mode colors alternate with transactions: If selected, configures the register window to alternate between the primary and secondary colors with each transaction, instead of each row.

- Draw horizontal lines between rows: If selected, GnuCash will draw a horizontal line between each row.

- Draw vertical lines between columns: If selected, GnuCash will draw a vertical line between the cells in each row.

Register Defaults

Figure 10.9. The Preferences window, Register Defaults tab

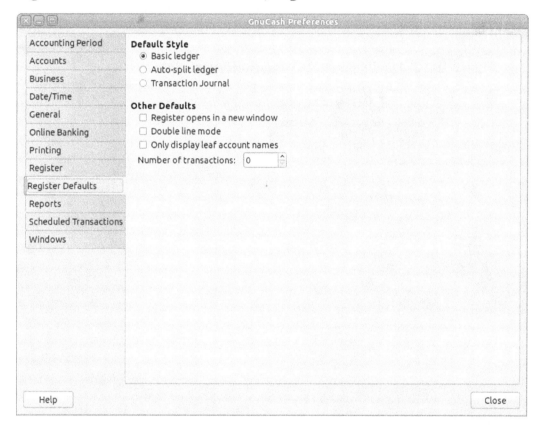

The Register Defaults tab preferences affect the behavior of the transaction register windows.

- Default Style

  Here you can choose from 3 different styles for register windows:

  - Basic ledger: Show all transactions on one line. (Two in double line mode.)

  - Auto-split ledger: Automatically expand the current transaction to show all splits. All other transactions are shown on one line. (Two in double line mode.)

  - Transaction journal: All transactions are expanded to show all splits.

- Other Defaults

  - Register opens in a new window: If selected, register will be in a separate window instead of in a tab.

  - Double line mode: If selected, show two lines of information for each transaction instead of one.

  - Only display leaf account names: If selected, only the name of the leaf accounts will be displayed in the Account selection popup. The default behavior is to display the full account name including the path in the account tree.

    ### Warning

    Enabling this option implies that you use unique leaf account names.

  - Number of transactions: How many transactions to show in a register. Set to 0 to show all transactions.

Reports

Figure 10.10. The Preferences window, Reports tab

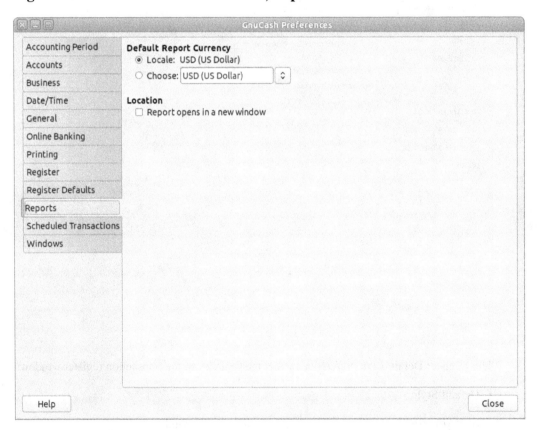

The Reports tab preferences affect the behavior of GnuCash reports.

- Default Report Currency: This item determines which currency will be used by default when creating reports. You can choose:

  - Locale: Use the system locale currency for all newly created reports.

  - Choose: Use the specified currency for all newly created reports.

- Location

  - Report opens in a new window: if you select this option, the reports will open up in a new window, instead of in a tab.

Scheduled Transactions

Figure 10.11. The Preferences window, Scheduled Transactions tab

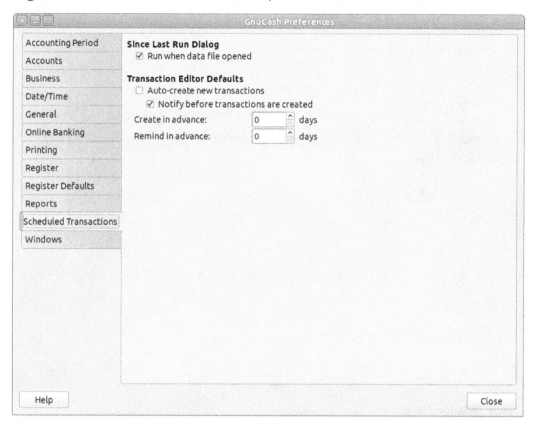

The Scheduled Transactions tab preferences affect the behavior of GnuCash for scheduling transactions. More information about scheduled transactions can be found in the section called "Scheduling Transactions".

- Since Last Run Dialog

  - Run when data file opened: If selected, the Since Last Run screen will appear when GnuCash opens the file.

  - Show notification window: If selected, a list of scheduled and created transactions will appear when GnuCash opens the file.

- Transaction Editor Defaults

  - Auto-Create new transactions: If selected, new scheduled transactions will automatically be entered into the register. If the auto-create option is enabled, you can also check Notify before transactions are created so that you will be able to confirm creating the transactions.

  - Create in advance: The default number of days in advance to create the registered scheduled transactions.

- Remind in advance: The default number of days in advance to remind about new scheduled transactions.

Windows

Figure 10.12. The Preferences window, Windows tab

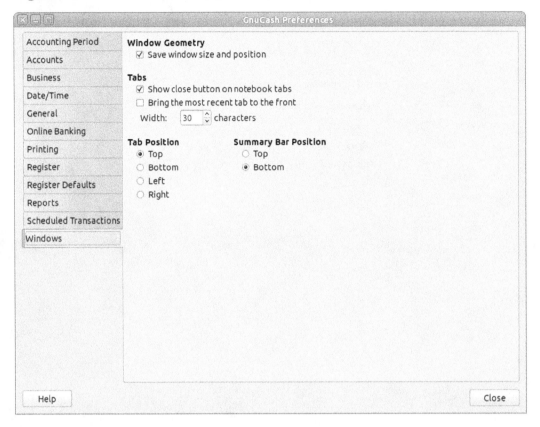

- Window Geometry

  - Save window size and position: If selected, next time GnuCash starts it will re-use the window size and position configured in the last run.

- Tabs

  - Show close button on notebook tabs: Adds a small close icon on each tab, to make it easier to close the various tabs.

  - Bring the most recent tab to the front: If selected, the newly created tab will be shown over the other tabs.

  - Width: The width of tab label expressed in characters.

    ## Note

    If the text in the tab is longer than this value (the test is approximate) then the tab label will have the middle cut and replaced with an ellipsis.

- Tab Position

Position the tabs at the Top (default), Bottom, Left or Right.

- Summary Bar Position

Position the Summary Bar at the Top or at the Bottom (default) of the GnuCash main window.

Book Options

The File → Properties menu item is used to set or modify choices that affect how a specific GnuCash file (also referred to as a Book) operates. Selecting this menu item brings up the Book Options dialog. This dialog also appears in situations where you are importing transactions into a new book, with the title New Book Options. It is automatically raised in these 'new book' situations because these settings can affect how imported data are converted to GnuCash transactions and so should be considered and set before your first import (specifically, the the section called "Use Split Action Field for Number" setting).

The settings in this dialog are kept with, and are part of, the file (or Book). This is in contrast to the settings described in the section called "Setting Preferences", which are set per user and not stored with the file. So Book Options settings are shared by all users who use a given file and any changes made by one user will affect all users of that file.

Tip

Pausing the cursor for a couple of seconds over options in these tabs will display a tooltip with a more detailed description of the choice.

The Book Options dialog has five buttons that are common to all tabs. The Reset defaults button takes all items on the visible tab and sets their value to the default setting; it only affects the visible tab. The Help button opens up a help window to this section. The Cancel button closes the dialog, making no changes to the saved settings for Book Options. The Apply button is initially insensitive but becomes sensitive when any setting is set or changed. Selecting it saves the setting(s) for the book but keeps the Book Options dialog open. Typically, the changes are reflected in the affected areas of GnuCash as soon as the button is pressed, so it can be used to 'see' the effect of a given option without having to re-open the dialog. The Apply button is not sensitive on the dialog if it appears during transaction import (that is, 'new book') situations. The OK button behaves like the Apply button except that it immediately *closes* the dialog, as well.

Accounts Book Options Tab

The Accounts tab of this dialog allows the selection of options that affect how accounting registers function.

Use Trading Accounts

Check the Use Trading Accounts checkbox to have trading accounts used for transactions involving more than one currency or commodity.

Day Threshold for Read-Only Transactions

Use the Day Threshold for Read-Only Transactions spin-box to choose the number of days before today, prior to which, transactions will be read-only and cannot be edited anymore in the registers. This threshold is marked by a red line in the account register windows. If zero, all transactions can be edited and none are read-only. This feature is intended to be used to guard against accidental changes to non-current transactions.

Use Split Action Field for Number

Note

This option is only available in GnuCash version 2.6 or later.

Check the Use Split Action Field for Number checkbox to have the split action field of the anchor split used for the 'Num' column in registers, reports and import/export functions, where applicable, in place of the transaction number; the transaction number is then shown as 'T-Num' on reports and on the second line of registers. This choice has a corresponding effect on business features.

The difference between the two is that with the checkbox not selected, the same 'Num' is displayed for a given transaction regardless of what register it is viewed in and with the checkbox selected, a different 'Num' can be entered/displayed for a given transaction in each register it is viewed in. In both cases, the 'next number logic' of the 'Num' cell is based on the account of the register the transaction is entered to or viewed from but in one case it fills the transaction number, in the other, it fills the split action field of the anchor split. In both cases, both fields are visible and can be viewed and used as free-form text in double-line mode for any value the user wants.

Warning

Initial setup of GnuCash: It is expected that, after careful consideration of the consequences, this option will be set when a new GnuCash file is created and not changed thereafter (see next warning). For this reason, a preference is provided (see Setting Preferences - General) that can establish an initial default setting for new files, so that if you will have more than one file, it is easier to set them all up consistently. You may wish to set up a test file and experiment with the two settings to understand the differences before establishing your first real GnuCash file.

Tip

Moving from Quicken: For users that are switching from other personal accounting applications, such as Quicken, selecting this option may be more consistent with the numbering approach used there and can preserve the numbering of historical data brought over; this option should be set before performing the initial import.

Warning

Changing this option for an existing GnuCash file: If you change this option for an existing file, historical data will not be changed. This means that if you set the option one way, enter (or import) transactions, then change the option and enter (or import) additional transactions and switch back-and-forth, you will end up with a file that will appear to have inconsistent treatment of numbers in registers, reports and exports. This is because the setting of this option at the time of data entry/import determines where the number data is stored and the setting at the time of data display/reporting/exporting determines which field is displayed as number.

There is no reason to avoid changing this option for an existing GnuCash file if you understand the implications. If you elect to make this change, it should probably be done between accounting periods with the understanding that number data prior to the date the option is changed will be displayed/reported/exported differently from that after the date.

Warning

If you change this option, and press Apply or OK, open registers and labels on query and sorting dialogs will be refreshed to reflect the new option immediately. But open reports need to be individually reloaded by the user to have the change reflected on the report.

Warning

This option is only available in GnuCash version 2.6 or later. If a GnuCash file from an earlier version is opened in version 2.6 or later, and this feature is not used, this feature will not prevent the file from being opened in the earlier version of GnuCash. However, if the option is set, the file will not be able to be opened by the earlier version, even if the option is set back to its original setting. A warning dialog will be displayed from the earlier version. Do not set this option if you want to open the file with an earlier version.

Budgeting Book Options Tab

The Budgeting tab allows you to specify the budget to be used for reports when none has otherwise been specified.

Business Book Options Tab

The Business tab allows you to enter values that are in turn used by the business features of GnuCash:

Company Name
The name of the company.

Company Contact Person
The name of the contact person to print on invoices.

Company Phone, Fax, Email Address
The references of your business.

Company Website URL
The internet address of the company's website.

Company ID
The tax ID of your company.

Default Customer TaxTable
The default taxtable applicable to your most common customers.

Default Vendor TaxTable
The default taxtable applicable to your most common vendors.

Fancy Date Format
The default date format used for fancy printed dates (e.g. on invoices).

Reset Defaults
Press the button to reset all values to their defaults.

Note

None of the above values is required to use GnuCash but, if given, will be used throughout the program. (f.e. in reports, invoices etc...)

Counters Book Options Tab

The Counters tab allows you to set the 'previous' value for each number indicated: Bill, Customer, Employee, etc. These counters are used by the Chapter 7, *Business Features* of GnuCash.

The number entered here will be incremented when the various business features calculate a value for a corresponding field on a dialog. For example, if you leave the Customer Number field blank on the New Customer dialog, the customer will be assigned the number in the counter field plus 1. The numbers displayed in the tab are incremented as these business features are used. (But note that if you have the

Book Options dialog open, you need to close it and re-open it to see the changes; the displayed field values are not automatically refreshed.)

The corresponding format fields are used to specify printf-style format strings that are used to format the printing of the number. For example, to put the literal "C - " in front of the customer number, you would put "C - %li" (without the quotes) in the customer format string field. If the value in the customer number field was 5, the next customer added would be assigned the number "C - 6". As another example, if you wanted the number to be printed with leading zeros and 5 characters wide, you would enter "C - %05li" and the next customer number would be assigned the number "C - 00006".

Note

For historical reasons GnuCash accepts multiple format specifiers although they all yield the same end result. You can choose "li", "lli" or I64i".

Changing Style Sheets

GnuCash has four default style sheets for web-page reports. These style sheets can be altered by using the HTML Style Sheets editor. To access the editor go to Edit → Style Sheets...

Using the Style Sheet Editor you may display/modify the setting of a Style Sheet.

Note

Changing the Style Sheet will change the appearance of all reports that have selected that Style Sheet. A Reload is required to view the changes, if the report(s) are currently displayed.

To add a new Style Sheet click the New... button in the Style Sheet pane. The New Style Sheet dialog will appear. Fill in the name field with the name of the new Style Sheet and choose a template. To remove a Style Sheet select the Style Sheet from the list and click Delete.

Default Style Sheet

The Default Style Sheet has four tabs to alter the appearance of reports utilizing it, Colors, Fonts, General and Tables.

Colors Tab

- Alternate Table Cell Color: Opens the color picker to choose a color that will be applied to alternate table rows.

Fonts Tab

- Title: Select the font and size for Titles.

- Account Link: Select the font and size for Account Links.

- Number Cell: Select the font and size for Number Cells.

- Negative Values in Red: Select to have negative values displayed in red.

- Text Cell: Select the font and size for Text Cells.

- Total Number Cell: Select the font and size for Total Number Cells.

- Total Label Cell: Select the font and size for Total Label Cells.

- Centered Label Cell: Select the font and size for Centered Label Cells.

General Tab

- Background Color: Opens the color picker to choose a new background color.

- Background Pixmap: Use the Browse button to select a picture to use as the background in reports.

- Enable Links: Select this to enable blue hyperlinks in reports.

Tables Tab

- Table cell spacing: Sets the space between table cells

- Table cell padding: Sets the space between table cell edges and contents

- Table border width: Sets the width of the borders on tables.

Easy Style Sheet

The Easy Style Sheet has five tabs to alter the appearance of reports: Colors, Fonts, General, Images and Tables.

Colors

- Background Color: Opens the color picker to choose a new background color.

- Text Color: Opens the color picker to choose a new text color.

- Text Cell Color: Opens the color picker to choose a new text cell color.

- Link Color: Opens the color picker to choose a new link color.

- Alternate Table Cell Color: Opens the color picker to choose a new color for alternate table rows.

- Subheading/Subtotal Cell Color: Opens the color picker to choose a new color for subheading/subtotal table rows.

- Sub-subheading/total Cell Color: Opens the color picker to choose a new color for sub-subheading/total table rows.

- Grand Total Cell Color: Opens the color picker to choose a new color for grand total rows.

Fonts

- Title: Select the font and size for Titles.

- Account Link: Select the font and size for Account Links.

- Number Cell: Select the font and size for Number Cells.

- Negative Values in Red: Select to have negative values displayed in red.

- Number Header: Select the font and size for Number Header table rows.

- Text Cell: Select the font and size for Text Cells.

- Total Number Cell: Select the font and size for Total Number Cells.

- Total Label Cell: Select the font and size for Total Label Cells.

- Centered Label Cell: Select the font and size for Centered Label Cells.

General

- Preparer: Name of the person preparing the report.

- Prepared for: Name of Organization or Company the report is prepared for.

- Show preparer info: Show the Preparer information in the report.

- Enable Links: Select this to enable blue hyperlinks in reports.

Images

- Background Tile: Use the Browse button to select a picture to use as the background in reports. The Clear button will clear the selection.

- Heading Banner: Use the Browse button to select a picture to use as the heading in reports. The Clear button will clear the selection.

- Heading Alignment: Select from pull-down list; Left, Right, Center, to specify the alignment of the banner at the top of report(s).

- Logo: Use the Browse button to select a picture to use as the logo in reports. The Clear button will clear the selection.

Tables

- Table cell spacing: Sets the space between table cells

- Table cell padding: Sets the space between table cell edges and contents

- Table border width: Sets the width of the borders on tables.

Footer Style Sheet

The Footer Style Sheet has the same five tabs to alter the appearance of reports as the Easy Style Sheets: Colors, Fonts, General, Images and Tables.

Colors

- Background Color: Opens the color picker to choose a new background color.

- Text Color: Opens the color picker to choose a new text color.

- Text Cell Color: Opens the color picker to choose a new text cell color.

- Link Color: Opens the color picker to choose a new link color.

- Alternate Table Cell Color: Opens the color picker to choose a new color for alternate table rows.

- Subheading/Subtotal Cell Color: Opens the color picker to choose a new color for subheading/subtotal table rows.

- Sub-subheading/total Cell Color: Opens the color picker to choose a new color for sub-subheading/total table rows.

- Grand Total Cell Color: Opens the color picker to choose a new color for grand total rows.

Fonts

- Title: Select the font and size for Titles.

- Account Link: Select the font and size for Account Links.

- Number Cell: Select the font and size for Number Cells.

- Negative Values in Red: Select to have negative values displayed in red.

- Number Header: Select the font and size for Number Header table rows.

- Text Cell: Select the font and size for Text Cells.

- Total Number Cell: Select the font and size for Total Number Cells.

- Total Label Cell: Select the font and size for Total Label Cells.

- Centered Label Cell: Select the font and size for Centered Label Cells.

General

- Preparer: Name of the person preparing the report.

- Prepared for: Name of Organization or Company the report is prepared for.

- Show preparer info: Show the Preparer information in the report.

- Enable Links: Select this to enable blue hyperlinks in reports.

- Footer: Text to be included in report footer.

Images

- Background Tile: Use the Browse button to select a picture to use as the background in reports. The Clear button will clear the selection.

- Heading Banner: Use the Browse button to select a picture to use as the heading in reports. The Clear button will clear the selection.

- Heading Alignment: Select from pull-down list; Left, Right, Center, to specify the alignment of the banner at the top of report(s).

- Logo: Use the Browse button to select a picture to use as the logo in reports. The Clear button will clear the selection.

Tables

- Table cell spacing: Sets the space between table cells

- Table cell padding: Sets the space between table cell edges and contents

- Table border width: Sets the width of the borders on tables.

Technicolor Style Sheet

The Technicolor Style Sheet has has five tabs to alter the appearance of reports: Colors, Fonts, General, Images and Tables.

Colors

- Background Color: Opens the color picker to choose a new background color.

- Text Color: Opens the color picker to choose a new text color.

- Text Cell Color: Opens the color picker to choose a new text cell color.

- Link Color: Opens the color picker to choose a new link color.

- Alternate Table Cell Color: Opens the color picker to choose a new color for alternate table rows.

- Subheading/Subtotal Cell Color: Opens the color picker to choose a new color for subheading/subtotal table rows.

- Sub-subheading/total Cell Color: Opens the color picker to choose a new color for sub-subheading/total table rows.

- Grand Total Cell Color: Opens the color picker to choose a new color for grand total rows.

Fonts

- Title: Select the font and size for Titles.

- Account Link: Select the font and size for Account Links.

- Number Cell: Select the font and size for Number Cells.

- Negative Values in Red: Select to have negative values displayed in red.

- Number Header: Select the font and size for Number Header table rows.

- Text Cell: Select the font and size for Text Cells.

- Total Number Cell: Select the font and size for Total Number Cells.

- Total Label Cell: Select the font and size for Total Label Cells.

- Centered Label Cell: Select the font and size for Centered Label Cells.

General

- Preparer: Name of the person preparing the report.

- Prepared for: Name of Organization or Company the report is prepared for.

- Show preparer info: Show the Preparer information in the report.

- Enable Links: Select this to enable blue hyperlinks in reports.

Images

- Background Tile: Use the Browse button to select a picture to use as the background in reports. The Clear button will clear the selection.

- Heading Banner: Use the Browse button to select a picture to use as the heading in reports. The Clear button will clear the selection.

- Heading Alignment: Select from pull-down list; Left, Right, Center, to specify the alignment of the banner at the top of report(s).

- Logo: Use the Browse button to select a picture to use as the logo in reports. The Clear button will clear the selection.

Tables

- Table cell spacing: Sets the space between table cells

- Table cell padding: Sets the space between table cell edges and cell contents

- Table border width: Sets the width of the borders on tables.

Setting Tax Report Options

The Income Tax Information dialog is used to set Tax Report Options. The settings on accounts in this dialog are used by the TXF Export function in reports to select the accounts for export. To access this dialog go to Edit → Tax Report Options.

If the Income Tax features are used, it is strongly recommended that the Tax Info column be made visible on the accounts tab (click large downward-pointing arrow and select Tax Info check box). The Tax Info column will display the Form/Schedule and tax category (e.g., Schedule D Dividend, cap gain distrib.) assigned to an account, if any. Alternatively, it will display the following error messages which can be corrected through Edit → Tax Report Options

- Tax-related but has no tax code

- Tax entity type not specified

- Tax type "tax_type": invalid code "code" for account type"

- Not tax-related; tax type "tax_type": invalid code "code" for account type

- Invalid code "code" for tax type "tax_type"

- Not tax-related; invalid code "code" for tax type "tax_type"

- No form: code "code", tax type "tax_type"

- Not tax-related; no form: code "code", tax type "tax_type"

- No description: form "form", code "code", tax type "tax_type"

- Not tax-related; no description: form "form", code "code", tax type "tax_type"

- Not tax-related; "form"("copy") "desc" (code "code", tax type "tax_type")

The Income Tax Identity must be set in order to assign codes to individual accounts. Click Edit to set the identity. The Tax Name is optional. If entered, it will be printed at the top of the report. A Type must be selected in order to activate the tax category selections. The choices are:

- Individual, Joint, etc. - Files US Form 1040 Tax Return

- Partnership - Files US Form 1065 Tax Return

- Corporation - Files US Form 1120 Tax Return

- S Corporation - Files US Form 1120S Tax Return

- None - No Income Tax Options Provided

While the Income Tax Entity Type can be changed after tax categories have been assigned to accounts, you should be cautioned that you will need to manually change each one if you do so, which could be quite tedious. The tax categories are unique for each Income Tax Entity Type, so changing the type will make all previously assigned categories invalid. It is assumed (and highly recommended) that each GnuCash file is for only one tax entity and this is where you specify its type of tax entity. You should not keep, for example, personal and partnership accounts mixed in one GnuCash file if you plan to use the Income Tax Reporting features.

A given TXF code can be assigned to multiple accounts. The Tax Schedule Report will combine accounts by code and generate a detailed TXF record for each account and a summary TXF record for the total as calculated by the report.

For codes for which the "Payer Name Source" is not grayed, the payer on the TXF record will be based on what is specified here, either the account name of the account or the account name of the account's parent account. This feature is typically used for interest accounts or stocks or mutual funds that pay dividends where the individual payees are shown on the tax schedule. For example, if the parent account's name is the name of your broker and the sub-account's names are the names of individual stocks that pay dividends and the name on the 1099-DIV received is that of the broker, in order to match that name, you would select 'Parent Account'; the total dividends from the broker would be exported and, if you had several brokers, there would be an amount exported and a subtotal for each broker, along with each brokers name. Alternatively, if you had a parent account named *Directly Held*, for example, and below it sub-accounts for one or more stocks, you would receive a 1099-DIV from the issuer of each stock separately and, in order to match that name, you would select Current Account; the total dividends from each stock would be exported and, if you had several stocks, there would be an amount exported and a subtotal for each stock, along with each stock's name as the payer.

Some tax Forms/Schedules need to have multiple copies filed under some circumstances (for example, Schedule C if a taxpayer and spouse have separate businesses). For tax categories on these Forms/Schedules, the Copy Number is not grayed out and can be used to segregate accounts by copy number.

- Accounts: This pane contains the list of accounts. Select an account to set a TXF category. If no account is selected nothing is changed. If multiple accounts are selected, all of the accounts will be set to the selected item.

- Tax Related: Select this check-box to add tax information to an account then select the TXF Category below. This setting is displayed on the account edit dialogue but cannot be changed from there.

- TXF Categories: Select the desired one. A detailed description appears just below (if available, otherwise it says No help available), along with the TXF code for the category and information about what line number on the form or schedule the amounts are included in by tax year (used for detailed sort on report).

- Payer Name Source: Select an option to determine where the text description that is exported along with the value of the account is derived from, as described above. This is usually the name of a bank, stock, or mutual fund that pays dividends or interest. Occasionally, it is a description of a deduction.

- Copy Number: A copy number that is exported along with the value of the account. This is used to segregate amounts between different copies of the same Form/Schedule that may need to be filed (e.g., Schedule C(1), Schedule C(2), etc.). This is also used to sort the report.

TXF Export - Known Anomalies and Limitations

TaxCut 1999

- Code: N488 "^ Sched B \ Div. income, cap gain distrib."

- Code: N286 "^ Sched B \ Dividend income"

These two codes, from the same payer, are not correlated. The user will have to adjust for this after import.

TaxCut 1999, 2000

- Code: N521 " F1040 \ Federal estimated tax, quarterly"

Does not accept the date field and does not import the individual payment amounts, only the total. The date and individual payment amounts, only matter if you have to compute the penalty. (this may be a TurboTax enhancement)

- Code: N460 " W-2 \ Salary or wages, self"

- Code: N506 " W-2 \ Salary or wages, spouse"

- and other related codes.

Use Copy Number to separate information from more than one job.

TurboTax 1999, 2000

- Code: N521 " F1040 \ Federal estimated tax, quarterly"

Does not accept the dates outside of the tax year. This is a problem for the last payment that is due Jan 15. GnuCash changes the the date of the last payment to Dec 31 for the export unless the "Do not use special date processing" option is selected in the report options display tab. The user will have to adjust for this after import. The date only matters if you have to compute the penalty.

TXF Tax eXport Format

- Duplicate Codes

Codes can be assigned to multiple accounts and the amounts will be summed for all the accounts generating one detail TXF record per account and one summary TXF record for the sum. Codes that let you select "Payer Name Source" will generate a separate summary TXF account with each change in payer. Selecting the "Print TXF export parameters" option will cause the report to show to which codes this applies (Payer Name Source option Y) and, for the accounts assigned to those codes, the Name Source each account is set to and the TXF item number that will be assigned to each. A summary TXF record will be generated for each change in assigned item line number. These may not be handled the same by TaxCut and TurboTax.

- Code: N673 "Short/Long gain or loss"

Short term or long term gain or loss from the sale of a security; generates TXF output for only the date sold and sales amount, with the date acquired and cost basis information left blank (to be separately added in the tax software). The code can be assigned to either a short-, long-, or mixed-term gain/loss income account and the security sales transaction should be entered as illustrated in Section 8.7, Selling Shares, of the GnuCash Tutorial and Concepts Guide. The report uses the transaction split of the gain/loss account to find one or more other splits in the same transaction with negative share quantities. For each of these found, it generates a detailed TXF output record with the quantity sold, the name of the security, the date sold, and the sales amount. Note that if, for a given transaction, more than one transaction split is to a gain/loss income account assigned to code 673, TXF output data will be erroneously repeated. That is because the report will fetch the same data, and re-output it, for each transaction split set to a gain/loss income account within the same transaction. For this reason, there should be no more than one gain/loss account entered per transaction to use this tax reporting code properly. (Note that no amounts are used from GnuCash's lot-tracking; a future enhancement is expected to use this data to provide capital gain reporting).

Detailed TXF Category Descriptions

Table 32. Detailed TXF Category Descriptions

Table 10.1. Detailed TXF Category Descriptions

Tax Form \ TXF Code Description	Extended TXF Help messages
< help \ H001 Name of Current account is exported.	Categories marked with a "<" or a "^", require a Payer identification to be exported. "<" indicates that the name of this account is exported as this Payer ID. Typically, this is a bank, stock, or mutual fund name.
^ help \ H002 Name of Parent account is exported.	Categories marked with a "<" or a "^", require a Payer identification to be exported. "^" indicates that the name of the PARENT of this account is exported as this Payer ID. Typically, this is a bank, stock, or mutual fund name.
# help \ H003 Not implemented yet, Do NOT Use!	Categories marked with a "#" not fully implemented yet! Do not use these codes!
none \ N000 Tax Report Only - No TXF Export	This is a dummy category and only shows up on the tax report, but is not exported.
Help F1040 \ H256 Form 1040 - the main tax form	Form 1040 is the main form of your tax return.
F1040 \ N261 Alimony received	Amounts received as alimony or separate maintenance. Note: child support is not considered alimony.
F1040 \ N257 Other income, misc.	Miscellaneous income such as: a hobby or a farm you operate mostly for recreation and pleasure, jury duty pay. Exclude self employment income, gambling winnings, prizes and awards.
F1040 \ N258 Sick pay or disability pay	Amounts you receive from your employer while you are sick or injured are part of your salary or wages. Exclude workers' compensation, accident or health insurance policy benefits, if you paid the premiums.
F1040 \ N260 State and local tax refunds	Refund of state or local income tax refund (or credit or offset) which you deducted or took a credit for in an earlier year. You should receive a statement, Form 1099-G. Not reportable if you didn't itemize last year.
F1040 \ N262 IRA contribution, self	Contribution to a qualified IRA. If you or your spouse are covered by a company retirement plan, this amount could be limited or eliminated.
F1040 \ N263 Keogh deduction, self	Contributions to a Keogh or HR 10 plan of a sole proprietor or a partnership.
F1040 \ N264 Alimony paid	Amounts payed as alimony or separate maintenance. Note: child support is not considered alimony.

Tax Form \ TXF Code **Description**	**Extended TXF Help messages**
< F1040 \ N265 Early withdrawal penalty	Penalty on Early Withdrawal of Savings from CD's or similar instruments. This is reported on Form 1099-INT or Form 1099-OID.
F1040 \ N266 Social Security income, self	The part of any monthly benefit under title II of the Social Security Act. These will be reported on Form SSA-1099.
F1040 \ N269 Taxable fringe benefits	Fringe benefits you receive in connection with the performance of your services are included in your gross income as compensation. Examples: Accident or Health Plan, Educational Assistance, Group-Term Life Insurance, Transportation (company car).
F1040 \ N481 IRA contribution, spouse	Contribution of a working spouse to a qualified IRA. If you or your spouse are covered by a company retirement plan, the deductible contribution could be limited or eliminated.
F1040 \ N482 IRA contrib., non-work spouse	IRA contribution for a non-working spouse.
F1040 \ N483 Social Security inc., spouse	Spouse's part of any monthly benefit under title II of the Social Security Act. These will be reported on Form SSA-1099.
F1040 \ N516 Keogh deduction, spouse	Spouse Contributions to a Keogh or HR 10 plan of a sole proprietor or a partnership.
F1040 \ N517 SEP-IRA deduction, self	Contributions made to a simplified employee pension plan (SEP-IRA).
F1040 \ N518 SEP-IRA deduction, spouse	Spouse contributions made to a simplified employee pension plan (SEP-IRA).
F1040 \ N519 RR retirement income, self	The part of tier I railroad retirement benefits, which are treated as a social security benefits. These will be reported on Form RRB-1099.
F1040 \ N520 RR retirement inc., spouse	Spouse's part of tier I railroad retirement benefits, which are treated as a social security benefits. These will be reported on Form RRB-1099.
F1040 \ N521 Federal estimated tax, quarterly	The quarterly payments you made on your estimated Federal income tax (Form 1040-ES). Include any overpay from your previous year return that you applied to your estimated tax. NOTE: If a full year (Jan 1, YEAR to Dec 31, YEAR) is specified, GnuCash adjusts the date to Mar 1, YEAR to Feb 28, YEAR +1. Thus, the payment due Jan 15 is exported for the correct year.
F1040 \ N607	Contributions made to your medical savings account that were not reported on your Form W-2.

Tax Form \ TXF Code Description	Extended TXF Help messages
Medical savings contribution, self	
F1040 \ N608 Medical savings contribution, spouse	Contributions made to your spouse's medical savings account that were not reported on their Form W-2.
F1040 \ N609 SIMPLE contribution, self	Contributions made to your SIMPLE retirement plan that were not reported on your Form W-2.
F1040 \ N610 SIMPLE contribution, spouse	Contributions made to your spouse's SIMPLE retirement plan that were not reported on your spouse's Form W-2.
F1040 \ N611 Fed tax withheld, Social Security, self	The amount of federal income taxes withheld from your part of any monthly benefit under title II of the Social Security Act.
F1040 \ N612 Fed tax withheld, Social Security, spouse	The amount of federal income taxes withheld from your spouse's part of any monthly benefit under title II of the Social Security Act.
F1040 \ N613 Fed tax withheld, RR retire, self	The amount of federal income taxes withheld from your part of tier I railroad retirement benefits, which are treated as a social security benefits.
F1040 \ N614 Fed tax withheld, RR retire, spouse	The amount of federal income taxes withheld from your spouse's part of tier I railroad retirement benefits, which are treated as a social security benefits.
F1040 \ N636 Student loan interest	The amount of interest you paid this year on qualified student loans.
Help F1099-G \ H634 Form 1099-G - certain Government payments	Form 1099-G is used to report certain government payments from federal, state, or local governments.
F1099-G \ N260 State and local tax refunds	Refund of state or local income tax refund (or credit or offset) which you deducted or took a credit for in an earlier year. You should receive a statement, Form 1099-G. Not reportable if you didn't itemize last year.
F1099-G \ N479 Unemployment compensation	Total unemployment compensation paid to you this year. Reported on Form 1099-G.
F1099-G \ N605 Unemployment comp repaid	If you received an overpayment of unemployment compensation this year or last and you repaid any of it this year, subtract the amount you repaid from the total amount you received.
F1099-G \ N606 Fed tax withheld, unemployment comp	The amount of federal income taxes withheld from your unemployment compensation.
F1099-G \ N672 Qualified state tuition earnings	Qualified state tuition program earnings you received this year.

Tax Form \ TXF Code **Description**	**Extended TXF Help messages**
Help F1099-MISC \ H553 Form 1099-MISC - MISCellaneous income	Form 1099-MISC is used to report miscellaneous income received and direct sales of consumer goods for resale.
^ *F1099-MISC* \ N259 Prizes and awards	The amount of prizes and awards that are not for services performed. Included is the fair market value of merchandise won on game shows.
^ *F1099-MISC* \ N557 Other income	The amount of prizes and awards that are not for services performed. Included is the fair market value of merchandise won on game shows. Included is all punitive damages, any damages for nonphysical injuries or sickness, and any other taxable damages, Deceased employee's wages paid to estate or beneficiary.
^ *F1099-MISC* \ N555 Rents	Amounts received for all types of rents, such as real estate rentals for office space, machine rentals, and pasture rentals.
^ *F1099-MISC* \ N556 Royalties	The gross royalty payments received from a publisher or literary agent.
^ *F1099-MISC* \ N558 Federal tax withheld	The amount of federal income tax withheld (backup withholding) from 1099-MISC income.
^ *F1099-MISC* \ N559 Fishing boat proceeds	Your share of all proceeds from the sale of a catch or the fair market value of a distribution in kind that you received as a crew member of a fishing boat.
^ *F1099-MISC* \ N560 Medical/health payments	The amount of payments received as a physician or other supplier or provider of medical or health care services. This includes payments made by medical and health care insurers under health, accident, and sickness insurance programs.
^ *F1099-MISC* \ N561 Non employee compensation	The amount of non-employee compensation received. This includes fees, commissions, prizes and awards for services performed, other forms of compensation for services you performed for a trade or business by which you are not employed. Also include oil and gas payments for a working interest.
^ *F1099-MISC* \ N562 Crop insurance proceeds	The amount of crop insurance proceeds as the result of crop damage.
^ *F1099-MISC* \ N563 State tax withheld	The amount of state income tax withheld (state backup withholding) from 1099-MISC income.
Help F1099=MSA \ H629 Form 1099-MSA Medical Savings Account	Form 1099-MSA is used to report medical savings account distributions.

Tax Form \ TXF Code Description	Extended TXF Help messages
F1099-MSA \ N631 MSA gross distribution	The amount you received this year from a Medical Savings Account. The amount may have been a direct payment to the medical service provider or distributed to you.
F1099-MSA \ N632 MSA earnings on excess contrib	The earnings on any excess contributions you withdrew from an MSA by the due date of your income tax return. If you withdrew the excess, plus any earnings, by the due date of your income tax return, you must include the earnings in your income in the year you received the distribution even if you used it to pay qualified medical expenses.
Help F1099-R \ H473 Form 1099-R - Retirement distributions	Form 1099-R is used to report taxable and non-taxable retirement distributions from retirement, pension, profit-sharing, or annuity plans. Use a separate Form 1099-R for each payer.
^ *F1099-R* \ N475 Total pension gross distribution	The gross amount of a distribution from a qualified pension or annuity plan. Note: IRA distributions are not included here.
^ *F1099-R* \ N476 Total pension taxable distribution	The taxable amount of a distribution from a qualified pension or annuity plan. Note: IRA distributions are not included here.
^ *F1099-R* \ N477 Total IRA gross distribution	The gross amount of a distribution from a qualified Individual Retirement Arrangement (IRA) plan.
^ *F1099-R* \ N478 Total IRA taxable distribution	The taxable amount of a distribution from a qualified Individual Retirement Arrangement (IRA) plan.
^ *F1099-R* \ N529 Pension federal tax withheld	The amount of federal income taxes withheld from your pension distribution.
^ *F1099-R* \ N530 Pension state tax withheld	The amount of state income taxes withheld from your pension distribution.
^ *F1099-R* \ N531 Pension local tax withheld	The amount of local income taxes withheld from your pension distribution.
^ *F1099-R* \ N532 IRA federal tax withheld	The amount of federal income taxes withheld from your IRA distribution.
^ *F1099-R* \ N533 IRA state tax withheld	The amount of state income taxes withheld from your IRA distribution.
^ *F1099-R* \ N534 IRA local tax withheld	The amount of local income taxes withheld from your IRA distribution.

Tax Form \ TXF Code **Description**	**Extended TXF Help messages**
^ *F1099-R* \ N623 SIMPLE total gross distribution	The gross amount of a distribution received from a qualified SIMPLE pension plan.
^ *F1099-R* \ N624 SIMPLE total taxable distribution	The taxable amount of a distribution received from a qualified SIMPLE plan. This amount may be subject to a federal penalty of up to 25%.
^ *F1099-R* \ N625 SIMPLE federal tax withheld	The amount of federal income taxes withheld from a SIMPLE distribution received.
^ *F1099-R* \ N626 SIMPLE state tax withheld	The amount of state income taxes withheld from a SIMPLE distribution received.
^ *F1099-R* \ N627 SIMPLE local tax withheld	The amount of local income taxes withheld from a SIMPLE distribution received.
Help F2106 \ H380 employee business expenses	Form 2106 is used to deduct employee business expenses. You must file this form if you were reimbursed by your employer or claim job-related travel, transportation, meal, or entertainment expenses. Use a separate Form 2106 for your spouse's expenses.
F2106 \ N381 Education expenses	Cost of tuition, books, supplies, laboratory fees, and similar items, and certain transportation costs if the education maintains or improves skills required in your present work or is required by your employer or the law to keep your salary, status, or job, and the requirement serves a business purpose of your employer. Expenses are not deductible if they are needed to meet the minimum educational requirements to qualify you in your work or business or will lead to qualifying you in a new trade or business.
F2106 \ N382 Automobile expenses	Total annual expenses for gasoline, oil, repairs, insurance, tires, license plates, or similar items.
F2106 \ N384 Local transportation expenses	Local transportation expenses are the expenses of getting from one workplace to another when you are not traveling away from home. They include the cost of transportation by air, rail, bus, taxi, and the cost of using your car. Generally, the cost of commuting to and from your regular place of work is not deductible.
F2106 \ N385 Other business expenses	Other job-related expenses, including expenses for business gifts, trade publications, etc.
F2106 \ N386 Meal/entertainment expenses	Allowable meals and entertainment expense, including meals while away from your tax home

Tax Form \ TXF Code Description	Extended TXF Help messages
	overnight and other business meals and entertainment.
F2106 \ N387 Reimb. business expenses (non-meal/ent.)	Reimbursement for business expenses from your employer that is NOT included on your Form W-2. Note: meals and entertainment are NOT included here.
F2106 \ N388 Reimb. meal/entertainment expenses	Reimbursement for meal and entertainment expenses from your employer that is NOT included on your Form W-2.
F2106 \ N389 Job seeking expenses	Fees to employment agencies and other costs to look for a new job in your present occupation, even if you do not get a new job.
F2106 \ N390 Special clothing expenses	cost and upkeep of work clothes, if you must wear them as a condition of your employment, and the clothes are not suitable for everyday wear. Include the cost of protective clothing required in your work, such as safety shoes or boots, safety glasses, hard hats, and work gloves.
F2106 \ N391 Employee home office expenses	Your use of the business part of your home must be: exclusive, regular, for your trade or business, AND The business part of your home must be one of the following: your principal place of business, a place where you meet or deal with patients, clients, or customers in the normal course of your trade or business, or a separate structure (not attached to your home) you use in connection with your trade or business. Additionally, Your business use must be for the convenience of your employer, and You do not rent all or part of your home to your employer and use the rented portion to perform services as an employee. See IRS Pub 587.
F2106 \ N383 Travel (away from home)	Travel expenses are those incurred while traveling away from home for your employer. The cost of getting to and from your business destination (air, rail, bus, car, etc.), taxi fares, baggage charges, and cleaning and laundry expenses. Note: meal and entertainment expenses are not included here.
Help F4137 \ H503 Form 4137 - tips not reported	Form 4137 is used to compute social security and Medicare tax owed on tips you did not report to your employer.
F4137 \ N505 Total cash/tips not reported to employer	The amount of tips you did not report to your employer.
Help F2441 \ H400 Form 2441 - child and dependent credit	Form 2441 is used to claim a credit for child and dependent care expenses.

Tax Form \ TXF Code Description	Extended TXF Help messages
< *F2441* \ N401 Qualifying child/dependent care expenses	The total amount you actually paid to the care provider. Also, include amounts your employer paid to a third party on your behalf.
< *F2441* \ N402 Qualifying household expenses	The cost of services needed to care for the qualifying person as well as to run the home. They include the services of a babysitter, cleaning person, cook, maid, or housekeeper if the services were partly for the care of the qualifying person.
Help F3903 \ H403 Form 3903 - moving expenses	Form 3903 is used to claim moving expenses.
F3903 \ N406 Transport/storage of goods	The amount you paid to pack, crate and move your household goods and personal effects. You may include the cost to store and insure household goods and personal effects within any period of 30 days in a row after the items were moved from your old home.
F3903 \ N407 Travel/lodging, except meals	The amount you paid to travel from your old home to your new home. This includes transportation and lodging on the way. Although not all members of your household must travel together, you may only include expenses for one trip per person. Do not include meals.
Help F4684 \ H412 Form 4684 - casualties and thefts	Form 4684 is used to report gains and losses from casualties and thefts.
F4684 \ N416 FMV after casualty	The fair market value (FMV) is the price at which the property would change hands between a willing buyer and seller, each having knowledge of the relevant facts. The FMV after a theft is zero if the property is not recovered. The FMV is generally determined by competent appraisal.
F4684 \ N413 Basis of casualty property	Cost or other basis usually means original cost plus improvements. Subtract any postponed gain from the sale of a previous main home. Special rules apply to property received as a gift or inheritance. See Pub 551, Basis of Assets, for details.
F4684 \ N414 Insurance/reimbursement	The amount of insurance or other reimbursement you received expect to receive.
F4684 \ N415 FMV before casualty	The fair market value (FMV) is the price at which the property would change hands between a willing buyer and seller, each having knowledge of the relevant facts. FMV is generally determined by competent appraisal.
Help F4835 \ H569	Form 4835 is used to report farm rental income received as a share of crops or livestock produced by

Tax Form \ TXF Code Description	Extended TXF Help messages
Form 4835 - farm rental income	your tenant if you did not materially participate in the operation or management of the farm. Use a different copy of Form 4835 for each farm rented.
F4835 \ N572 Total cooperative distributions	Distributions received from a cooperative. This includes patronage dividends, non patronage distributions, per-unit retain allocations, and redemption of non qualified notices and per unit retain allocations. Reported on Form 1099-PATR.
F4835 \ N571 Sale of livestock/produce	Income you received from livestock, produce, grains, and other crops based on production. Under both the cash and the accrual methods of reporting, you must report livestock or crop share rentals received in the year you convert them into money or its equivalent.
F4835 \ N573 Agricultural program payments	Government payments received for: price support payments, market gain from the repayment of a secured Commodity Credit Corporation (CCC) loan for less than the original loan amount, diversion payments, cost-share payments (sight drafts), payments in the form of materials (such as fertilizer or lime) or services (such as grading or building dams). Reported on Form 1099-G.
F4835 \ N574 CCC loans reported/election	Generally, you do not report CCC loan proceeds as income. However, if you pledge part or all of your production to secure a CCC loan, you may elect to report the loan proceeds as income in the year you receive them, instead of the year you sell the crop.
F4835 \ N575 CCC loans forfeited/repaid	The full amount forfeited or repaid with certificates, even if you reported the loan proceeds as income. See IRS Pub 225.
F4835 \ N576 Crop insurance proceeds received	You generally include crop insurance proceeds in the year you receive them. Treat as crop insurance proceeds the crop disaster payments you receive from the federal government.
F4835 \ N577 Crop insurance proceeds deferred	If you use the cash method of accounting and receive crop insurance proceeds in the same tax year in which the crops are damaged, you can choose to postpone reporting the proceeds as income until the following tax year. A statement must also be attached to your return. See IRS Pub 225.
F4835 \ N578 Other income	Illegal Federal irrigation subsidies, bartering income, income from discharge of indebtedness, state gasoline or fuel tax refund, the gain or loss on the sale of commodity futures contracts, etc.
F4835 \ N579 Car and truck expenses	The business portion of car or truck expenses, such as, for gasoline, oil, repairs, insurance, tires, license plates, etc.

Tax Form \ **TXF Code** **Description**	**Extended TXF Help messages**
F4835 \ N580 Chemicals	Chemicals used in operating your farm, such as insect sprays and dusts.
F4835 \ N581 Conservation expenses	Your expenses for soil or water conservation or for the prevention of erosion of land used in farming. To take this deduction, your expenses must be consistent with a plan approved by the Natural Resources Conservation Service (NRCS) of the Department of Agriculture.
F4835 \ N582 Custom hire expenses	Amounts you paid for custom hire (machine work) (the machine operator furnished the equipment). Do not include amounts paid for rental or lease of equipment you operated yourself.
F4835 \ N583 Employee benefit programs	Contributions to employee benefit programs, such as accident and health plans, group-term life insurance, and dependent care assistance programs. Do not include contributions that are a incidental part of a pension or profit-sharing plan.
F4835 \ N584 Feed purchased	The cost of feed for your livestock. Generally, you cannot currently deduct expenses for feed to be consumed by your livestock in a later tax year. See instructions for Schedule F.
F4835 \ N585 Fertilizers and lime	The cost of fertilizer, lime, and other materials applied to farm land to enrich, neutralize, or condition it. You can also deduct the cost of applying these materials. However, see Prepaid Farm Supplies, in Pub 225, for a rule that may limit your deduction for these materials.
F4835 \ N586 Freight and trucking	The costs of freight or trucking of produce or livestock.
F4835 \ N587 Gasoline, fuel, and oil	The costs of gas, fuel, oil, etc. for farm equipment.
F4835 \ N588 Insurance (other than health)	Premiums paid for farm business insurance, such as: fire, storm, crop, theft and liability protection of farm assets. Do not include premiums for employee accident and health insurance.
F4835 \ N589 Interest expense, mortgage	The interest you paid to banks or other financial institutions for which you received a Form 1098, for a mortgage on real property used in your farming business (other than your main home). If you paid interest on a debt secured by your main home, and any proceeds from that debt were used in your farming operation, refer to IRS Pub 225.
F4835 \ N590	The interest you paid for which you did not receive a Form 1098 (perhaps someone else did, and you are

Tax Form \ TXF Code Description	Extended TXF Help messages
Interest expense, other	liable too), for a mortgage or other loans for your farm business.
F4835 \ N591 Labor hired	The amounts you paid for farm labor. Do not include amounts paid to yourself. Count the cost of boarding farm labor but not the value of any products they used from the farm. Count only what you paid house-hold help to care for farm laborers.
F4835 \ N592 Pension/profit-sharing plans	Enter your deduction for contributions to employee pension, profit-sharing, or annuity plans. If the plan included you as a self-employed person, see the instructions for Schedule C (Form 1040).
F4835 \ N593 Rent/lease vehicles, equip.	The business portion of your rental cost, for rented or leased vehicles, machinery, or equipment. But if you leased a vehicle for a term of 30 days or more, you may have to reduce your deduction by an inclusion amount. For details, see the instructions for Schedule C (Form 1040).
F4835 \ N594 Rent/lease land, animals	Amounts paid to rent or lease property such as pasture or farm land.
F4835 \ N595 Repairs and maintenance	Amounts you paid for repairs and maintenance of farm buildings, machinery, and equipment. You can also include what you paid for tools of short life or minimal cost, such as shovels and rakes.
F4835 \ N596 Seeds and plants purchased	The amounts paid for seeds and plants purchased for farming.
F4835 \ N597 Storage and warehousing	Amounts paid for storage and warehousing of crops, grains, etc.
F4835 \ N598 Supplies purchased	Livestock supplies and other supplies, including bedding, office supplies, etc.
F4835 \ N599 Taxes	Real estate and personal property taxes on farm business assets; Social security and Medicare taxes you paid to match what you are required to withhold from farm employees' wages and any Federal unemployment tax paid; Federal highway use tax.
F4835 \ N600 Utilities	Amounts you paid for gas, electricity, water, etc., for business use on the farm. Do not include personal utilities. You cannot deduct the base rate (including taxes) of the first telephone line into your residence, even if you use it for business.
F4835 \ N601 Vet, breeding, medicine	The costs of veterinary services, medicine and breeding fees.

Tax Form \ TXF Code **Description**	**Extended TXF Help messages**
F4835 \ N602 Other farm expenses	Include all ordinary and necessary farm rental expenses not deducted elsewhere on Form 4835, such as advertising, office supplies, etc. Do not include fines or penalties paid to a government for violating any law.
Help F4952 \ H425 Form 4952 - investment interest	Form 4952 is used to compute the amount of investment interest expense deductible for the current year and the amount, if any, to carry forward to future years.
F4952 \ N426 Investment interest expense	The investment interest paid or accrued during the tax year, regardless of when you incurred the indebtedness. Investment interest is interest paid or accrued on a loan (or part of a loan) that is allocable to property held for investment.
Help F6252 \ H427 Form 6252 - income from casual sales	Form 6252 is used to report income from casual sales of real or personal property when you will receive any payments in a tax year after the year of sale (i.e., installment sale).
F6252 \ N428 Selling price	Enter the total of any money, face amount of the installment obligation, and the FMV of other property that you received or will receive in exchange for the property sold.
F6252 \ N429 Debt assumed by buyer	Enter only mortgages or other debts the buyer assumed from the seller or took the property subject to. Do not include new mortgages the buyer gets from a bank, the seller, or other sources.
F6252 \ N431 Depreciation allowed	Enter all depreciation or amortization you deducted or should have deducted from the date of purchase until the date of sale. Add any section 179 expense deduction. Several other adjustments are allowed, See Form 6252 instructions.
F6252 \ N432 Expenses of sale	Enter sales commissions, advertising expenses, attorney and legal fees, etc., in selling the property.
F6252 \ N434 Payments received this year	Enter all money and the fair market value (FMV) of any property you received in this tax year. Include as payments any amount withheld to pay off a mortgage or other debt, such as broker and legal fees. Do not include interest whether stated or unstated.
F6252 \ N435 Payments received prior years	Enter all money and the fair market value (FMV) of property you received before this tax year from the sale. Include allocable installment income and any other deemed payments from prior years. Do not include interest whether stated or unstated.
Help F8815 \ H441	Form 8815 is used to compute the amount of interest you may exclude if you cashed series EE U.S.

Tax Form \ **TXF Code** **Description**	**Extended TXF Help messages**
Form 8815 - EE U.S. savings bonds sold for education	savings bonds this year that were issued after 1989 to pay for qualified higher education costs.
F8815 \ N442 Qualified higher education expenses	Qualified higher education expenses include tuition and fees required for the enrollment or attendance of the person(s). Do not include expenses for room and board, or courses involving sports, games, or hobbies that are not part of a degree or certificate granting program.
F8815 \ N443 Nontaxable education benefits	Nontaxable educational benefits. These benefits include: Scholarship or fellowship grants excludable from income under section 117; Veterans' educational assistance benefits; Employer-provided educational assistance benefits that are not included in box 1 of your W-2 form(s); Any other payments (but not gifts, bequests, or inheritances) for educational expenses that are exempt from income tax by any U.S. law. Do not include nontaxable educational benefits paid directly to, or by, the educational institution.
F8815 \ N444 EE US savings bonds proceeds	Enter the total proceeds (principal and interest) from all series EE and I U.S. savings bonds issued after 1989 that you cashed during this tax year.
F8815 \ N445 Post-89 EE bond face value	The face value of all post-1989 series EE bonds cashed this tax year.
Help F8863 \ H639 Form 8863 - Hope and Lifetime Learning education credits	Form 8863 is used to compute the Hope and Lifetime Learning education credits. IRS rules are stringent for these credits. Refer to IRS Publication 970 for more information.
F8863 \ N637 Hope credit	Expenses qualified for the Hope credit are amounts paid this tax year for tuition and fees required for the student's enrollment or attendance at an eligible educational institution.
F8863 \ N638 Lifetime learning credit	Expenses qualified for the Lifetime Learning credit are amounts paid this tax year for tuition and fees required for the student's enrollment or attendance at an eligible educational institution.
Help F8829 \ H536 Form 8829 - business use of your home	Form 8829 is used only if you file a Schedule C, Profit or Loss from Business, and you meet specific requirements to deduct expenses for the business use of your home. IRS rules are stringent for this deduction. Refer to IRS Publication 587.
F8829 \ N537 Deductible mortgage interest	The total amount of mortgage interest that would be deductible whether or not you used your home for business (i.e., amounts allowable as itemized deductions on Schedule A, Form 1040). Form 8829 computes the deductible business portion.

Tax Form \ TXF Code Description	Extended TXF Help messages
F8829 \ N538 Real estate taxes	The total amount of real estate taxes that would be deductible whether or not you used your home for business (i.e., amounts allowable as itemized deductions on Schedule A, Form 1040). Form 8829 computes the deductible business portion.
F8829 \ N539 Insurance	The total amount of insurance paid for your home, in which an area or room is used regularly and exclusively for business. Form 8829 computes the deductible business portion.
F8829 \ N540 Repairs and maintenance	The total amount of repairs and maintenance paid for your home, in which an area or room is used regularly and exclusively for business. Form 8829 computes the deductible business portion.
F8829 \ N541 Utilities	The total amount of utilities paid for your home, in which an area or room is used regularly and exclusively for business. Form 8829 computes the deductible business portion.
F8829 \ N542 Other expenses	If you rent rather than own your home, include rent paid for your home, in which an area or room is used regularly and exclusively for business. Form 8829 computes the deductible business portion.
Help F8839 \ H617 Form 8839 - adoption expenses	Form 8839 is used to report qualified adoption expenses.
F8839 \ N618 Adoption fees	Adoption fees that are reasonable and necessary, directly related to, and for the principal purpose of, the legal adoption of an eligible child.
F8839 \ N619 Court costs	Court costs that are reasonable and necessary, directly related to, and for the principal purpose of, the legal adoption of an eligible child.
F8839 \ N620 Attorney fees	Attorney fees that are reasonable and necessary, directly related to, and for the principal purpose of, the legal adoption of an eligible child.
F8839 \ N621 Traveling expenses	Traveling expenses (including meals and lodging) while away from home, directly related to, and for the principal purpose of, the legal adoption of an eligible child.
F8839 \ N622 Other expenses	Other expenses that are reasonable and necessary, directly related to, and for the principal purpose of, the legal adoption of an eligible child.
Home Sale \ N392 Home Sale worksheets (was F2119)	Home Sale worksheets (replaces Form 2119) are used to report the sale of your personal residence. See IRS Pub 523.
Home Sale \ N393 Selling price of old home	The selling price is the total amount you receive for your home. It includes money, all notes, mortgages, or other debts assumed by the buyer as part of the

Tax Form \ **TXF Code** **Description**	**Extended TXF Help messages**
	sale, and the fair market value of any other property or any services you receive. Reported on Form 1099-S.
Home Sale \ N394 Expense of sale	Selling expenses include commissions, advertising fees, legal fees, title insurance, and loan charges paid by the seller, such as loan placement fees or "points."
Home Sale \ N396 Fixing-up expenses	Fixing-up expenses are decorating and repair costs that you paid to sell your old home. For example, the costs of painting the home, planting flowers, and replacing broken windows are fixing-up expenses. Fixing-up expenses must meet all the following conditions. The expenses: Must be for work done during the 90-day period ending on the day you sign the contract of sale with the buyer; Must be paid no later than 30 days after the date of sale; Cannot be deductible in arriving at your taxable in-come; Must not be used in figuring the amount realized; and Must not be capital expenditures or improvements.
Home Sale \ N397 Cost of new home	The cost of your new home includes costs incurred within the replacement period (beginning 2 years before and ending 2 years after the date of sale) for the following items: Buying or building the home; Rebuilding the home; and Capital improvements or additions.
Help Sched A \ H270 Schedule A - itemized deductions	Schedule A is used to report your itemized deductions.
Sched A \ N271 Subscriptions	Amounts paid for subscriptions to magazines or services that are directly related to the production or collection of taxable income. (example: subscriptions to investment publications, stock newsletters, etc.).
Sched A \ N272 Gambling losses	Gambling losses, but only to the extent of gambling winnings reported on Form 1040. Note: not subject to the 2% AGI of limitation.
Sched A \ N273 Medicine and drugs	Prescription medicines, eyeglasses, contact lenses, hearing aids. Over-the-counter medicines are not deductible.
Sched A \ N274 Medical travel and lodging	Lodging expenses while away from home to receive medical care in a hospital or a medical care facility related to a hospital. Do not include more than $50 a night for each eligible person. Ambulance service and other travel costs to get medical care.

Tax Form \ TXF Code **Description**	**Extended TXF Help messages**
Sched A \ N275 State income taxes	State income taxes paid this year for a prior year. Include any part of a prior year refund that you chose to have credited to this years state income taxes.
Sched A \ N276 Real estate taxes	Include taxes (state, local, or foreign) you paid on real estate you own that was not used for business, but only if the taxes are based on the assessed value of the property. Do not include taxes charged for improvements that tend to increase the value of your property (for example, an assessment to build a new sidewalk).
Sched A \ N277 Other taxes	Other taxes paid not included under state and local income taxes, real estate taxes, or personal property taxes. You may want to take a credit for the foreign tax instead of a deduction.
Sched A \ N280 Cash charity contributions	Contributions or gifts by cash or check you gave to organizations that are religious, charitable, educational, scientific, or literary in purpose. You may also deduct what you gave to organizations that work to prevent cruelty to children or animals. For donations of $250 or more, you must have a statement from the charitable organization showing the amount donated and the value of goods or services you received.
Sched A \ N281 Tax preparation fees	Fees you paid for preparation of your tax return, including fees paid for filing your return electronically.
Sched A \ N282 Investment management fees	Investment interest is interest paid on money you borrowed that is allocable to property held for investment. It does not include any interest allocable to passive activities or to securities that generate tax-exempt income.
Sched A \ N283 Home mortgage interest (1098)	Home mortgage interest and points reported to you on Form 1098. The interest could be on a first or second mortgage, home equity loan, or refinanced mortgage.
Sched A \ N284 Points paid (no 1098)	Generally, you must deduct points you paid to refinance a mortgage over the life of the loan. If you used part of the proceeds to improve your main home, you may be able to deduct the part of the points related to the improvement in the year paid. See Pub. 936 Use this line for points not reported on Form 1098.
Sched A \ N484 Doctors, dentists, hospitals	Insurance premiums for medical and dental care, medical doctors, dentists, eye doctors, surgeons, X-ray, laboratory services, hospital care, etc. See IRS Pub 502.

Tax Form \ TXF Code **Description**	**Extended TXF Help messages**
Sched A \ N486 Misc., subject to 2% AGI limit	Safety equipment, small tools, and supplies you needed for your job; Uniforms required by your employer and which you may not usually wear away from work; subscriptions to professional journals; job search expenses; certain educational expenses. You may need to file Form 2106.
Sched A \ N485 Non-cash charity contributions	The fair market value of donated property, such as used clothing or furniture.
Sched A \ N522 State estimated tax, quarterly	State estimated tax payments made this year.
Sched A \ N523 Misc., no 2% AGI limit	Other miscellaneous itemized deductions that are not reduced by 2% of adjusted gross income, such as casualty and theft losses from income-producing, amortizable bond premium on bonds acquired before October 23, 1986, federal estate tax on income in respect to a decedent, certain unrecovered investment in a pension, impairment-related work expenses of a disabled person.
Sched A \ N535 Personal property taxes	Enter personal property tax you paid, but only if it is based on value alone. Example: You paid a fee for the registration of your car. Part of the fee was based on the car s value and part was based on its weight. You may deduct only the part of the fee that is based on the car s value.
Sched A \ N544 Local income taxes	Local income taxes that were not withheld from your salary, such as local income taxes you paid this year for a prior year.
Sched A \ N545 Home mortgage interest (no 1098)	Home mortgage interest paid, for which you did not receive a Form 1098 from the recipient. The interest could be on a first or second mortgage, home equity loan, or refinanced mortgage.
Help Sched B \ H285 Schedule B - interest and dividend income	Schedule B is used to report your interest and dividend income.
^ *Sched B* \ N286 Dividend income, Ordinary	Ordinary dividends from mutual funds, stocks, etc., are reported to you on a 1099-DIV. Note: these are sometimes called short term capital gain distributions. Do not include (long term) capital gain distributions or non-taxable dividends here, these go on Sched D
< *Sched B* \ N287 Interest income	Taxable interest includes interest you receive from bank accounts, credit unions, loans you made to others. There are several categories of interest, be sure you select the correct one!

Tax Form \ TXF Code Description	Extended TXF Help messages
< Sched B \ N288 Interest income, US government	Interest on U.S. obligations, such as U.S. Treasury bills, notes, and bonds issued by any agency of the United States. This income is exempt from all state and local income taxes. There are several categories of interest, be sure you select the correct one!
< Sched B \ N289 Interest income, State and municipal bond	Interest on bonds or notes of states, counties, cities, the District of Columbia, or possessions of the United States is generally free of federal income tax (but you may pay state income tax). There are several categories of interest, be sure you select the correct one!
< Sched B \ N290 Interest income, tax-exempt private activity bond	Interest income from a qualified tax-exempt private activity bond is not taxable if it meets all requirements. This income is included on your Schedule B as non-taxable interest income. There are several categories of interest, be sure you select the correct one!
< Sched B \ N487 Dividend income, non-taxable	Some mutual funds pay shareholders non-taxable dividends. The amount of non-taxable dividends are indicated on your monthly statements or Form 1099-DIV.
< Sched B \ N489 Interest income, non-taxable	Non-taxable interest income other than from bonds or notes of states, counties, cities, the District of Columbia, or a possession of the United States, or from a qualified private activity bond. There are several categories of interest, be sure you select the correct one!
< Sched B \ N490 Interest income, taxed only by fed	Interest income that is taxed on your federal return, but not on your state income tax return - other than interest paid on U.S. obligations. There are several categories of interest, be sure you select the correct one!
< Sched B \ N491 Interest income, taxed only by state	Interest income that is not taxed on your federal return, but is taxed on your state income tax return - other than interest income from state bonds or notes, the District of Columbia, or a possession of the United States. There are several categories of interest, be sure you select the correct one!
< Sched B \ N492 Interest income, OID bonds	Interest income from Original Issue Discount (OID) bonds will be reported to you on Form 1099-OID. There are several categories of interest, be sure you select the correct one!
< Sched B \ N524 Interest income, Seller-financed mortgage	Interest the buyer paid you on a mortgage or other form of seller financing, for your home or other property and the buyer used the property as a personal residence. There are several categories of interest, be sure you select the correct one!

Tax Form \ TXF Code Description	Extended TXF Help messages
< Sched B \ N615 Fed tax withheld, dividend income	The amount of federal income taxes withheld from dividend income. This is usually reported on Form 1099-DIV.
< Sched B \ N616 Fed tax withheld, interest income	The amount of federal income taxes withheld from interest income. This is usually reported on Form 1099-INT.
Help Sched C \ H291 Schedule C - self-employment income	Schedule C is used to report income from self-employment. Use a separate Schedule C to report income and expenses from different businesses.
Sched C \ N293 Gross receipts or sales	The amount of gross receipts from your trade or business. Include amounts you received in your trade or business that were properly shown on Forms 1099-MISC.
Sched C \ N294 Meals and entertainment	Total business meal and entertainment expenses. Business meal expenses are deductible only if they are (a) directly related to or associated with the active conduct of your trade or business, (b) not lavish or extravagant, and (c) incurred while you or your employee is present at the meal.
Sched C \ N296 Returns and allowances	Credits you allow customers for returned merchandise and any other allowances you make on sales.
Sched C \ N297 Wages paid	The total amount of salaries and wages for the tax year. Do not include amounts paid to yourself.
Sched C \ N298 Legal and professional fees	Accountant's or legal fees for tax advice related to your business and for preparation of the tax forms related to your business.
Sched C \ N299 Rent/lease vehicles, equip.	The amount paid to rent or lease vehicles, machinery, or equipment, for your business. If you leased a vehicle for a term of 30 days or more, you may have to reduce your deduction by an amount called the inclusion amount. See Pub. 463.
Sched C \ N300 Rent/lease other business property	The amounts paid to rent or lease real estate or property, such as office space in a building.
Sched C \ N301 Supplies (not from Cost of Goods Sold)	The cost of supplies not reported under Cost Of Goods Sold.
Sched C \ N302 Other business expenses	Other costs not specified on other lines of Schedule C, such as: Clean-fuel vehicles and refueling property; Donations to business organizations; Educational expenses; Environmental cleanup costs; Impairment-related expenses; Interview expense allowances; Licenses and regulatory fees; Moving machinery; Outplacement services; Penalties and fines you pay for late performance or nonperfor-

Tax Form \ TXF Code Description	Extended TXF Help messages
	mance of a contract; Subscriptions to trade or professional publications.
Sched C \ N303 Other business income	The amounts from finance reserve income, scrap sales, bad debts you recovered, interest (such as on notes and accounts receivable), state gasoline or fuel tax refunds you got this year, prizes and awards related to your trade or business, and other kinds of miscellaneous business income.
Sched C \ N304 Advertising	The amounts paid for advertising your trade or business in newspapers, publications, radio or television. Also include the cost of brochures, business cards, or other promotional material.
Sched C \ N305 Bad debts from sales/services	Include debts and partial debts from sales or services that were included in income and are definitely known to be worthless.
Sched C \ N306 Car and truck expenses	You can deduct the actual expenses of running your car or truck, or take the standard mileage rate.
Sched C \ N307 Commissions and fees	The amounts of commissions or fees paid to independent contractors (non employees) for their services.
Sched C \ N308 Employee benefit programs	Contributions to employee benefit programs that are not an incidental part of a pension or profit-sharing plan. Examples are accident and health plans, group-term life insurance, and dependent care assistance programs.
Sched C \ N309 Depletion	The amounts for depletion. If you have timber depletion, attach Form T. See Pub. 535.
Sched C \ N310 Insurance, other than health	Premiums paid for business insurance. Do not include amounts paid for employee accident and health insurance. nor amounts credited to a reserve for self-insurance or premiums paid for a policy that pays for your lost earnings due to sickness or disability. See Pub. 535.
Sched C \ N311 Interest expense, mortgage	The interest you paid to banks or other financial institutions for which you received a Form 1098, for a mortgage on real property used in your business (other than your main home).
Sched C \ N312 Interest expense, other	The interest you paid for which you did not receive a Form 1098 (perhaps someone else did, and you are liable too), for a mortgage or other loans for your business.
Sched C \ N313 Office expenses	The cost of consumable office supplies such as business cards, computer supplies, pencils, pens, postage stamps, rental of postal box or postage

Tax Form \ TXF Code Description	Extended TXF Help messages
	machines, stationery, Federal Express and UPS charges, etc.
Sched C \ N314 Pension/profit sharing plans	You can set up and maintain the following small business retirement plans for yourself and your employees, such as: SEP (Simplified Employee Pension) plans; SIMPLE (Savings Incentive Match Plan for Employees) plans; Qualified plans (including Keogh or H.R. 10 plans). You deduct contributions you make to the plan for yourself on Form 1040.
Sched C \ N315 Repairs and maintenance	The cost of repairs and maintenance. Include labor, supplies, and other items that do not add to the value or increase the life of the property. Do not include the value of your own labor. Do not include amounts spent to restore or replace property; they must be capitalized.
Sched C \ N316 Taxes and licenses	Include the following taxes: State and local sales taxes imposed on you as the seller of goods or services; Real estate and personal property taxes on business assets; Social security and Medicare taxes paid to match required withholding from your employees' wages; Also, Federal unemployment tax paid; Federal highway use tax.
Sched C \ N317 Travel	Expenses for lodging and transportation connected with overnight travel for business while away from your tax home.
Sched C \ N318 Utilities	The costs of electricity, gas, telephone, etc. for your business property.
Sched C \ N493 Cost of Goods Sold - Purchases	If you are a merchant, use the cost of all merchandise you bought for sale. If you are a manufacturer or producer, this includes the cost of all raw materials or parts purchased for manufacture into a finished product. You must exclude the cost of merchandise you withdraw for your personal or family use.
Sched C \ N494 Cost of Goods Sold - Labor	Labor costs are usually an element of cost of goods sold only in a manufacturing or mining business. In a manufacturing business, labor costs that are properly allocable to the cost of goods sold include both the direct and indirect labor used in fabricating the raw material into a finished, salable product.
Sched C \ N495 Cost of Goods Sold - Materials/supplies	Materials and supplies, such as hardware and chemicals, used in manufacturing goods are charged to cost of goods sold. Those that are not used in the manufacturing process are treated as deferred charges. You deduct them as a business expense when you use them.

Tax Form \ TXF Code Description	Extended TXF Help messages
Sched C \ N496 Cost of Goods Sold - Other costs	Other costs incurred in a manufacturing or mining process that you charge to your cost of goods sold are containers, freight-in, overhead expenses.
Help Sched D \ H320 Schedule D - capital gains and losses	Schedule D is used to report gains and losses from the sale of capital assets.
# *Sched D \ N321* Short Term gain/loss - security	Short term gain or loss from the sale of a security. Not yet implemented in GnuCash.
# *Sched D \ N323* Long Term gain/loss - security	Long term gain or loss from the sale of a security. Not yet implemented in GnuCash.
^ *Sched D \ N488* Dividend income, capital gain distributions	Sometimes called long term capital gain distributions. These are from mutual funds, other regulated investment companies, or real estate investment trusts. These are reported on your monthly statements or Form 1099-DIV. Note: short term capital gain distributions are reported on Sched B as ordinary dividends
# *Sched D \ N673* Short/Long Term gain or loss	Short term or long term gain or loss from the sale of a security; for use when only the date sold and net sales amount are available and the date acquired and cost basis information is not available and will be separately added in the tax software.
Help Sched E \ H325 Schedule E - rental and royalty income	Schedule E is used to report income or loss from rental real estate, royalties, and residual interest in REMIC's. Use a different copy for each rental or royalty. Use the Schedule K-1 categories for partnership rental income and loss amounts.
Sched E \ N326 Rents received	The amounts received as rental income from real estate (including personal property leased with real estate) but you were not in the real estate business. (If you are in the business of renting personal property, use Schedule C.)
Sched E \ N327 Royalties received	Royalties received from oil, gas, or mineral properties (not including operating interests); copyrights; and patents.
Sched E \ N328 Advertising	Amounts paid to advertise rental unit(s) in newspapers or other media or paid to realtor's to obtain tenants.
Sched E \ N329 Auto and travel	The ordinary and necessary amounts of auto and travel expenses related to your rental activities, including 50% of meal expenses incurred while traveling away from home.
Sched E \ N330 Cleaning and maintenance	The amounts paid for cleaning services (carpet, drapes), cleaning supplies, locks and keys, pest con-

Tax Form \ TXF Code Description	Extended TXF Help messages
	trol, pool service, and general cost of upkeep of the rental property.
Sched E \ N331 Commissions	The amounts paid as Commissions to realtor's or management companies to collect rent.
Sched E \ N332 Insurance	Insurance premiums paid for fire, theft, liability.
Sched E \ N333 Legal and professional fees	The amounts of fees for tax advice and the preparation of tax forms related to your rental real estate or royalty properties.
Sched E \ N334 Mortgage interest expense	Interest paid to banks or other financial institutions for a mortgage on your rental property, and you received a Form 1098.
Sched E \ N335 Other interest expense	Interest paid for a mortgage on your rental property, not paid to banks or other financial institutions or you did not receive a Form 1098.
Sched E \ N336 Repairs	You may deduct the cost of repairs made to keep your property in good working condition. Repairs generally do not add significant value to the property or extend its life.
Sched E \ N337 Supplies	Miscellaneous items needed to maintain the property, such as: brooms, cleaning supplies, nails, paint brushes, etc.
Sched E \ N338 Taxes	The amounts paid for real estate and personal property taxes. Also include the portion of any payroll taxes you paid for your employees.
Sched E \ N339 Utilities	The costs of electricity, gas, telephone, etc. for your rental property.
Sched E \ N341 Other expenses	Other expenses that are not listed on other tax lines of Schedule E. These might include the cost of gardening and/or snow removal services, association dues, bank charges, etc.
Sched E \ N502 Management fees	The amount of fees to a manager or property management company to oversee your rental or royalty property.
Help Sched F \ H343 Schedule F - Farm income and expense	Schedule F is used to report farm income and expense. Use a different copy of Schedule F for each farm you own.
Sched F \ N344 Labor hired	The amounts you paid for farm labor. Do not include amounts paid to yourself. Count the cost of boarding farm labor but not the value of any products they used from the farm. Count only what you paid house-hold help to care for farm laborers.

Tax Form \ TXF Code Description	Extended TXF Help messages
Sched F \ N345 Repairs and maintenance	Amounts you paid for repairs and maintenance of farm buildings, machinery, and equipment. You can also include what you paid for tools of short life or minimal cost, such as shovels and rakes.
Sched F \ N346 Interest expense, mortgage	The interest you paid to banks or other financial institutions for which you received a Form 1098, for a mortgage on real property used in your farming business (other than your main home). If you paid interest on a debt secured by your main home, and any proceeds from that debt were used in your farming operation, refer to IRS Pub 225.
Sched F \ N347 Interest expense, other	The interest you paid for which you did not receive a Form 1098 (perhaps someone else did, and you are liable too), for a mortgage or other loans for your farm business.
Sched F \ N348 Rent/lease land, animals	Amounts paid to rent or lease property such as pasture or farm land.
Sched F \ N349 Rent/lease vehicles, equip.	The business portion of your rental cost, for rented or leased vehicles, machinery, or equipment. But if you leased a vehicle for a term of 30 days or more, you may have to reduce your deduction by an inclusion amount. For details, see the instructions for Schedule C (Form 1040).
Sched F \ N350 Feed purchased	The cost of feed for your livestock. Generally, you cannot currently deduct expenses for feed to be consumed by your livestock in a later tax year. See instructions for Schedule F.
Sched F \ N351 Seeds and plants purchased	The amounts paid for seeds and plants purchased for farming.
Sched F \ N352 Fertilizers and lime	The cost of fertilizer, lime, and other materials applied to farm land to enrich, neutralize, or condition it. You can also deduct the cost of applying these materials. However, see Prepaid Farm Supplies, in Pub 225, for a rule that may limit your deduction for these materials.
Sched F \ N353 Supplies purchased	Livestock supplies and other supplies, including bedding, office supplies, etc.
Sched F \ N355 Vet, breeding, and medicine	The costs of veterinary services, medicine and breeding fees.
Sched F \ N356 Gasoline, fuel, and oil	The costs of gas, fuel, oil, etc. for farm equipment.

Tax Form \ TXF Code Description	Extended TXF Help messages
Sched F \ N357 Storage and warehousing	Amounts paid for storage and warehousing of crops, grains, etc.
Sched F \ N358 Taxes	Real estate and personal property taxes on farm business assets; Social security and Medicare taxes you paid to match what you are required to withhold from farm employees' wages and any Federal unemployment tax paid; Federal highway use tax.
Sched F \ N359 Insurance, other than health	Premiums paid for farm business insurance, such as: fire, storm, crop, theft and liability protection of farm assets. Do not include premiums for employee accident and health insurance.
Sched F \ N360 Utilities	Amounts you paid for gas, electricity, water, etc., for business use on the farm. Do not include personal utilities. You cannot deduct the base rate (including taxes) of the first telephone line into your residence, even if you use it for business.
Sched F \ N361 Freight and trucking	The costs of freight or trucking of produce or livestock.
Sched F \ N362 Conservation expenses	Your expenses for soil or water conservation or for the prevention of erosion of land used in farming. To take this deduction, your expenses must be consistent with a plan approved by the Natural Resources Conservation Service (NRCS) of the Department of Agriculture.
Sched F \ N363 Pension/profit sharing plans	Enter your deduction for contributions to employee pension, profit-sharing, or annuity plans. If the plan included you as a self-employed person, see the instructions for Schedule C (Form 1040).
Sched F \ N364 Employee benefit programs	Contributions to employee benefit programs, such as accident and health plans, group-term life insurance, and dependent care assistance programs. Do not include contributions that are a incidental part of a pension or profit-sharing plan.
Sched F \ N365 Other farm expenses	Include all ordinary and necessary farm expenses not deducted elsewhere on Schedule F, such as advertising, office supplies, etc. Do not include fines or penalties paid to a government for violating any law.
Sched F \ N366 Chemicals	Chemicals used in operating your farm, such as insect sprays and dusts.
Sched F \ N367 Custom hire expenses	Amounts you paid for custom hire (machine work) (the machine operator furnished the equipment). Do not include amounts paid for rental or lease of equipment you operated yourself.

Tax Form \ **TXF Code** **Description**	**Extended TXF Help messages**
Sched F \ N372 Agricultural program payments	Government payments received for: price support payments, market gain from the repayment of a secured Commodity Credit Corporation (CCC) loan for less than the original loan amount, diversion payments, cost-share payments (sight drafts), payments in the form of materials (such as fertilizer or lime) or services (such as grading or building dams). Reported on Form 1099-G.
Sched F \ N373 CCC loans reported/election	Generally, you do not report CCC loan proceeds as income. However, if you pledge part or all of your production to secure a CCC loan, you may elect to report the loan proceeds as income in the year you receive them, instead of the year you sell the crop.
Sched F \ N374 CCC loans forfeited or repaid	The amount forfeited or repaid with certificates, even if you reported the loan proceeds as income. See IRS Pub 225.
Sched F \ N375 Crop insurance proceeds received	You generally include crop insurance proceeds in the year you receive them. Treat as crop insurance proceeds the crop disaster payments you receive from the federal government.
Sched F \ N376 Crop insurance proceeds deferred	If you use the cash method of accounting and receive crop insurance proceeds in the same tax year in which the crops are damaged, you can choose to postpone reporting the proceeds as income until the following tax year. A statement must also be attached to your return. See IRS Pub 225.
Sched F \ N377 Other farm income	Illegal Federal irrigation subsidies, bartering income, income from discharge of indebtedness, state gasoline or fuel tax refund, the gain or loss on the sale of commodity futures contracts, etc.
Sched F \ N368 Sales livestock/product raised	Amounts you received from the sale of livestock, produce, grains, and other products you raised.
Sched F \ N369 Resales of livestock/items	Amounts you received from the sales of livestock and other items you bought specifically for resale. Do not include sales of livestock held for breeding, dairy purposes, draft, or sport. These are reported on Form 4797, Sales of Business Property.
Sched F \ N370 Custom hire income	The income you received for custom hire (machine work).
Sched F \ N371 Total cooperative distributions	Distributions received from a cooperative. This includes patronage dividends, non patronage distributions, per-unit retain allocations, and redemption of non qualified notices and per unit retain allocations. Reported on Form 1099-PATR.

Tax Form \ **TXF Code** **Description**	**Extended TXF Help messages**
Sched F \ N378 Cost of resale livestock/items	The cost or other basis of the livestock and other items you actually sold.
Sched F \ N543 Car and truck expenses	The business portion of car or truck expenses, such as, for gasoline, oil, repairs, insurance, tires, license plates, etc.
Help Sched H \ H565 Schedule H - Household employees	Schedule H is used to report Federal employment taxes on cash wages paid this year to household employees. Federal employment taxes include social security, Medicare, withheld Federal income, and Federal unemployment (FUTA) taxes.
^ *Sched H* \ N567 Cash wages paid	For household employees to whom you paid $1,100 (as of 1999) or more each of cash wages that are subject to social security and Medicare taxes. To find out if the wages are subject to these taxes, see the instructions for Schedule H.
^ *Sched H* \ N568 Federal tax withheld	Federal income tax withheld from total cash wages paid to household employees during the year.
Help Sched K-1 \ H446 Schedule K-1 - partnership income, credits, deductions	Schedule K-1 is used to report your share of a partnership's income, credits, deductions, etc. Use a separate copy of Schedule K-1 for each partnership.
# *Sched K-1* \ N448 Ordinary income or loss	Your share of the ordinary income (loss) from the trade or business activities of the partnership. This is reported to you on Schedule K-1. (You usually report this on Schedule E, See instructions for Schedule K-1)
# *Sched K-1* \ N449 Rental real estate income or loss	The income or (loss) from rental real estate activities engaged in by the partnership. This is reported to you on Schedule K-1. (You usually report this on Schedule E, See instructions for Schedule K-1)
# *Sched K-1* \ N450 Other rental income or loss	The income or (loss) from rental activities, other than the rental of real estate. This is reported to you on Schedule K-1. (You usually report this on Schedule E, See instructions for Schedule K-1)
Sched K-1 \ N451 Interest income	The amount of interest income the partnership reported to you on Schedule K-1. (You report this on Schedule B)
Sched K-1 \ N452 Dividends, ordinary	The amount of dividend income the partnership reported to you on Schedule K-1. (You report this on Schedule B)
# *Sched K-1* \ N453 Net ST capital gain or loss	The short-term gain or (loss) from sale of assets the partnership reported to you on K-1. (You report this on Schedule D)

Tax Form \ TXF Code **Description**	**Extended TXF Help messages**
# Sched K-1 \ N454 Net LT capital gain or loss	The long-term gain or (loss) from the sale of assets the partnership reported to you on Schedule K-1. (You report this on Schedule D)
Sched K-1 \ N455 Guaranteed partner payments	A guaranteed payments the partnership reported to you on Schedule K-1. (You report this on Schedule E)
# Sched K-1 \ N456 Net Section 1231 gain or loss	The gain or (loss) from sale of Section 1231 assets the partnership reported to you on Schedule K-1. (You report this on Form 4797)
Sched K-1 \ N527 Royalties	The amount of the royalty income the partnership reported to you on Schedule K-1. (You report this on Schedule E)
Sched K-1 \ N528 Tax-exempt interest income	The amount of tax-exempt interest income the partnership reported to you on Schedule K-1. (You report this on Form 1040)
Help W-2 \ H458 Form W-2 - Wages earned and taxes withheld	Form W-2 is used by your employer to report the amount of wages and other compensation you earned as an employee, and the amount of federal and state taxes withheld and fringe benefits received. Use a separate copy of Form W-2 for each employer.
^ W-2 \ N267 Reimbursed moving expenses, self	Qualified moving expense reimbursements paid directly to you by an employer.
^ W-2 \ N460 Salary or wages, self	The total wages, tips, and other compensation, before any payroll deductions, you receive from your employer.
^ W-2 \ N461 Federal tax withheld, self	The amount of Federal income tax withheld from your wages for the year.
^ W-2 \ N462 Social Security tax withheld, self	The amount of social security taxes withheld from your wages.
^ W-2 \ N463 Local tax withheld, self	The amount of local taxes withheld from your wages.
^ W-2 \ N464 State tax withheld, self	The amount of state taxes withheld from your wages.
^ W-2 \ N465 Dependent care benefits, self	The amount dependent care benefits, including the fair market value of employer-provided or employer-sponsored day-care facilities you received.
^ W-2 \ N480 Medicare tax withheld, self	The amount of Medicare taxes withheld from your wages.

Tax Form \ TXF Code Description	Extended TXF Help messages
^ W-2 \ N506 Salary or wages, spouse	The total wages, tips, and other compensation, before any payroll deductions, your spouse receives from your spouse's employer.
^ W-2 \ N507 Federal tax withheld, spouse	The amount of Federal income tax withheld from your spouse's wages for the year.
^ W-2 \ N508 Social Security tax withheld, spouse	The amount of social security taxes withheld from your spouse's wages.
^ W-2 \ N509 Local tax withheld, spouse	The amount of local taxes withheld from your spouse's wages.
^ W-2 \ N510 Medicare tax withheld, spouse	The amount of Medicare taxes withheld from your spouse's wages.
^ W-2 \ N511 State tax withheld, spouse	The amount of state taxes withheld from your spouse's wages.
^ W-2 \ N512 Dependent care benefits, spouse	The amount dependent care benefits, including the fair market value of employer-provided or employer-sponsored day-care facilities your spouse received.
^ W-2 \ N546 Reimbursed moving expenses, spouse	Qualified moving expense reimbursements paid directly to your spouse by your spouse's employer.
Help W-2G \ H547 Form W-2G - gambling winnings	Form W-2G is used to report certain gambling winnings.
^ W-2G \ N549 Gross winnings	The amount of gross winnings from gambling. This may include winnings from horse racing, dog racing, jai alai, lotteries, keno, bingo, slot machines, sweepstakes, and wagering pools. If the amount is large enough, it will be reported on Form W-2G.
^ W-2G \ N550 Federal tax withheld	The amount of federal income taxes withheld from gross gambling winnings.
^ W-2G \ N551 State tax withheld	The amount of state income taxes withheld from gross gambling winnings.

Source: https://github.com/Gnucash/gnucash/blob/maint/src/tax/us/txf-help.scm

Reset Warnings...

GnuCash gives warnings when certain operations are attempted, such as removing a transaction or removing the splits of a transaction. The warning message gives you the option to not give you these warnings when attempting the operation. Check-boxes labeled Remember and don't ask me again and Remember and don't ask me again this session allow disabling the warnings. This option permits reseting the warnings to the default, IE make the warning happen. Warnings may be selectivly enabled.

Changing the Language

The language of the GnuCash user interface is not modifiable directly from the program's preferences.

The way you can change the language depends on the operating system you are running GnuCash on.

Linux
    In general you should set the LANGUAGE and LANG environment variables before starting GnuCash. To do this you need to open a terminal and run the following command:

    LANGUAGE=*ll_LL* LANG=*ll_LL* gnucash

    ll_LL is the locale you want to run GnuCash with (*de_DE* for Deutsch, *it_IT* for Italian etc.)

Note

    On some systems (e.g. Ubuntu) the encoding could be part of the locales name, like *ll_LL.UTF-8*. You can use these names as well.

MacOSX
    If you want to use a different translation from the one that is automatically selected, you can run the following in Terminal.app:

    defaults write $(mdls -name kMDItemCFBundleIdentifier -raw /Applications/GnuCash.app) AppleLanguages "(*de*, *en*)"

    Use whatever language codes you want, replacing Deutsch and English. It won't work if there isn't a translation file for the language you want.

    If you want to unset it (that is, return to using the system settings), run this:

    defaults delete $(mdls -name kMDItemCFBundleIdentifier -raw /Applications/GnuCash.app)

Windows™
    If you are running GnuCash 2.4.0 (or newer) on Windows, you can set the interface language by editing the file environment with a text editor (e.g. Notepad). By default this file is installed in c:\Program Files\gnucash\etc\gnucash. Change this file such that the last few lines are:

```
# If you wish GnuCash to use a different language, uncomment th
# below and set LANG to your preferred locale
LANG=ll_LL
LANGUAGE={LANG}
```

    ll_LL is the locale you want to run GnuCash with (*de_DE* for Deutsch, *it_IT* for Italian etc.)

Tip

More and updated information about this topic can be found on the Locale Settings page [http://wiki.gnucash.org/wiki/Locale_Settings] of the GnuCash wiki.

Appendix A. GnuCash Tips and tidbits

GnuCash Version 2.6.11 + Finance::Quote Version 1.38, February 2016

This chapter gives you some background information about Finance::Quote.

Finance::Quote Sources

There are 3 types of sources of which the first - currency - is hardcoded and responsible to fetch ISO currencies. The other two can be selected in the security editor.

Finance::Quote Sources - Currency source

Table A.1. Currency source for Finance::Quote

GnuCash Name	Finance::Quote Name	Notes
Currency	currency	In 2012 happened a modification on the website. Make sure, you updated F::Q to version 1.18.

Quote Sources - Individual sources

Table A.2. Individual sources for quotes

GnuCash Name	Finance::Quote Name	URL, Notes
Amsterdam Euronext eXchange, NL	aex	http://www.aex.nl includes Futures and Options
American International Assurance, HK	aiahk	http://www.aia.com.hk
Association of Mutual Funds In India, IN	amfiindia	http://www.amfiindia.com
Athens Stock Exchange, GR	asegr	http://www.ase.gr
Australian Stock Exchange, AU	asx	http://www.asx.com.au
BAMOSZ funds, HU	bamosz	http://www.bamosz.hu
BMO NesbittBurns, CA	bmonesbittburns	http://bmonesbittburns.com
Bucharest Stock Exchange (Bursa de Valori Bucuresti), RO	bsero	http://www.bvb.ro
Budapest Stock Exchange (BET), ex-BUX, HU	bse or bet	http://www.bet.hu
Citywire Funds, GB	citywire	http://citywire.co.uk
Colombo Stock Exchange, LK	cse	http://www.cse.lk
Cominvest Asset Management, ex-Adig, DE	cominvest	http://www.cominvest-am.de Obsolete, update: http://eggert.org/software/Comdirect.pm
Deka Investments, DE	deka	http://www.deka.de

GnuCash Name	Finance::Quote Name	URL, Notes
DWS, DE	dwsfunds	http://www.dws.de
Equinox Unit Trusts, ZA	za_unittrusts	http://www.equinox.co.za
Fidelity Investments, US	fidelity_direct	http://www.fidelity.com
Finance Canada	financecanada	http://finance.canada.com
Financial Times Funds service, GB	ftfunds	http://funds.ft.com
Finanzpartner, DE	finanzpartner	http://www.finanzpartner.de
First Trust Portfolios, US	ftportfolios_direct	http://www.ftportfolios.com
Fund Library, CA	fundlibrary	http://www.fundlibrary.com
GoldMoney spot rates, JE	goldmoney	http://www.goldmoney.com
HElsinki stock eXchange, FI	hex	http://www.hex.com
Man Investments, AU	maninv	http://www.maninvestments.com.au
Morningstar, GB	mstaruk	http://morningstar.co.uk
Morningstar, JP	morningstarjp	http://www.morningstar.co.jp
Morningstar, SE	morningstar	http://www.morningstar.se
Motley Fool, US	fool	http://www.fool.com
New Zealand stock eXchange, NZ	nzx	http://www.nzx.com
Paris Stock Exchange/Boursorama, FR	bourso	http://www.boursorama.com
Paris Stock Exchange/LeRevenu, FR	lerevenu	http://bourse.lerevenu.com
Platinum Asset Management, AU	platinum	http://www.platinum.com.au
SIX Swiss Exchange Funds, CH	sixfunds	http://www.six-swiss-exchange.com
SIX Swiss Exchange Shares, CH	sixshares	http://www.six-swiss-exchange.com
Skandinaviska Enskilda Banken funds, SE	seb_funds	http://www.seb.se Consult http://taz.vv.se-bank.se/cgi-bin/pts3/pow/Fonder/kurser/kurslista_body.asp for all available funds.
Sharenet, ZA	za	http://www.sharenet.co.za
StockHouse Canada, CA	stockhousecanada_fund	http://www.stockhouse.ca
TD Waterhouse Canada, CA	tdwaterhouse	http://www.tdwaterhouse.ca
TD Efunds, CA	tdefunds	http://www.stockhouse.ca
TIAA-CREF, US	tiaacref	http://www.tiaa-cref.org Also here were changes, which require at least F::Q 1.18.
Toronto Stock eXchange, CA	tsx	http://www.TMXmoney.com

GnuCash Name	Finance::Quote Name	URL, Notes
T. Rowe Price, US	troweprice_direct	http://www.troweprice.com
Trustnet, GB	trustnet	http://www.trustnet.co.uk
Union Investment, DE	unionfunds	http://www.union-invest.de
US Treasury Bonds, US	usfedbonds	http://www.publicdebt.treas.gov
US Govt. Thrift Savings Plan, US	tsp	http://www.tsp.gov
Vanguard, US	vanguard	part of yahoo_us module
VWD, DE (unmaintained)	vwd	See https://lists.gnu-cash.org/pipermail/gnu-cash-user/2008-February/023686.html
Yahoo USA	yahoo	http://finance.yahoo.com
Yahoo Asia	yahoo_asia	http://sg.finance.yahoo.com
Yahoo Australia	yahoo_australia	http://au.finance.yahoo.com
Yahoo Brasil	yahoo_brasil	http://br.finance.yahoo.com
Yahoo Europe	yahoo_europe	http://finance.uk.yahoo.com
Yahoo New Zealand	yahoo_nz	http://nz.finance.yahoo.com
Yahoo Finance through JSON call	yahoo_json	
Zuerich Investments (outdated)	zifunds	

Finance::Quote Sources - Multiple sources

Table A.3. Multiple sources for quotes

Name
Asia (Yahoo, ...)
Australia (ASX, Yahoo, ...)
Brasil (Yahoo, ...)
Canada (Yahoo, ...)
Canada Mutual (Fund Library, ...)
Dutch (AEX, ...)
Europe (Yahoo, ...)
Greece (ASE, ...)
India Mutual (AMFI, ...)
Fidelity (Fidelity, ...)
Finland (HEX, ...)
First Trust (First Trust, ...)
France (Boursorama, ...)
Nasdaq (Yahoo, ...)
New Zealand (Yahoo, ...)
NYSE (Yahoo, ...)

Name
Romania (bsero, ...)
T. Rowe Price
U.K. Unit Trusts
USA (Yahoo, Fool ...)

Sources: src/engine/gnc-commodity.c:gnc_quote_source (commit 05da881, which was adjusted for Finance::Quote 1.38), GnuCash-Wiki, bugzilla, mailing list archive.

Yahoo Specifics

Yahoo offers quotes from many exchanges and markets. If you are not asking for US markets, you have to specify where to look. A typical Yahoo symbol has the form <ISIN><markets suffix>.

Table A.4. Yahoo Codes for Exchanges and Markets

Country	Exchange	Suffix	Delay
Argentina	Buenos Aires Stock Exchange	.BA	30 min
Australia	Australian Stock Exchange	.AX	20 min
Austria	Vienna Stock Exchange	.VI	15 min
Brazil	BOVESPA - Sao Paolo Stock Exchange	.SA	15 min
Canada	Toronto Stock Exchange	.TO	15 min
Canada	TSX Venture Exchange	.V	15 min
Chile	Santiago Stock Exchange	.SN	15 min
China	Shanghai Stock Exchange	.SS	30 min
China	Shenzhen Stock Exchange	.SZ	30 min
Denmark	Copenhagen Stock Exchange	.CO	15 min
France	Euronext	.NX	15 min
France	Paris Stock Exchange	.PA	15 min
Germany	Berlin Stock Exchange	.BE	15 min
Germany	Bremen Stock Exchange	.BM	15 min
Germany	Dusseldorf Stock Exchange	.DU	15 min
Germany	Frankfurt Stock Exchange	.F	15 min
Germany	Hamburg Stock Exchange	.HM	15 min
Germany	Hanover Stock Exchange	.HA	15 min

Country	Exchange	Suffix	Delay
Germany	Munich Stock Exchange	.MU	15 min
Germany	Stuttgart Stock Exchange	.SG	15 min
Germany	XETRA Stock Exchange	.DE	15 min
Greece	Athens Stock Exchange	.AT	15 min
Hong Kong	Hong Kong Stock Exchange	.HK	15 min
India	Bombay Stock Exchange	.BO	15 min
India	National Stock Exchange of India	.NS	Real-time**
Indonesia	Jakarta Stock Exchange	JK	10 min
Israel	Tel Aviv Stock Exchange	.TA	20 min
Italy	Milan Stock Exchange	.MI	20 min
Japan	Nikkei Indices	N/A	30 min
Mexico	Mexico Stock Exchange	.MX	20 min
Netherlands	Amsterdam Stock Exchange	.AS	15 min
New Zealand	New Zealand Stock Exchange	.NZ	20 min
Norway	Oslo Stock Exchange	.OL	15 min
Russia	Moscow Interbank Currency Exchange (MICEX)	.ME	15 min
Singapore	Singapore Stock Exchange	.SI	20 min
South Korea	Korea Stock Exchange	.KS	20 min
South Korea	KOSDAQ	.KQ	20 min
Spain	Barcelona Stock Exchange	.BC	15 min
Spain	Bilbao Stock Exchange	.BI	15 min
Spain	Madrid Fixed Income Market	.MF	15 min
Spain	Madrid SE C.A.T.S.	.MC	15 min
Spain	Madrid Stock Exchange	.MA	15 min
Sweden	Stockholm Stock Exchange	.ST	15 min
Switzerland	Swiss Exchange	.SW	30 min
Taiwan	Taiwan OTC Exchange	.TWO	20 min
Taiwan	Taiwan Stock Exchange	.TW	20 min
United Kingdom	FTSE Indices	N/A	15 min
United Kingdom	London Stock Exchange	.L	20 min

Country	Exchange	Suffix	Delay
United Kingdom	London Stock Exchange	.IL	20 min
United States of America	BATS Exchange	N/A	Real-time
United States of America	Chicago Board of Trade	.CBT	10 min
United States of America	Chicago Mercantile Exchange	.CME	10 min
United States of America	Dow Jones Indexes	N/A	Real-time
United States of America	NASDAQ Stock Exchange	N/A	Real-time*
United States of America	New York Board of Trade	.NYB	30 min
United States of America	New York Commodities Exchange	.CMX	30 min
United States of America	New York Mercantile Exchange	.NYM	30 min
United States of America	New York Stock Exchange	N/A	Real-time*
United States of America	NYSE Mkt	N/A	Real-time*
United States of America	OTC Bulletin Board Market	N/A	Real-time*
United States of America	OTC Markets Group	N/A	15 min
United States of America	S & P Indices	N/A	Real-time

Source: http://help.yahoo.com/l/us/yahoo/finance/quotes/fitadelay.html queried at 2012-09-22.

TIAA-CREF Specifics

TIAA-CREF Annuities are not listed on any exchange, unlike their mutual funds TIAA-CREF provides unit values via a cgi on their website. The cgi returns a csv file in the format

```
bogus_symbol1,price1,date1
bogus_symbol2,price2,date2
..etc.
```

where bogus_symbol takes on the following values for the various annuities:

Note

The symbols are case-sensitive and changed their capitalization in the last time.

Table A.5. Pseudo-symbols that can be used for TIAA-CREF quotes

Name	Symbol	bogus
CREF Bond Market Account	CREFbond	41081991

Name	Symbol	bogus
CREF Equity Index Account	CREFequi	41082540
CREF Global Equities Account	CREFglob	41081992
CREF Growth Account	CREFgrow	41082544
CREF Inflation-Linked Bond Account	CREFinfb	41088773
CREF Money Market Account	CREFmony	41081993
CREF Social Choice Account	CREFsoci	41081994
CREF Stock Account	CREFstok	41081995
TIAA Real Estate Account	TIAAreal	41091375
TIAA-CREF Bond Fund (Retirement)	TIDRX	4530828
TIAA-CREF Bond Index Fund (Retirement)	TBIRX	20739662
TIAA-CREF Bond Plus Fund (Retirement)	TCBRX	4530816
TIAA-CREF Emerging Markets Equity Fund (Retirement)	TEMSX	26176543
TIAA-CREF Emerging Markets Equity Index Fund (Retirement)	TEQSX	26176547
TIAA-CREF Equity Index Fund (Retirement)	TIQRX	4530786
TIAA-CREF Global Natural Resources Fund (Retirement)	TNRRX	39444919
TIAA-CREF Growth & Income Fund (Retirement)	TRGIX	312536
TIAA-CREF High Yield Fund (Retirement)	TIHRX	4530821
TIAA-CREF Inflation-Linked Bond Fund (Retirement)	TIKRX	4530829
TIAA-CREF International Equity Fund (Retirement)	TRERX	302323
TIAA-CREF International Equity Index Fund (Retirement)	TRIEX	300269
TIAA-CREF Large-Cap Growth Fund (Retirement)	TILRX	4530785
TIAA-CREF Large-Cap Growth Index Fund (Retirement)	TRIRX	299525
TIAA-CREF Large-Cap Value Fund (Retirement)	TRLCX	301332
TIAA-CREF Large-Cap Value Index Fund (Retirement)	TRCVX	304333
TIAA-CREF Lifecycle 2010 Fund (Retirement)	TCLEX	302817

Name	Symbol	bogus
TIAA-CREF Lifecycle 2015 Fund (Retirement)	TCLIX	302393
TIAA-CREF Lifecycle 2020 Fund (Retirement)	TCLTX	307774
TIAA-CREF Lifecycle 2025 Fund (Retirement)	TCLFX	313994
TIAA-CREF Lifecycle 2030 Fund (Retirement)	TCLNX	307240
TIAA-CREF Lifecycle 2035 Fund (Retirement)	TCLRX	309003
TIAA-CREF Lifecycle 2040 Fund (Retirement)	TCLOX	300959
TIAA-CREF Lifecycle 2045 Fund (Retirement)	TTFRX	9467597
TIAA-CREF Lifecycle 2050 Fund (Retirement)	TLFRX	9467596
TIAA-CREF Lifecycle 2055 Fund (Retirement)	TTRLX	34211330
TIAA-CREF Lifecycle Index 2010 Fund (Retirement)	TLTRX	21066482
TIAA-CREF Lifecycle Index 2015 Fund (Retirement)	TLGRX	21066496
TIAA-CREF Lifecycle Index 2020 Fund (Retirement)	TLWRX	21066479
TIAA-CREF Lifecycle Index 2025 Fund (Retirement)	TLQRX	21066485
TIAA-CREF Lifecycle Index 2030 Fund (Retirement)	TLHRX	21066435
TIAA-CREF Lifecycle Index 2035 Fund (Retirement)	TLYRX	21066475
TIAA-CREF Lifecycle Index 2040 Fund (Retirement)	TLZRX	21066473
TIAA-CREF Lifecycle Index 2045 Fund (Retirement)	TLMRX	21066488
TIAA-CREF Lifecycle Index 2050 Fund (Retirement)	TLLRX	21066490
TIAA-CREF Lifecycle Index 2055 Fund (Retirement)	TTIRX	34211328
TIAA-CREF Lifecycle Index Retirement Income Fund (Retirement)	TRCIX	21066468
TIAA-CREF Lifecycle Retirement Income Fund (Retirement)	TLIRX	9467594

Name	Symbol	bogus
TIAA-CREF Lifestyle Aggressive Growth Fund (Retirement)	TSARX	40508431
TIAA-CREF Lifestyle Conservative Fund (Retirement)	TSCTX	40508433
TIAA-CREF Lifestyle Growth Fund (Retirement)	TSGRX	40508437
TIAA-CREF Lifestyle Income Fund (Retirement)	TLSRX	40508427
TIAA-CREF Lifestyle Moderate Fund (Retirement)	TSMTX	40508460
TIAA-CREF Managed Allocation Fund (Retirement)	TITRX	4530825
TIAA-CREF Mid-Cap Growth Fund (Retirement)	TRGMX	305499
TIAA-CREF Mid-Cap Value Fund (Retirement)	TRVRX	315272
TIAA-CREF Money Market Fund (Retirement)	TIEXX	4530771
TIAA-CREF Real Estate Securities Fund (Retirement)	TRRSX	300081
TIAA-CREF S&P 500 Index Fund (Retirement)	TRSPX	306105
TIAA-CREF Short-Term Bond Fund (Retirement)	TISRX	4530818
TIAA-CREF Small-Cap Blend Index Fund (Retirement)	TRBIX	314644
TIAA-CREF Small-Cap Equity Fund (Retirement)	TRSEX	299968
TIAA-CREF Social Choice Equity Fund (Retirement)	TRSCX	300078
TIAA-CREF Bond Fund (Institutional)	TIBDX	307276
TIAA-CREF Bond Index Fund (Institutional)	TBIIX	20739664
TIAA-CREF Bond Plus Fund (Institutional)	TIBFX	4530820
TIAA-CREF Emerging Markets Equity Fund (Institutional)	TEMLX	26176540
TIAA-CREF Emerging Markets Equity Index Fund (Institutional)	TEQLX	26176544
TIAA-CREF Enhanced International Equity Index Fund (Institutional)	TFIIX	9467603

Name	Symbol	bogus
TIAA-CREF Enhanced Large-Cap Growth Index Fund (Institutional)	TLIIX	9467602
TIAA-CREF Enhanced Large-Cap Value Index Fund (Institutional)	TEVIX	9467606
TIAA-CREF Equity Index Fund (Institutional)	TIEIX	301718
TIAA-CREF Global Natural Resources Fund (Institutional)	TNRIX	39444916
TIAA-CREF Growth & Income Fund (Institutional)	TIGRX	314719
TIAA-CREF High Yield Fund (Institutional)	TIHYX	4530798
TIAA-CREF Inflation-Linked Bond Fund (Institutional)	TIILX	316693
TIAA-CREF International Equity Fund (Institutional)	TIIEX	305980
TIAA-CREF International Equity Index Fund (Institutional)	TCIEX	303673
TIAA-CREF Large-Cap Growth Fund (Institutional)	TILGX	4530800
TIAA-CREF Large-Cap Growth Index Fund (Institutional)	TILIX	297809
TIAA-CREF Large-Cap Value Fund (Institutional)	TRLIX	300692
TIAA-CREF Large-Cap Value Index Fund (Institutional)	TILVX	302308
TIAA-CREF Lifecycle 2010 Fund (Institutional)	TCTIX	4912376
TIAA-CREF Lifecycle 2015 Fund (Institutional)	TCNIX	4912355
TIAA-CREF Lifecycle 2020 Fund (Institutional)	TCWIX	4912377
TIAA-CREF Lifecycle 2025 Fund (Institutional)	TCYIX	4912384
TIAA-CREF Lifecycle 2030 Fund (Institutional)	TCRIX	4912364
TIAA-CREF Lifecycle 2035 Fund (Institutional)	TCIIX	4912375
TIAA-CREF Lifecycle 2040 Fund (Institutional)	TCOIX	4912387
TIAA-CREF Lifecycle 2045 Fund (Institutional)	TTFIX	9467607

Name	Symbol	bogus
TIAA-CREF Lifecycle 2050 Fund (Institutional)	TFTIX	9467601
TIAA-CREF Lifecycle 2055 Fund (Institutional)	TTRIX	34211329
TIAA-CREF Lifecycle Index 2010 Fund (Institutional)	TLTIX	21066484
TIAA-CREF Lifecycle Index 2015 Fund (Institutional)	TLFIX	21066498
TIAA-CREF Lifecycle Index 2020 Fund (Institutional)	TLWIX	21066480
TIAA-CREF Lifecycle Index 2025 Fund (Institutional)	TLQIX	21066486
TIAA-CREF Lifecycle Index 2030 Fund (Institutional)	TLHIX	21066495
TIAA-CREF Lifecycle Index 2035 Fund (Institutional)	TLYIX	21066477
TIAA-CREF Lifecycle Index 2040 Fund (Institutional)	TLZIX	21066474
TIAA-CREF Lifecycle Index 2045 Fund (Institutional)	TLXIX	21066478
TIAA-CREF Lifecycle Index 2050 Fund (Institutional)	TLLIX	21066492
TIAA-CREF Lifecycle Index 2055 Fund (Institutional)	TTIIX	34211326
TIAA-CREF Lifecycle Index Retirement Income Fund (Institutional)	TRILX	21066463
TIAA-CREF Lifecycle Retirement Income Fund (Institutional)	TLRIX	9467595
TIAA-CREF Lifestyle Aggressive Growth Fund (Institutional)	TSAIX	40508428
TIAA-CREF Lifestyle Conservative Fund (Institutional)	TCSIX	40508425
TIAA-CREF Lifestyle Growth Fund (Institutional)	TSGGX	40508434
TIAA-CREF Lifestyle Income Fund (Institutional)	TSITX	40508450
TIAA-CREF Lifestyle Moderate Fund (Institutional)	TSIMX	40508443
TIAA-CREF Managed Allocation Fund (Institutional)	TIMIX	4530787
TIAA-CREF Mid-Cap Growth Fund (Institutional)	TRPWX	297210

Name	Symbol	bogus
TIAA-CREF Mid-Cap Value Fund (Institutional)	TIMVX	316178
TIAA-CREF Money Market Fund (Institutional)	TCIXX	313650
TIAA-CREF Real Estate Securities Fund (Institutional)	TIREX	303475
TIAA-CREF S&P 500 Index Fund (Institutional)	TISPX	306658
TIAA-CREF Short-Term Bond Fund (Institutional)	TISIX	4530784
TIAA-CREF Small-Cap Blend Index Fund (Institutional)	TISBX	309018
TIAA-CREF Small-Cap Equity Fund (Institutional)	TISEX	301622
TIAA-CREF Social Choice Equity Fund (Institutional)	TISCX	301897
TIAA-CREF Tax-Exempt Bond Fund (Institutional)	TITIX	4530819
TIAA-CREF Bond Fund (Retail)	TIORX	4530794
TIAA-CREF Bond Index Fund (Retail)	TBILX	20739663
TIAA-CREF Bond Plus Fund (Retail)	TCBPX	4530788
TIAA-CREF Emerging Markets Equity Fund (Retail)	TEMRX	26176542
TIAA-CREF Emerging Markets Equity Index Fund (Retail)	TEQKX	26176545
TIAA-CREF Equity Index Fund (Retail)	TINRX	4530797
TIAA-CREF Global Natural Resources Fund (Retail)	TNRLX	39444917
TIAA-CREF Growth & Income Fund (Retail)	TIIRX	4530790
TIAA-CREF High Yield Fund (Retail)	TIYRX	4530830
TIAA-CREF Inflation-Linked Bond Fund (Retail)	TCILX	313727
TIAA-CREF International Equity Fund (Retail)	TIERX	4530827
TIAA-CREF Large-Cap Growth Fund (Retail)	TIRTX	4530791
TIAA-CREF Large-Cap Value Fund (Retail)	TCLCX	302696

Name	Symbol	bogus
TIAA-CREF Lifecycle Retirement Income Fund (Retail)	TLRRX	9467600
TIAA-CREF Lifestyle Aggressive Growth Fund (Retail)	TSALX	40508429
TIAA-CREF Lifestyle Conservative Fund (Retail)	TSCLX	40508432
TIAA-CREF Lifestyle Growth Fund (Retail)	TSGLX	40508435
TIAA-CREF Lifestyle Income Fund (Retail)	TSILX	40508438
TIAA-CREF Lifestyle Moderate Fund (Retail)	TSMLX	40508453
TIAA-CREF Managed Allocation Fund (Retail)	TIMRX	4530817
TIAA-CREF Mid-Cap Growth Fund (Retail)	TCMGX	305208
TIAA-CREF Mid-Cap Value Fund (Retail)	TCMVX	313995
TIAA-CREF Money Market Fund (Retail)	TIRXX	4530775
TIAA-CREF Real Estate Securities Fund (Retail)	TCREX	309567
TIAA-CREF Short-Term Bond Fund (Retail)	TCTRX	4530822
TIAA-CREF Small-Cap Equity Fund (Retail)	TCSEX	297477
TIAA-CREF Social Choice Equity Fund (Retail)	TICRX	4530792
TIAA-CREF Tax-Exempt Bond Fund (Retail)	TIXRX	4530793
TIAA-CREF Bond Fund (Premier)	TIDPX	21066506
TIAA-CREF Bond Index Fund (Premier)	TBIPX	21066534
TIAA-CREF Bond Plus Fund (Premier)	TBPPX	21066533
TIAA-CREF Emerging Markets Equity Fund (Premier)	TEMPX	26176541
TIAA-CREF Emerging Markets Equity Index Fund (Premier)	TEQPX	26176546
TIAA-CREF Equity Index Fund (Premier)	TCEPX	21066530
TIAA-CREF Global Natural Resources Fund (Premier)	TNRPX	39444918

Name	Symbol	bogus
TIAA-CREF Growth & Income Fund (Premier)	TRPGX	21066461
TIAA-CREF High Yield Fund (Premier)	TIHPX	21066501
TIAA-CREF Inflation-Linked Bond Fund (Premier)	TIKPX	21066500
TIAA-CREF International Equity Fund (Premier)	TREPX	21066466
TIAA-CREF International Equity Index Fund (Premier)	TRIPX	21066462
TIAA-CREF Large-Cap Growth Fund (Premier)	TILPX	21066499
TIAA-CREF Large-Cap Value Fund (Premier)	TRCPX	21066467
TIAA-CREF Lifecycle 2010 Fund (Premier)	TCTPX	21066521
TIAA-CREF Lifecycle 2015 Fund (Premier)	TCFPX	21066528
TIAA-CREF Lifecycle 2020 Fund (Premier)	TCWPX	21066518
TIAA-CREF Lifecycle 2025 Fund (Premier)	TCQPX	21066522
TIAA-CREF Lifecycle 2030 Fund (Premier)	TCHPX	21066527
TIAA-CREF Lifecycle 2035 Fund (Premier)	TCYPX	21066517
TIAA-CREF Lifecycle 2040 Fund (Premier)	TCZPX	21066516
TIAA-CREF Lifecycle 2045 Fund (Premier)	TTFPX	21066444
TIAA-CREF Lifecycle 2050 Fund (Premier)	TCLPX	21066526
TIAA-CREF Lifecycle 2055 Fund (Premier)	TTRPX	34211331
TIAA-CREF Lifecycle Index 2010 Fund (Premier)	TLTPX	21066483
TIAA-CREF Lifecycle Index 2015 Fund (Premier)	TLFPX	21066497
TIAA-CREF Lifecycle Index 2020 Fund (Premier)	TLWPX	21066434
TIAA-CREF Lifecycle Index 2025 Fund (Premier)	TLVPX	21066481
TIAA-CREF Lifecycle Index 2030 Fund (Premier)	TLHPX	21066494

Name	Symbol	bogus
TIAA-CREF Lifecycle Index 2035 Fund (Premier)	TLYPX	21066476
TIAA-CREF Lifecycle Index 2040 Fund (Premier)	TLPRX	21066487
TIAA-CREF Lifecycle Index 2045 Fund (Premier)	TLMPX	21066489
TIAA-CREF Lifecycle Index 2050 Fund (Premier)	TLLPX	21066491
TIAA-CREF Lifecycle Index 2055 Fund (Premier)	TTIPX	34211327
TIAA-CREF Lifecycle Index Retirement Income Fund (Premier)	TLIPX	21066493
TIAA-CREF Lifecycle Retirement Income Fund (Premier)	TPILX	21066470
TIAA-CREF Lifestyle Aggressive Growth Fund (Premier)	TSAPX	40508430
TIAA-CREF Lifestyle Conservative Fund (Premier)	TLSPX	40508426
TIAA-CREF Lifestyle Growth Fund (Premier)	TSGPX	40508436
TIAA-CREF Lifestyle Income Fund (Premier)	TSIPX	40508451
TIAA-CREF Lifestyle Moderate Fund (Premier)	TSMPX	40508456
TIAA-CREF Mid-Cap Growth Fund (Premier)	TRGPX	21066464
TIAA-CREF Mid-Cap Value Fund (Premier)	TRVPX	21066455
TIAA-CREF Money Market Fund (Premier)	TPPXX	21066469
TIAA-CREF Real Estate Securities Fund (Premier)	TRRPX	21066459
TIAA-CREF Short-Term Bond Fund (Premier)	TSTPX	21066445
TIAA-CREF Small-Cap Equity Fund (Premier)	TSRPX	21066446
TIAA-CREF Social Choice Equity Fund (Premier)	TRPSX	21066460

Source: Comments in https://rt.cpan.org/Ticket/Attachment/1121440/589997/Tiaacref.pm.zip

Appendix B. GNU Free Documentation License

Version 1.1, March 2000
Copyright © 2000 Free Software Foundation, Inc.

Free Software Foundation, Inc. 59 Temple Place,
   Suite 330, Boston, MA
   02111-1307 USA

Everyone is permitted to copy and distribute verbatim copies of this license document, but changing it is not allowed.

0. PREAMBLE

The purpose of this License is to make a manual, textbook, or other written document "free" in the sense of freedom: to assure everyone the effective freedom to copy and redistribute it, with or without modifying it, either commercially or noncommercially. Secondarily, this License preserves for the author and publisher a way to get credit for their work, while not being considered responsible for modifications made by others.

This License is a kind of "copyleft", which means that derivative works of the document must themselves be free in the same sense. It complements the GNU General Public License, which is a copyleft license designed for free software.

We have designed this License in order to use it for manuals for free software, because free software needs free documentation: a free program should come with manuals providing the same freedoms that the software does. But this License is not limited to software manuals; it can be used for any textual work, regardless of subject matter or whether it is published as a printed book. We recommend this License principally for works whose purpose is instruction or reference.

1. APPLICABILITY AND DEFINITIONS

This License applies to any manual or other work that contains a notice placed by the copyright holder saying it can be distributed under the terms of this License. The "Document", below, refers to any such manual or work. Any member of the public is a licensee, and is addressed as "you".

A "Modified Version" of the Document means any work containing the Document or a portion of it, either copied verbatim, or with modifications and/or translated into another language.

A "Secondary Section" is a named appendix or a front-matter section of the Document [209] that deals exclusively with the relationship of the publishers or authors of the Document to the Document's overall subject (or to related matters) and contains nothing that could fall directly within that overall subject. (For example, if the Document is in part a textbook of mathematics, a Secondary Section may not explain any mathematics.) The relationship could be a matter of historical connection with the subject or with related matters, or of legal, commercial, philosophical, ethical or political position regarding them.

The "Invariant Sections" are certain Secondary Sections [209] whose titles are designated, as being those of Invariant Sections, in the notice that says that the Document [209] is released under this License.

The "Cover Texts" are certain short passages of text that are listed, as Front-Cover Texts or Back-Cover Texts, in the notice that says that the Document [209] is released under this License.

A "Transparent" copy of the Document [209] means a machine-readable copy, represented in a format whose specification is available to the general public, whose contents can be viewed and edited directly and straightforwardly with generic text editors or (for images composed of pixels) generic paint programs or (for drawings) some widely available drawing editor, and that is suitable for input to text formatters or for automatic translation to a variety of formats suitable for input to text formatters. A copy made in an otherwise Transparent file format whose markup has been designed to thwart or discourage subsequent modification by readers is not Transparent. A copy that is not "Transparent" is called "Opaque".

Examples of suitable formats for Transparent copies include plain ASCII without markup, Texinfo input format, LaTeX input format, SGML or XML using a publicly available DTD, and standard-conforming simple HTML designed for human modification. Opaque formats include PostScript, PDF, proprietary formats that can be read and edited only by proprietary word processors, SGML or XML for which the DTD and/or processing tools are not generally available, and the machine-generated HTML produced by some word processors for output purposes only.

The "Title Page" means, for a printed book, the title page itself, plus such following pages as are needed to hold, legibly, the material this License requires to appear in the title page. For works in formats which do not have any title page as such, "Title Page" means the text near the most prominent appearance of the work's title, preceding the beginning of the body of the text.

2. VERBATIM COPYING

You may copy and distribute the Document [209] in any medium, either commercially or noncommercially, provided that this License, the copyright notices, and the license notice saying this License applies to the Document are reproduced in all copies, and that you add no other conditions whatsoever to those of this License. You may not use technical measures to obstruct or control the reading or further copying of the copies you make or distribute. However, you may accept compensation in exchange for copies. If you distribute a large enough number of copies you must also follow the conditions in section 3.

You may also lend copies, under the same conditions stated above, and you may publicly display copies.

3. COPYING IN QUANTITY

If you publish printed copies of the Document [209] numbering more than 100, and the Document's license notice requires Cover Texts [209], you must enclose the copies in covers that carry, clearly and legibly, all these Cover Texts: Front-Cover Texts on the front cover, and Back-Cover Texts on the back cover. Both covers must also clearly and legibly identify you as the publisher of these copies. The front cover must present the full title with all words of the title equally prominent and visible. You may add other material on the covers in addition. Copying with changes limited to the covers, as long as they preserve the title of the Document [209] and satisfy these conditions, can be treated as verbatim copying in other respects.

If the required texts for either cover are too voluminous to fit legibly, you should put the first ones listed (as many as fit reasonably) on the actual cover, and continue the rest onto adjacent pages.

If you publish or distribute Opaque [210] copies of the Document [209] numbering more than 100, you must either include a machine-readable Transparent [210] copy along with each Opaque copy, or state in or with each Opaque copy a publicly-accessible computer-network location containing a complete Transparent copy of the Document, free of added material, which the general network-using public has access to download anonymously at no charge using public-standard network protocols. If you use the latter option, you must take reasonably prudent steps, when you begin distribution of Opaque copies in quantity, to ensure that this Transparent copy will remain thus accessible at the stated location until at least one year after the last time you distribute an Opaque copy (directly or through your agents or retailers) of that edition to the public.

It is requested, but not required, that you contact the authors of the Document [209] well before redistributing any large number of copies, to give them a chance to provide you with an updated version of the Document.

4. MODIFICATIONS

You may copy and distribute a Modified Version [209] of the Document [209] under the conditions of sections 2 and 3 above, provided that you release the Modified Version under precisely this License, with the Modified Version filling the role of the Document, thus licensing distribution and modification of the Modified Version to whoever possesses a copy of it. In addition, you must do these things in the Modified Version:

- **A.**   Use in the Title Page [210] (and on the covers, if any) a title distinct from that of the Document [209], and from those of previous versions (which should, if there were any, be listed in the History section of the Document). You may use the same title as a previous version if the original publisher of that version gives permission.

- **B.**   List on the Title Page [210], as authors, one or more persons or entities responsible for authorship of the modifications in the Modified Version [209], together with at least five of the principal authors of the Document [209] (all of its principal authors, if it has less than five).

- **C.**   State on the Title Page [210] the name of the publisher of the Modified Version [209], as the publisher.

- **D.**   Preserve all the copyright notices of the Document [209].

- **E.**   Add an appropriate copyright notice for your modifications adjacent to the other copyright notices.

- **F.**   Include, immediately after the copyright notices, a license notice giving the public permission to use the Modified Version [209] under the terms of this License, in the form shown in the Addendum below.

- **G.**   Preserve in that license notice the full lists of Invariant Sections [209] and required Cover Texts [209] given in the Document's [209] license notice.

- **H.**   Include an unaltered copy of this License.

- **I.**   Preserve the section entitled "History", and its title, and add to it an item stating at least the title, year, new authors, and publisher of the Modified Version [209]as given on the Title Page [210]. If there is no section entitled "History" in the Document [209], create one stating the title, year, authors, and publisher of the Document as given on its Title Page, then add an item describing the Modified Version as stated in the previous sentence.

- **J.**   Preserve the network location, if any, given in the Document [209] for public access to a Transparent [210] copy of the Document, and likewise the network locations given in the Document for previous versions it was based on. These may be placed in the "History" section. You may omit a network location for a work that was published at least four years before the Document itself, or if the original publisher of the version it refers to gives permission.

- **K.**   In any section entitled "Acknowledgements" or "Dedications", preserve the section's title, and preserve in the section all the substance and tone of each of the contributor acknowledgements and/or dedications given therein.

- **L.**   Preserve all the Invariant Sections [209] of the Document [209], unaltered in their text and in their titles. Section numbers or the equivalent are not considered part of the section titles.

- **M.**   Delete any section entitled "Endorsements". Such a section may not be included in the Modified Version [209].

- **N.**   Do not retitle any existing section as "Endorsements" or to conflict in title with any Invariant Section [209].

If the Modified Version [209] includes new front-matter sections or appendices that qualify as Secondary Sections [209] and contain no material copied from the Document, you may at your option designate some or all of these sections as invariant. To do this, add their titles to the list of Invariant Sections [209] in the Modified Version's license notice. These titles must be distinct from any other section titles.

You may add a section entitled "Endorsements", provided it contains nothing but endorsements of your Modified Version [209] by various parties--for example, statements of peer review or that the text has been approved by an organization as the authoritative definition of a standard.

You may add a passage of up to five words as a Front-Cover Text [209], and a passage of up to 25 words as a Back-Cover Text [209], to the end of the list of Cover Texts [209] in the Modified Version [209]. Only one passage of Front-Cover Text and one of Back-Cover Text may be added by (or through arrangements made by) any one entity. If the Document [209] already includes a cover text for the same cover, previously added by you or by arrangement made by the same entity you are acting on behalf of, you may not add another; but you may replace the old one, on explicit permission from the previous publisher that added the old one.

The author(s) and publisher(s) of the Document [209] do not by this License give permission to use their names for publicity for or to assert or imply endorsement of any Modified Version [209].

5. COMBINING DOCUMENTS

You may combine the Document [209] with other documents released under this License, under the terms defined in section 4 above for modified versions, provided that you include in the combination all of the Invariant Sections [209] of all of the original documents, unmodified, and list them all as Invariant Sections of your combined work in its license notice.

The combined work need only contain one copy of this License, and multiple identical Invariant Sections [209] may be replaced with a single copy. If there are multiple Invariant Sections with the same name but different contents, make the title of each such section unique by adding at the end of it, in parentheses, the name of the original author or publisher of that section if known, or else a unique number. Make the same adjustment to the section titles in the list of Invariant Sections in the license notice of the combined work.

In the combination, you must combine any sections entitled "History" in the various original documents, forming one section entitled "History"; likewise combine any sections entitled "Acknowledgements", and any sections entitled "Dedications". You must delete all sections entitled "Endorsements."

6. COLLECTIONS OF DOCUMENTS

You may make a collection consisting of the Document [209] and other documents released under this License, and replace the individual copies of this License in the various documents with a single copy that is included in the collection, provided that you follow the rules of this License for verbatim copying of each of the documents in all other respects.

You may extract a single document from such a collection, and dispbibute it individually under this License, provided you insert a copy of this License into the extracted document, and follow this License in all other respects regarding verbatim copying of that document.

7. AGGREGATION WITH INDEPENDENT WORKS

A compilation of the Document [209] or its derivatives with other separate and independent documents or works, in or on a volume of a storage or distribution medium, does not as a whole count as a Modified Version [209] of the Document, provided no compilation copyright is claimed for the compilation. Such a compilation is called an "aggregate", and this License does not apply to the other self-contained works thus compiled with the Document , on account of their being thus compiled, if they are not themselves derivative works of the Document. If the Cover Text [209] requirement of section 3 is applicable to these copies of the Document, then if the Document is less than one quarter of the entire aggregate, the Document's Cover Texts may be placed on covers that surround only the Document within the aggregate. Otherwise they must appear on covers around the whole aggregate.

8. TRANSLATION

Translation is considered a kind of modification, so you may distribute translations of the Document [209] under the terms of section 4. Replacing Invariant Sections [209] with translations requires special permission from their copyright holders, but you may include translations of some or all Invariant Sections in addition to the original versions of these Invariant Sections. You may include a translation of this License provided that you also include the original English version of this License. In case of a disagreement between the translation and the original English version of this License, the original English version will prevail.

9. TERMINATION

You may not copy, modify, sublicense, or distribute the Document [209] except as expressly provided for under this License. Any other attempt to copy, modify, sublicense or distribute the Document is void, and will automatically terminate your rights under this License. However, parties who have received copies, or rights, from you under this License will not have their licenses terminated so long as such parties remain in full compliance.

10. FUTURE REVISIONS OF THIS LICENSE

The Free Software Foundation [http://www.gnu.org/fsf/fsf.html] may publish new, revised versions of the GNU Free Documentation License from time to time. Such new versions will be similar in spirit to the present version, but may differ in detail to address new problems or concerns. See http://www.gnu.org/copyleft/ [http://www.gnu.org/copyleft].

Each version of the License is given a distinguishing version number. If the Document [209] specifies that a particular numbered version of this License "or any later version" applies to it, you have the option of following the terms and conditions either of that specified version or of any later version that has been published (not as a draft) by the Free Software Foundation. If the Document does not specify a version number of this License, you may choose any version ever published (not as a draft) by the Free Software Foundation.

Addendum

To use this License in a document you have written, include a copy of the License in the document and put the following copyright and license notices just after the title page:

Copyright YEAR YOUR NAME.

Permission is granted to copy, distribute and/or modify this document under the terms of the GNU Free Documentation License, Version 1.1 or any later version published by the Free Software Foundation; with the Invariant Sections [209] being LIST THEIR TITLES, with the Front-Cover Texts [209] being LIST, and with the Back-Cover Texts [209] being LIST. A copy of the license is included in the section entitled "GNU Free Documentation License".

If you have no Invariant Sections [209], write "with no Invariant Sections" instead of saying which ones are invariant. If you have no Front-Cover Texts [209], write "no Front-Cover Texts" instead of "Front-Cover Texts being LIST"; likewise for Back-Cover Texts [209].

If your document contains nontrivial examples of program code, we recommend releasing these examples in parallel under your choice of free software license, such as the GNU General Public License [http://www.gnu.org/copyleft/gpl.html], to permit their use in free software.

www.ingramcontent.com/pod-product-compliance
Lightning Source LLC
Chambersburg PA
CBHW060551060326
40690CB00017B/3672